Complete
Fish and Game Cookery
of
North America

Complete
Fish and Game Cookery
of
North America

FRANCES MacILQUHAM

Special photography by Sylvia and Jim Bashline
Decorative drawings by E. B. Sanders

Winchester Press

Library of Congress Cataloging in Publication Data

MacIlquham, Frances, 1915–
    Complete fish and game cookery of North America.

    Includes index.
    1. Cookery (Fish) 2. Cookery (Game) 3. Fishes—
North America. 4. Game and game-birds—North America.
I. Title.
TX747.M217   641.6'92   82-4789
ISBN 0-8329-0284-5   AACR2

Published by Winchester Press
An imprint of New Century Publishers, Inc.

Contents

Acknowledgments

Without the generous cooperation of others, I could never have compiled a work of this scope. I wish it were possible to name all who have given unstintingly of their knowledge, skills, and time. Over the years they have come to number in scores.

I remain indebted to all those whose assistance was acknowledged in my earlier books, *Canadian Game Cookery* (1966, McClelland and Stewart, Toronto) and *Fish Cookery of North America* (1974, Winchester Press, New York); their help has had a bearing on material in this book.

There have been many others since. Government agencies—federal, provincial, state, and municipal—were involved to varying degrees. I am particularly indebted to the United States Travel Service of the U.S. Department of Commerce and to their Toronto agents, who not only made possible most of the research in the continental United States but whose assistance in planning productive field work was invaluable to me, and to the many state and local agencies who in consequence aided my research.

To the Explorers Highroad group of the Manitoba, Minnesota, and North Dakota tourism departments, who showed me the vastness of the Red River Valley and introduced me to its lore.

To Indian and Northern Affairs, Canada, for permission to quote from the brochure *Arctic Recipes* and from a collection of Indian and Eskimo recipes by the Ladies' Auxiliary of the Church of the Ascension, Inuvik, Northwest Territories.

To others who have assisted in various ways: Dr. R. W. "Bill" Altman, wildlife biologist, Oklahoma State University, Cooperative Extension Service, Stillwater; Frank Ashida, Westours, Seattle, Washington; Ellen Ayotte, district home economist, Cooperative Extension Service, University of Alaska, Fairbanks; Cynthia Bayer, angler (and tireless chauffeuse), Clearwater, Florida; Victor E. Bergeron (better known as Trader Vic), sportsman and restaurateur, San Francisco, California; Wes Bower, outdoor writer, Pennsylvania Game Commission, Huntingdon, Pennsylvania; Joseph Caringulla, Lassco Smoke-Cure Fishing Co., Los Angeles, California; Stephanie Cincotta, Seafood Affairs, San Francisco, California; Terry D. Combs, director of tourism, Cherokee Nation, Tahlequah, Oklahoma; Tod Ghio, Anthony's Fish Grottos, San Diego, California; Charles J. "Chuck" Keim, sportsman, Fairbanks, Alaska; Dr. Walter A. Kenyon, curator, New World Archaeology, Royal Ontario Museum, Toronto, Ontario; J. A. "Kip" and Beryl Kippan, Souris, British Columbia; Fay McCotter, home economist, North Carolina Department of Natural and Economic Resources, Raleigh; Charly and Pat McTee, Schertz, Texas; Joyce and Jim Milner, skippers of *The Californian*, Long Beach, California; Jim Mosley, game-cooking expert, G & M Catering Services, Austin, Texas; Paul Paddlety (Sate-Ah-Tay), Indian City U.S.A., Anadarko, Oklahoma; Ada Peachey, Belleville, Pennsylvania; Mr. and Mrs. Red Corn, Pawhuska, Tribal Seat of Osage Nation in Oklahoma; Bob Rossolini, restaurateur and game farmer, Seattle and Bangor, Washington; Don Sawatsky, historian and sportsman, Whitehorse, Yukon; and the Sportman's Clubs of Texas, Inc., and Texas Outdoor Writers Association, if I may thank them *en groupe* for my initiation into southwestern game cooking.

My special thanks to the many generous contributors of recipes, those who gave from their personal repertoires and fellow authors who kindly permitted me to use their published recipes. These are acknowledged individually in the text.

I am indebted to Norm Lee, chef and sportsman of The Pas, Manitoba, for a fine demonstration of filleting walleye, and to my good friend and colleague John Power, outdoor writer of the *Toronto Star*, who photographed the procedure for me.

To my friends and neighbors Jean Collins, Linda Foote, Corinne McMillan, and Meika VanHaagen for kindly and patiently reading thousands of words of manuscript, and to Jeannie Carothers who typed them, my gratitude. All are of Toronto.

Encouragement (not to mention solvency) has been important. I am indebted to the editors of *Outdoor Canada*, *The Globe and Mail* (Toronto), and, over the past three years, the *Toronto Star*, who have published my articles on cooking fish and game. Many of the recipes in this book have appeared previously in these publications.

To Cookbook Publishers, Inc., Lenexa, Kansas, for permission to use material from *What's Cooking in Our National Parks*.

Preface

When it was decided that I revise my two earlier books on the cookery of game and fish, the thought was simply to select the best recipes from each, include new recipes since acquired to broaden the scope, and combine it all into one straightforward cookbook of North American fish and game. However, as the work developed the project took its own direction, overrode the cookbook, and ordained a book of cookery.

To tell how this happened, I must first explain how I distinguish one from the other. A cookbook is simply a collection of practical, tested recipes and information pertinent to their preparation. A book of cookery is a story of the art of preparing food, with its cultural and economic ramifications, like threads, woven into the social history of a people.

In assessing the contents of my previous books and the volumes of notes, recipes, and other materials gathered since writing them, it became evident that the preparation of game, which here includes fish, birds, and mammals, was historically an important part of the social fabric of North America, both to the aboriginals whose ancestors crossed the Bering Strait from Asia and to the newcomers who learned from them how to eat while they developed the "New World." To try to isolate recipes from the total cookery would be like trying to separate the weft from the warp of the fabric.

What my research has uncovered since the publication of *Canadian Game Cookery*, with its geographic limitations, is the extent to which the variety and abundance of wildlife figured in the building of all of North America. For those who settled the coasts from Canada to Mexico, down the Atlantic, through the Gulf of Mexico and up the Pacific to Alaska, the wealth of the sea provided. Game meats and freshwater fish fed the colonists of the East, the settlers of the West, and the prospectors and traders en route. Buffalo, or bison, were a source of staple meats on the Plains from Texas to the Canadian Prairie provinces, as beef is today. Venison meats filled the pots from Mexico to the Arctic. Wild meats, particularly, sustained the exploration of the entire continent, not to mention the building of its railroads.

Nor was the game all venison and buffalo. Reptiles, from alligators in Florida to rattlesnakes in the Southwest (still considered a delicacy), provided meat. Panther was described as "surpassing delicious"; sea otter provided meat for the Russian traders in Alaska. Champlain mentioned otter and wildcat among meats for the table of his Order of Good Cheer. Gwen Lewis' delightful *Buckskin Cookery*, about the early days in the Cariboo in British Columbia, tells of a trapper's dinner guest whose enthusiasm for the fine stew she'd just been served was dampened when, exiting through the woodshed, she noticed a freshly skinned coyote—its bared teeth glinting in a moonbeam—with one of its hindquarters missing. Recipes from the Northwest Territories' trappers recommend boiled lynx as good to eat with muktuk.

In fact, almost any healthy wild animal of this continent, properly dressed and cooked, is edible, even if some are considered less aesthetically agreeable than others. (I have a childhood memory of my father rendering out skunk oil for some purpose known only to himself and frying a couple of pieces of the meat for my brother and me so we could say, should the occasion ever arise, that we had eaten skunk. I don't remember what it tasted like, so it must have been all right.)

Both *Canadian Game Cookery* and *Fish Cookery of North America* were written on the premise that hunting and fishing are important tools in effective wildlife management, that cooking the fruits of field and stream is the final phase of a conservation program, and that the end is defeated unless the game reaches the table in edible condition—that is to say, the best cook in the world, armed with the greatest recipes, cannot transform bad meat into table fare. Though my belief in these assertions has strengthened with each year, this volume concerns itself less with the practical aspects of field care and dressing than did my previous books. Given the scope of this book, the variables involved (especially in handling big game) are infinite; and the subject is too broad and too important to treat superficially. Besides, others have done the job more competently than I could. Nonetheless, it's up to the hunters and anglers who would justify their sport to deliver good meat; it's in the field that the recipe begins. All recipes in this book are for properly dressed and cared-for game only.

The recipes and methods included come from all over North America, and range from primitive *al fresco* to *haute cuisine*. Except perhaps for Mexican cooking and its Tex-Mex spinoff, I have not found regionality to be clear-cut in the cooking of game. Rather, it is a matter of applying universal basic methods to local fauna, flora, and facilities. Indeed, to call this collection North American is even somewhat misleading; like the roots of the North American people, including the aboriginals, the methods and most of the recipes in this and my previous works may be found in some form in other parts of the world.

The thread that ties this account of North American cookery together is the inherent hospitality peculiar to people with a tradition of providing their tables by their own efforts with the harvests of the land and water.

Frances MacIlquham
Toronto, Ontario

PART ONE

A Heritage of Cookery

At the time of year when they are in the habit of feasting each
other, they employ cooks, who are chosen on purpose for the
business. These, first of all, take a great round earthen vessel (which
they know how to make and to burn so that water can be
boiled in it as well as in our kettles), and place it over a large wood-
fire, which one of them drives with a fan, very effectively holding
it in the hand. The head cook now puts things to be cooked into
the great pot; others put water for washing into a hole in the
ground; another brings water in a utensil that serves for a bucket;
another pounds on a stone the aromatics that are to be used for
seasoning; while the women are picking over or preparing
the viands.... Although they have great festivities after their
manner, yet they are very temperate in eating.

LeMoyne
"Preparations for a Feast"
Narrative of LeMoyne, 1564

1

The Order of Good Cheer

Seven wild fowl carefully boned . . . a goose was stuffed into a turkey, a partridge into the goose, a duck into the partridge, quail into duck, dove into quail, and lark into dove. Slow baked with wine basting, it was served cross-sliced so that light and dark meat alternated
—Legend

When Samuel de Champlain established *l'Ordre de Bon Temps* at Port Royal in Acadia in 1606, he launched the first social club on record in North America and inspired a game cookery that was to become legendary in the New World.

As Champlain's companion Marc Lecarbot explained in his *History of New France*, the Order of Good Cheer (*l'Ordre de Bon Temps*) was designed to keep the tables "joyous and well served" through the winters for the scurvy-haunted little band of homesick men in a strange land.

In the Order each man was appointed *mâitre d'hôtel*, or chief steward, for a day in his turn, which came around once a fortnight. He was to see that his table was "well and honorably provided for." The exercise in the applied psychology of food was effective, and the men joined in *l'esprit de corps*. Each set out to hunt or fish to add a delicacy to the fare. Zealous rivalry resulted in a well-laden table, and in the process a nutritious diet was assured.

There were fish, waterfowl, grouse, larks, and other birds. There were moose, deer, beaver, otter, rabbits, wildcats, and raccoons. Of meats, it was recorded that there was "none so tender as the moose meat (wherefrom we also made excellent pasties) and nothing so delicate as a beaver's tail."

There were wild fruits and plants from the surrounding land, and eventually Champlain's garden, planted with seeds from home, yielded "vegetables as fine and as well formed as in France." Wines from Bordeaux were in generous store.

Morning and midday had their offerings of fish and flesh but the evening meal was the grand regale. Into the refectory marched the steward of the day, napkin on shoulder, wand of office in hand, and around his neck the Collar of the Order of Good Cheer. After him came the members of the Order, each bearing a dish. Before offering thanks, the steward handed over to his successor the Collar of the Order, and with a cup of wine they drank to each other.

The Indians, drawn by the convivial scene, came to gaze in wonder. Their chiefs were persuaded to join in the feasting. Almost nightly they were colorful guests, and the Frenchmen were saddened when their Indian friends were absent, away on their winter hunts

Champlain wrote, "All vied, one with the other, to see who could do the best, and bring back the finest game—we did not find ourselves badly off, nor did the Indians who were with us."

2

A Native Heritage

Iron wares were acceptable as gifts.
—Jacques Cartier
Cape Breton Island, 1534

Jacques Cartier, or perhaps some Basque fishermen before him, first offered metal wares to the natives of northeastern North America, but it was not until the next century, when the *coureurs de bois* began actively trading iron and copper kettles for the Indians' beaver pelts, that change in an impressive native cookery already thousands of years old really got under way. Metal cookware materially enhanced the way of life of the natives of North America and was to have a lasting impact on the cookery across the continent.

In the trading process, the white man acquired the contents of the kettles—fish and game meats of the finest quality in the world, and wild rice, roots, fruits, nuts, and berries to enhance them, not to mention corn, squash, pumpkin, and sweet potatoes—and unique ways of cooking them all.

THE INHABITANTS

When the white man arrived, the natives of North America were living on what the land and sea provided. They hunted and fished, and where cultural tradition dictated and the soil was favorable, they farmed.

Hunters followed the game, and farmers, like farmers everywhere, tended to stay settled. This is not to say that hunters ignored the fruits of the soil or that farmers didn't hunt and fish. Hunters used edible wild plants and traded with farmers for produce. Farmlands were surrounded by game, and farmers hunted and fished seasonally as farmers are wont to do anywhere. Trade was common, and through a series of exchanges, goods and commodities moved up, down, and across the land.

Buffalo, deer, and fish were the main sources of animal meat inland; fish and other seafoods were principal on the coasts; and fish, sea mammals, and caribou provided not only meat but most material needs across the top of the continent from the Atlantic to the Pacific. For the natives of the East and West coasts, the wealth of the seas was at their doorstep. "When the tide went out, the table was set," the saying goes; and everywhere small game and wildfowl rounded out the meat supply.

The Hunters: From east to west and north to the Arctic, Indian or Eskimo, the nomadic hunters all had one thing in common: The manner in which they prepared food was a matter of expediency. A particular method was not confined to any one tribe or nation. Cooking was done by the means suitable to the raw materials at hand.

Fish and game were cooked in beautiful clay pots or in underground pits, roasted on a spit or broiled on a rack over coals, or wrapped in mud, clay, or wet leaves and buried in the coals. Food was hot-stone boiled in baskets, boxes, earthen pots, bags of hide or paunch, or in a hide-lined hole in a tree stump or in the ground. Everywhere meats and fish were hung to dry in sun and smoke to preserve them for the leaner days to come.

The cooking method used depended largely on the availability of fuels, which in the absence of forest, could be anything with latent heat from buffalo chips (dried dung) in the West to seal oil or peat moss in the North.

In general these early North Americans preferred most of their foods cooked. The Eskimos' liking for raw meat and fish (the word *Eskimo* means "raw meat eater") was probably conditioned by thousands of years of coping with the sparse and/or inefficient fuels of their environment.

In their manner of living, these primitive hunters and fishermen across the country set a survival pattern for the early explorers and settlers, and for the woodsmen and sportsmen who have followed in the pursuit of their vocations and recreation.

The Farmers: Where the land was fertile, the Indians cultivated it. Plains tribes farmed the area now known as the Midwest, raising corn, beans, and squashes; as mentioned earlier they also hunted and fished the local fields and streams. They traded corn, beans, and wild rice with the hunters for buffalo meat and hides, and eventually for horses. They cooked by stone boiling.

In the Southwest, the agricultural Pueblos cultivated corn and vegetables indigenous to the region. They lived chiefly from their harvests and were not dependent on hunting. They ground

corn into flour and made their tortillas on hot slabs of stone. (They grew the chili peppers that were to give the one-, two-, and three-alarm ratings to Texas' famous dish. See The McTees' Two-Alarm Chili.)

In the Northeast, from the lower Great Lakes region and the St. Lawrence Valley southward, farming was done extensively. The Iroquois—the Five Nations occupying what is now New York State—and their enemy kinsmen the Huron and the Neutrals of Southern Ontario farmed on a large scale.

With established domiciles and hardwood plentiful, the Iroquois were masters of open-hearth cooking. They cultivated numerous vegetables, among them many varieties of corn, beans, and squashes, and they used wild plant foods as well. They hunted and trapped deer, ducks, turkeys, pigeons, beaver, and small game in the woods around them; they fished the teeming lakes and streams as well. The Iroquois larder was well stocked. The Iroquois gave considerable attention to the preparation of food, and to them we owe the basic principles of big- and small-game cookery.

To the southern Indian farmers, we owe what has become synonymous with cooking of the Old South—the many uses of corn, such as in clambakes, chowder, corn breads, fish fries, and turkey stuffings.

A Provident People: Before the white man came, the Indians of North America on the whole, and certainly the Eskimos, were of necessity provident people. Though not consciously conservative of wildlife, they generally ate everything edible of their quarry and utilized the rest in various ways.

The blood was made into pudding and other confections. In his journals the explorer Samuel Hearne described a dish called "beattee": "Handy to make . . . a kind of haggis made with blood, a good quantity of fat shred small, some of the tenderest of the flesh, together with the heart and lungs of the animal cut or torn into small shivers, all of which is put into the stomach and roasted by being suspended before the fire with a string. . . . it is a most delicious morsel, even without pepper, salt or any seasoning." Hearne warned of the importance of not overfilling the stomach lest it burst during cooking.

"Caribou moss" is still used in the far Northwest. The first stomach of the freshly killed caribou is left undisturbed for three days, and then the contents are used like sauerkraut. This is considered the only way to eat caribou moss, which is a scurvy preventive.

The brain, another delicacy, was used in the processing of buckskin as well. Implements were made from the antlers, drumheads from buckskin, hair oil from shinbone marrow, snowshoe laces from sinew. As one historian put it, "These native Americans used everything from the deer except its vocal sounds, and these were imitated in tribal rites" (W.P. Taylor, ed., *Deer of North America*, 1956, The Stackpole Company).

Many of the natives' religious principles dictated a natural economy. The trapper was never to throw the skinned body of an animal on the ground—that meant bad hunting. The porcupine was not to be molested, as it was the bearer of news.

Most Indians used the oils of animals and birds for medicinal purposes. The hoof of the left hind foot of an elk* was said to possess such remarkable properties that miraculous cures were credited to it.

---

*Probably a moose. The Latin *alces* or French *élan* was the word for the European elk and was given by the early explorers to the moose, which resembled it. To add to the confusion, the wapiti, known since the time of the first settlers as the North American elk, is really a big deer. French settlers were inclined to call any unfamiliar member of the deer family *élan*. Fortunately, when it comes to cooking, it's all venison.

THE METHODS OF COOKING

In the East

Pits and Pots: When the *coureurs de bois* joined the Indians in the woods of New France, they encountered a strange cuisine. This was the ancient pit method of underground cooking. Pits, dug deep in sandy ground and floored with stones, were fired with hardwoods until there was a deep bed of coals and the surrounding sand sizzled to water. The pits ranged in size from sand holes to accommodate a bird or a fish to deep pits big enough for joints of moose.

The meat, fish, or fowl encased in clay was buried in the coals and covered with the hot sand. Another fire was built over the covered pit and allowed to burn out. The food was then left to cook slowly in its own juices, with full retention of moisture and flavor. A simple, weatherproof method, its great advantage was that all preparations could be made beforehand, whether for full-dress feasting, for dinner to be ready on return from the day's hunt, or for breakfasting on fish or fowl.

All we know of these deep pits of the Northeast, other than what has come to us through tradition and legend, has come to light through artifacts and relics uncovered in recent archaeological excavations. In 1957 excavations at Inverhuron Provincial Park in Bruce County, Ontario, uncovered

pits, dated at around 1000 B.C., used by an ancient pre-Iroquois culture. Some were big enough to accommodate large joints of meat and had been used only once. This is probably because when the huntsmen brought down a large animal, they found it more convenient to move the camp to the kill than to undertake the arduous task of bringing the animal back to camp.

Champlain wrote of the squaws emerging from the woods at the site of a kill and setting up camp. Here the Indians gathered and feasted as long as meat remained. (They were a very convivial people, and the kill itself was occasion for a *tabagie*, or feast. So was any event—even the piercing of a new baby's ears.) It is said that the Algonquins kept their tents closed until all had eaten so the animals would not be offended by the waste of meat.

In Algonquin Park in Ontario and throughout northern Quebec, loggers, trappers, and sportsmen have reported finding small sand holes of undetermined age that bore signs of repeated use, indicating a campsite. (It should be noted that sand-hole beans, favored to this day by Quebec woodsmen, was originally an Indian dish, cooked underground in earthen pots.)

The superiority of the *coureurs de bois'* metal cookware over stone, wood, clay, or birch bark quickly became apparent to the Indians. For their part, the French always knew a fine method of cooking when they saw it, and with their native culinary flair, they extended pit cooking to pot roasts and stews, and added their potions to the pot. In the meeting to the two remote cultures, the combination of pits and pots marked the beginning of an exciting northern outdoor cookery that has survived for 300 years by virtue of its simplicity, excellence, and expediency.

However novel it was to the *coureurs de bois*, pit cooking is, of course, of prehistoric origin, universally practiced. No doubt it came with the first North Americans across the Alaskan land link from Asia and followed the paths of their migrations, adapting along the way. From the clambakes on the East Coast to the underground ovens of the West Coast Indians 5,000 miles away, pits were used in one form or another. As we'll see later, somewhere en route they met the barbecue moving up from the South and merged to give us that culinary spectacular of the North American West, the deep-pit barbecue.

On the Open Hearth: Fur trade with the French and metal cookwares reached the Iroquois farming tribes at about the same time, during the seventeenth century. Prior to this the Indian farmer hunted for festive or practical needs, but it seems the hunt and the feast were of double benefit. That is, the kill was occasion for a feast, and the feast occasion for a kill.

The Iroquois cooked by dry heat on the open hearth and boiled in lovely pottery suspended over the fire. Three basic cooking procedures were determined by the meat to be cooked. These three procedures are a guide to successful North American game cookery, outdoors or in the kitchen (see Iroquois open-hearth cookery table).

Like most Indians, the Iroquois were skilled in boning game meats, birds, and fish. The tenderizing properties of pine and cedar (they wrapped the meat in the branches) and juniper berries certainly were known to them.

Maple sap (and syrup or sugar) flavored the soups, basted the roasts, and sweetened the general diet of the eastern natives. It was used not by the Iroquois alone but wherever the maple tree occurred. The northeastern Indians used maple smoke to cure meat in much the same way that maple smoke was later used to make Quebec maple-cured bacon and ham products of worldwide prestige.

IROQUOIS OPEN-HEARTH COOKERY

Method	Meat	Procedure
Twice-boiling*	*Tough cuts* Big game such as venison and bear; old small game.	Meat parboiled in first pot; fat and oils saved; soup made from stock. Meat transferred to second pot and made into stews.

Method	Meat	Procedure
Once-boiling* and broiling over coals	*Oily or fat meats* Fall bear, owl, and aquatics such as beaver, muskrat, otter, and fat waterfowl.	Meat boiled in pot; fat and oils saved; soup made from stock. Meat removed and broiled over coals. "Boiling out" excessive oils improves flavor and texture.
Roasting or broiling over coals	*Fine tender meats* *Lean*: venison, fowl, small animals. *Fat*: young fall bear and small fat animals.	Meat dry-roasted, quickly, over coals on stick or green hardwood spit. Lean meat larded and seared to preserve moisture. Fat meat self-larded, excess fat is rendered out.

*Boiling done with maple sap when it's available.

The iron kettle marked a major advance in sugaring over the evaporation and freeze-drying methods in use. The last was described by Samuel Drake in 1799: "Squaws began to make sugar. We

had no large kettles with us this year, and they made the frost in some measure supply the place of fire in making sugar. Shallow pans—take off ice. I asked them if they were not taking away the sugar. They said no; it was water they were casting away—sugar did not freeze and there was scarcely any in the ice."

The iron and copper kettles, or *chaudières*, gave title to the robust soups now identified with New England. It isn't known from whom the New England settlers learned to make their clam and fish chowders. The Indians of the Carolinas already had a hearty stew of clams, with fish and/or small game and fowl and vegetables, and a seasonal stew they called succotash,* simmering in an earthen pot over the fire when the white people arrived. In any event, it appears that the clam chowder borrowed its substance from the Algonquian stew and its name from the Frenchman's *chaudière*, the huge kettle that replaced the beautiful but less durable earthenware on the hearth.

In the West

For the Plains people, hunter and farmer, the buffalo was the source of meat. The quarry did not come easily, and the hunt, regardless of the manner of the kill, was only for food, clothing, shelter, and the other material needs that the buffalo fulfilled.

Fresh meat was hot-stone boiled in earthen pots where convenient or in the more durable, portable bags of hide. Stone boiling was not confined to the Plains; it was used anywhere that fuel was sparse or simply as a booster to the fire. Stone boiling is believed to be the earliest method of boiling, predating the use of pottery for boiling. Hot-stone boiling still provides a practical aid in outdoor cooking, even where fuel is no problem.

As elsewhere, drying of meat was done extensively by the Plains Indians. Indeed, dried wild buffalo sustained the explorers of the North American West.

Buffalo tongues were a delicacy then as now. After a successful hunt, the Comanche held a ceremonial feast called the Buffalo Tongue Dance, which was actually a thanksgiving dinner but with no dancing. The rest of the buffalo meat was used fresh or dried into jerky and pounded into pemmican to provide against lean days or for hunters' provisions.

When the overland explorers and traders from the East arrived with iron and copper kettles in which to cook the Indians' buffalo meat, they also brought an insatiable market for the hide of the buffalo, an extravagant appetite for its tongue and hump, and firearms. With swift horses moving up from the South, all this hunting attracted white men and neighboring Indian tribes alike, and the buffalo was no match for the onslaught. By the end of the nineteenth century, on the plains and prairies, the Indians' kettle was empty.

From the South

Meanwhile, the barbecue had been working its way northward. *Barbecue*, a word rooted in the tongue of a West Indian Carib tribe, means a rack of interwoven poles used for drying and smoking meats and fish and, among other practical uses, for sleeping. It seems that its current use as a device for broiling first came to light in Virginia.

The French artist LeMoyne, who accompanied French explorers to Florida in 1564, described the barbecue as used for smoke-drying fish and meat. Another artist, John White, who was with

---

*A nourishing, tasty concoction of tender corn cut from the cob at the milk stage, stewed with beans, and with fish or dog meat added for flavor.

Raleigh in Roanoke in 1585, described a similar arrangement: "Laying their fish vppon this hurdle, they made a fyre vnderneathe to broile the same, not after the manner of the people of Florida, which do but schorte [salt] and harden their meat in the smoke only to reserve the same duringe all the winter. For this people [in Roanoke] reservinge nothinge for store, they do broile . . . and when as the hurdle cannot holde all the fishes, they hange the rest by the fyres on sticks sett upp on the grounde against the fyre. . . . They take good heede that they bee not burntt."

The arrangement for cooking involved a grid or a rack of green poles supported by stones over a wood fire. It offered great versatility and maneuverability (similar to a kitchen range). Fish and game were broiled directly over the fire, doubtless picking up a flavor of smoke, or were cooked in earthen pottery on the rack.

Whether the method of barbecuing moved northward through the Southwest and the Midwest via the peculiar system of intertribal communication, or whether the exploring La Salle and LeMoyne brothers recognized it as a superior setup for open-fire cooking, is uncertain. It is likely that the replacement of the wood poles with iron grating, which made the barbecue more practical in timberless country, had a lot to do with its northward course through the plains. In any event, from the southwestern states to the Prairie provinces, westerners took the barbecue to their hearts and hearths. In fact, it has traveled the plains, hills, and seashores of North America to become a fixture at our back doors.

To the West Coast

As explorers from the East moved into the Rocky Mountains, others had already reached the Pacific shores by sea, bringing trade goods and metal wares which soon made their way inland.

The Indians of the Northwest Coast from northern California to the Alaska panhandle region lived on the generous bounty of land and sea, but the diets and cooking methods of the Indians living in the interior differed somewhat from those of the Indians along the seashore.

In the Interior: The natives of the interior lived along river drainage systems and followed the salmon as their seasonal migrations dictated. They hunted deer, elk, mountain goat and sheep, bears, and small game. They hunted caribou and moose in the northerly regions and crossed onto the prairies in search of buffalo.

Though cooking techniques were few, they were effective and the menu never wanted for variety. An abundance of fruits and vegetables flourished in the lush valleys and on the mountainsides. Underground baking was used mostly for roots, though meats and anything else that required long cooking also went into the underground oven. The method differed from the eastern hardwood charcoal pits in that softwoods and hot stones were used.

On a festive scale, this baking was a remarkable affair. A pit, about 2½ feet deep, was dug; it was made large enough in area so that all the food to be cooked could be spread out. The bottom was covered with large, flat stones, the pit was filled with a great heap of dry firewood, and small stones were scattered over all. The wood was kindled, and as it burned down, the small hot stones and embers fell through to the bottom. The unburned wood was then removed, and the red-hot stones covered with a thin layer of damp earth. Next were added layers of berry-bush branches, broken firewood branches, pine needles, and fir branches. The food was spread evenly over the top layer and covered with more fir branches, pine needles, and then fir branches again. The whole thing was covered with earth, and a huge fire was kindled on top. Enormous quantities of food cooked in 12 to 24 hours.

Sometimes poles were worked through to the hot stones, then withdrawn, and as water was poured into the holes, the food steamed.

By the Seashore: The Indians along the Pacific coast rarely hunted inland; indeed, they tended to avoid the forests, and only festive needs might occasion a big-game hunt in the mountains. Fish, easily come by, were the mainstay of the diet. Waterfowl furnished variety, especially the ducks, which were netted in great quantities. Shellfish were plucked from the sea. Whales provided oil and meat (the blubber, when dried, was highly esteemed). Seals yielded meat as well as oils and luxurious furs. Roots, fruits, and berries grew on the coast in the same profusion as inland, and they were used, both fresh and dried, with extravagant flair in cooking.

Indoors and out, the women broiled food over an open fire and hot-stone boiled in beautiful woven baskets and carved wooden boxes—the same ancient cooking vessels that were used before the iron kettle dominated the hearth. They baked outdoors in underground ovens.

As across the continent, a significant event was occasion for a feast. After a hunter had caught about five whales, and had trophies to prove it, he gave a feast out of deference to his quarry. This meant a *potlatch*. By giving away as much as 500 gallons of whale oil at one affair, the whaler secured his standing in the community, at least for the time being. He was also fairly certain that his own material needs would be taken care of, since his guests were obliged to return the invitation and out-do him in gift giving or suffer a loss in their own prestige.

The method of underground cooking on the coast was a more refined version of the method used in the interior. On a small scale, it was similar to the clambakes on the eastern seaboard, but the underground arrangement was more like a pressure cooker than an oven. The procedure, used for cooking roots, fish, and game, was as follows: A deep hole was dug in sandy ground, and into it red-hot stones were loaded. The stones were covered with wet seaweed or grass, on which were laid the roots or the cleaned and oiled fish, fowl, or other meats, and all was covered with more seaweed. A long pole was pushed straight down through the middle to the stones and the pit was filled with earth. Then the pole was withdrawn and water was poured into the opening, which was immediately plugged with more earth. A good head of steam formed and cooking was done in a short time.

Service was elegant—food was served in exquisitely carved bowls laid on long tablecloths with napkins woven from shredded cedar bark, fine and soft as silk.

North to the Arctic

The goose, plucked and cleaned, hangs by a string from a pole over a bed of coals—a twist of the string in passing keeps the bird turning, until done. The Swampy Cree Indians of the Hudson Bay region call this "Goose on a String."

—Walter Kenyon
Curator, New World Archaeology
Royal Ontario Museum, Toronto

As with all coastal peoples, food from the sea held a place in the Arctic diet, but with a difference. Fat was (and is) as important as meat. The Eskimo hunted the mammals of the Arctic waters and disposed of the quarry with impressive economy.

The polar bear, seal, walrus, and sea otter furnished food, fuels, and furs for the Eskimos' clothing, skins for their boats, and furnishings for their homes. The whale supplied food, ribs for their canoes and carvings, and baleen for multiple uses. Whale oil preserved their muktuk and served as winter fuel.

Nothing was overlooked as a source of food or other commodity. To the Eskimos up Greenland way, sea birds' eggs were an important dietary source, and the egg hunt was an annual expedition. After the hunt, the eggs were stuffed into an animal intestine and cached hanging from cliffs to ripen.

To the Indians of the Northwest Coast up to the Bering Sea, the oil of the olechan, or eulachon, (or hooligan, as it's called in Alaska), was an important item of barter. The tiny, smeltlike fish were scooped into baskets and boats as they entered the rivers to spawn. The olechan was so oily that when dried, fitted with a wick, and lighted, it burned like a candle; hence its nickname "candlefish."

In their igloos, the Eskimos cooked over a soapstone lamp, fueling it with oils from the blubber of sea mammals and burning the fuel with wicks of Arctic cotton (a sedge with tufted spikes), an arrangement that gave a beautiful, soft illumination but not the most efficient heat for cooking. Eskimos often ate meat raw, and they still do, even as they now avail themselves of modern fuels and facilities.

On the move, the Eskimos and their Indian neighbors cooked over an open fire, using fuels as they found them. (They still do this, although today many a Coleman campstove travels the tundra.) They cured fish and meats in the ancient universal ways, and still do. Although caribou of the barren lands were vital in the diet of the North, the inhabitants have always been trappers and much of their daily food continues to come from small game.

The old traditional cooking methods are still in use, but today the Eskimo and Indian women inside the Arctic Circle are as much at home over a kitchen range with its pots and pans, cutting the meat with a steel ulu, as they are over a moss fire on the tundra.

Whether it's a Seminole's iron kettle of soffkee (a meat stew, usually of venison) simmering on the metal grate over a wagon-wheel fire under a chickee in the Florida Everglades, or an Eskimo's muktuk curing in a 45-gallon steel drum full of whale oil, iron wares have altered the mode of North American outdoor food preparation.

Dry-Smoke Curing

Hanging up the fish and flesh with withes to drie in the ayre; they also lay them on raftes
and hurdles and make a smoake under them of a softe fire and so drie them as the Sauages
use to doe in Virginia.

—Richard Fisher
Letter from Cape Breton, 1593

Everywhere in North America the natives dried meats and fish in air and sun and smoke. Since antiquity wild meats have been preserved by dry curing, and the successful methods survived with the peoples who developed them—or more likely, those peoples survived who devised the successful methods of curing the meats. So ancient and universal is the practice of drying meats over smoke that one may speculate that its benefits were accidentally discovered as people learned that a smoky smudge kept the insects away and incidentally hastened the drying of their meat and fish. From the Tropics to the Arctic, the smoke-drying principle was the same. Fish and strips of meat were hung to dry in sun and air over smoke as provision against lean days ahead.

As the scene shifted northward and long periods of drying weather became less dependable, shelter was arranged to contain the smoke and keep things dry. The shelter might be anything from a tepee of brush or hide to a large permanent smokehouse.

On the breezy, arid plains, long strips of buffalo meat were dried and hardened into jerky. *Jerky*, an American word, comes from the Peruvian *charqui*, meaning "cut in thin strips and dried in air and breeze," or "jerked," and refers to all meat so processed in North America. The virtually indestructible meat, relieved of 80 to 90 percent of its original weight, was (and still is) pounded to a soft, stringy powder in a leather bag between stones. Blended with fat, often with berries mixed in, it became pemmican (from Cree *pimmi*, "meat"; *kan*, "fat"), the basis of our elegant potted meats, or pâtés.

Light and nourishing, jerky and pemmican sustained the nomads, including the explorers of North America and the builders of railroads. The product itself is ancient and universal. It was credited with giving the ancient Magyars of Hungary an edge over their adversaries on the march, who trailed livestock along with them.

3

Cooking by Woodfire

They found the spittes of Oke of the Sauages which had roasted meat a little before.
—Richard Fisher
Letter from Cape Breton, 1593

The cookery methods and recipes that appear in this chapter may involve the use of wood fires. When planning to use an open fire in or near bushland or any high-risk area, consult local authorities regarding safety conditions, which can change from day to day. Obtain required permissions and full information on how to build fires and how to put them out. (Also obtain information on garbage disposal.) In very dry weather, or where there is a risk of a forest fire, campfires may be forbidden, and only an approved campstove or properly controlled charcoal barbecue may be allowed.

Choose a campsite with a safe fireplace in mind. Never build a fire on rocks with crevices. Fire can travel unnoticed along the dry, rotted vegetable matter in the crevices to erupt weeks later and miles away. Don't build a fire near a rotten or fallen log or tree, under overhanging branches, on or near dry muskeg, or on dry grassland.

The best spot for a campfire is close to water, on the sandy mineral soil or smooth, clean stones and rocks of a stream or lake shore. Clear the area of all debris. Inshore or on grassland, turn over a circular area of soil or sod about 6 feet in diameter, and build the fire in the center.

The fire should be no bigger than the size required for the cooking to be done. On the trail, a very small fire will cook a few fish and boil a tea pail for lunch. Build it between two logs or stones to create a draft and support a frying pan. Drive two forked poles upright into the ground and place a crosspiece in the fork to hold the tea pail over the fire. A little fast-burning, dry softwood or small wood debris will rapidly give sufficient heat, and the fire can be quickly extinguished. Never leave a site until a fire is *out*, wet and cold to the hand.

For prolonged use, the wagon-wheel fire of the Seminoles and Miccosukees of the Florida Everglades is practical. Logs are arranged like spokes of a wheel, with the fire at the hub. As the hub ends of the logs burn, they are pushed into the fire. Fresh logs can be introduced to keep the fire going indefinitely. Called the "circle of life," this arrangement gives continuous heat with minimal effort.

If you are a novice and unsure about your ability to start a fire, take along a box of commercial barbecue fire-starters. *Never* use gasoline or campstove fuel on an outdoor (or indoor) wood fire. Use kerosene with extreme caution. Don't throw it on the fire; dip small twigs or branches in the fuel and bury them in the kindling *before* lighting.

Carry a campstove, no matter how small, for the times when it may be the only source of cooking heat allowed.

Wood-fire cookery of fish or game is divided here into three categories: deep-pit cooking, open-hearth cooking, and smoking. All three are a matter of method rather than recipe; each has its peculiar techniques, and various combinations of all three may be used.

Outdoor cooking appliances, from the campstove to the many barbecue devices, are merely substitutes for, or adaptations or modifications of, the primitive methods of applying heat to food. The fashionable terra cotta fish or chicken brick is but an adaptation of the clay pack. The slow-cooker appliance differs little in principle from the ancient sand hole or from the less ancient but old-fashioned hotbox (a well-insulated wooden chest, in which a pot of food was placed to slow-cook between two intensely heated stone disks).

DEEP-PIT COOKING

Several techniques of deep-pit, or sand-hole, cooking have evolved from the early methods used by natives in various parts of North America. Depending on the particular method, foods may be placed in an iron pot, or simply wrapped in mud or clay, and then baked in a pit or sand hole.

Pot-in-a-Pit Method (or Sand-hole Cooking)

A Dutch oven or a covered iron kettle with a bail (half-loop) handle is used in deep-pit, or sand-hole, cooking. Cooking time is overnight, up to 16 to 18 hours.

First, dig a pit in sandy ground 2 feet deep and just wide enough to accommodate the Dutch oven, then scatter small stones or loose gravel over the bottom to let the fire breathe. During the evening, fire the pit with green hardwood until the walls of sand are hot enough to spit back to water. This takes all evening. Meanwhile, prepare the food to be cooked and place it in the pot. When the pot is filled, cover it and seal the lid with a thick flour-and-water paste or with clay.

Using a spade, scoop out the fire, leaving coals in the bottom of the pit. Lower the Dutch oven into the pit, and cover it completely with hot sand from the sides of the pit. Rake the remaining fire back over the pit and allow it to burn out.

Build the next morning's fire over the pit. Be sure the fire is out before leaving the site. Dinner will be ready at noon, and still hot by late afternoon.

The sand-hole cooking of the *coureurs de bois* is still a favorite of eastern guides and trappers. Today the method is the same, but the modern food industry has changed the bill of fare. Soup and sauce mixes, dehydrated vegetables, instant fare of all sorts are now the wonder foods of the bush. Once limited in variety because of their bulk and weight, provisions now travel in pocket packets, flavored with seasonings and spices that have traveled halfway around the world to enrich the woodsman's kettle.

Partridge and Cabbage Casserole

2 partridges, cleaned, skinned or plucked, and split
2 tablespoons bacon fat
½ pound salt pork, diced
½ cup flour, seasoned with salt and pepper
1 tablespoon onion flakes, or 1 or 2 onions, sliced
2 small cabbages, quartered

Heat the bacon fat in a Dutch oven and brown the salt pork. Dredge the partridge in the flour mixture and brown in the hot fat. Add the quartered cabbage and onion flakes. Cover with water and add a dash of whiskey, if handy. Seal the Dutch oven as directed and cook by deep-pit method.

Variation: Use 1 partridge and 1 rabbit, dressed and jointed. Or use 2 small rabbits.

Pot roasts and stews of big and small game may be cooked in the sand hole. See recipes for venison and small game. Prepare as usual, seal the pot, and cook in the sand hole as directed.

Sand-Hole Clay Baking

Wrapping a fish or fowl in clay and baking it in a sand hole is an ancient method used wherever wood and clay or mud occur. Hardwood with its long lasting coals is desirable. Where softwood fuels and their short-lived coals are used, stones are heated in the fire and used to boost the heat in the pit. The clay considered best is the blue-gray clay from riverbeds or from under the sand at water's edge of lake or bay. Where clay is lacking, a heavy malleable mud substitutes as second best.

Only a freshly caught fish, or a freshly killed bird cleanly shot in the neck or head, should be cooked by this method. Bleed the fish through the throat; bleed the bird by cutting off the head. Don't clean the fish, or pluck or draw the bird. Let either drain while preparing the pit.

Dig a pit in sandy soil, big enough to hold the game with several inches to spare. Fire the pit with hardwood until there are enough coals to bury the bird or fish in its clay coating.

Meanwhile encase the entire bird or fish in wet clay. Scoop a hole in the coals and bury the package. Cover the coals with clay. Build a fire over the clay and let it die *out*. Leave while away for the day, or 5 to 8 hours. Break away the clay—the feathers or scales and skin will come with it. Split the bird or slit the fish, and the innards will fall out in pebble form. Cooked in its own juices, the flesh is sweet and succulent.

Shallow Pit Mud Pack

Make a shallow pit in sandy soil and in it build a fire. Add hardwood to build up a deep bed of coals. Throw in a few small stones, about 2 inches in diameter.

Dress the fish, leaving on the head and tail. Rub the cavity with bacon fat. Fill with damp fresh wild herbs or clean grass. Tuck in two or three of the hot stones, then close the cavity with twigs. Coat the fish well with thick wet mud or slick clay. Rake back the coals making room for the fish, leaving a layer of coals in the bottom of the pit. Place the fish in the coals and rake the surrounding coals over top. Add some small wood and let it burn down. When the fish is ready, in about an hour, remove it from the coals and crack away the mud—the skin comes with it. Remove the herbs and stones from the cavity. Serve with salt, pepper, and lemon juice.

OPEN-HEARTH COOKING

Wherever fuel is available, the open hearth is the most common means of wood-fire cookery. Its scope and versatility are boundless. Depending on the size of the hearth, you can broil a bird or roast a haunch of venison on it. You can fry fish in a pan or bury them to bake in the coals, wrapped in leaves and mud or foil—or sandwiched prospector style between two gold pans. Put a barbecue rack over the fire, and besides barbecuing, you can make soups, stews, or pot roasts. In fact, if you have the ingredients, most pot and kettle recipes given in the general cookery chapters can be used on the rack over the open fire. You can even bake a bannock.

Broiling over the Coals

The time-honored method of cooking by wood fire is simply the direct application of intense, dry heat—that is, broiling. It is a quick method, ideal for fish flesh and fine, tender young wild meats.

Broiling may be done over, under, and beside the fire—by any arrangement that exposes the flesh to, and within quick cooking distance of, the source of heat. This includes barbecuing, grilling, spit-roasting, planking, or any other method that fits the definition of broiling. While the desert nomads of the Middle East were shish-kabobing on their swords, the Indians of North America were skewer-broiling on their forked poles.

BROILING GAME

Lean game animals and wildfowl tend to dry out in dry heat and need to be well larded. Steaks and chops should be cut thick. And these, as well as cuts of hare and squirrel, and split birds, should be coated well with fat on all sides before broiling. Thick chunks of venison should be larded outside and inside. For whole fowl, small hare, or squirrel, stuff the cavities with rolled strips of bacon or chunks of fat salt pork, and lard the surfaces. Strips of fat bacon may be skewered or wired around the meat. Naturally fat game, such as fall bear and fat small animals, need no larding.

Small Cuts: Relatively small cuts of game may be impaled on a larded green pole and then cooked over deep coals. They also may be broiled in a wire toaster or on a barbecue rack.

For variety, skewer three or four small chunks of venison on a stick. Dip in brandy or whiskey and sear off in the fire. Brush the meat with fat and broil over the coals.

Large Cuts, Whole Fowl, and Small Game: Spit-broiling is used to cook large, thick cuts of meat, whole fowl, and small game animals over an open hearth. Cut a green hardwood pole strong enough to support the meat, and trim off the branches at an angle, leaving sharp barbs on which to secure the meat. Drive stout forked poles into the ground on either side of the fire to support the spit.

Run the barbed pole or spit through the larded bird or meat, giving the spit a backward jerk to set the barbs and hold the meat securely as it is turned. Arrange the spit over a bed of glowing coals, protected from the wind. The coals should be deep enough to last until the meat is cooked, and sufficient in area for the meat to be exposed to a fairly uniform heat.

Sear the meat quickly all over, quite close to the coals. Raise the spit so that the meat is close enough to the heat to cook but far enough from it to avoid scorching and flames from dripping fat. Turn frequently, basting the lean meats often with fat or a barbecue sauce. A chunk of fat impaled on a pole and stuck into the ground or a pile of rocks so as to hang over the roast will provide automatic basting as it melts over the cooking meat. Keep water handy (in a squirt or spray bottle) to extinguish flames from the dripping fat.

Note that small game and fat big game such as bear and pigs require thorough cooking. Bear is best broiled in individual, thinly cut portions until well done.

BROILING FISH

On a Forked Pole: Clean and scale a 1- to 2-pound fish leaving the head on. Cut a fresh, long, slender green hardwood pole. Cut off the end at about little-finger thickness; trim branches, leaving four or five sharp barbs ½ to 1 inch long, depending on the size of the fish.

Season the cavity of the fish; if there is wild sorrel, mint, or aromatic seaweed around, tuck some in the cavity. Slip the pole through the mouth of the fish, wrap the body around the pole, and close the body with wood skewers. Hold the fish in one hand and jerk the pole to set the barbs. Brush the fish with fat. Stick the pole in the ground, propping it securely with stones, beside a good campfire, or hold it over the coals, or spit-cook it as described above for small game. Turn frequently until cooked.

In the Round: Broiling fish in the round, ungutted, is a favorite method for pompano along the Florida beaches and for freshwater walleye and trout in northern Ontario.

Run the pole or skewer through the fish and hold it or put it on supports over the coals. Turn the fish so it cooks to a crisp gold on both sides. Then slit the fish up the middle; the innards and pole come away, leaving the succulent fish.

On a Skewer (Fillets): Scale and fillet a firm-fleshed fish, leaving the skin on. (The skin helps to hold the pieces of fish together.) Cut the fillets into chunks. Make a skewer from a slim, freshly peeled green hardwood pole, leaving small barbs at one end.

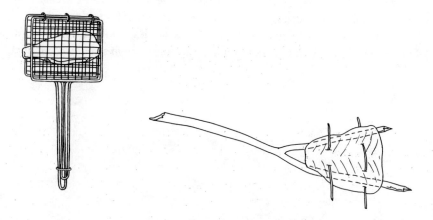

Skewer a couple of chunks of fish on the pole, giving them a little push to set the barbs. Brush the fish with fat, dust it lightly with flour, and hold it over the coals, turning it until nicely browned. Fish cooks very quickly; don't overcook it or it may fall into the fire. An elaborate form of this arrangement is the colorful, popular patio dish of *shish kabob*, cooked on stainless steel skewers, far removed from wood fires and forked poles.

Over the Coals (Fillets and Steaks): Wipe the fillets or steaks with a damp cloth or paper towel and cut them into serving-size portions. If the fish is lean, brush it well with oil or melted butter; if it's fat, sprinkle it with lemon juice or vinegar. Make a basting sauce of melted fat (or oil), lemon juice, salt, pepper, and a sharp sauce (optional), adding seasonings to taste. Mix in a few drops of vodka or whiskey.

Grease a hinged wire grill and put the fillets or steaks in it. Baste them well with the sauce, and grill them over the hot coals a few minutes on each side, basting frequently. A secure grill may be improvised from slim green forked poles or switches, the fillets or steaks "woven" into it with twigs.

Indian-Style Planked Fish: Clean the fish, rinse it, and wipe it dry. Cut through the ribs from the inside just to one side of the backbone and flatten the fish. Select a piece of heavy bark, or use a board about a foot longer than the fish. Heat the plank by the fire. Fasten the fish to it securely by the tail, scales next to the concave side of the bark. Season and baste the flesh with cooking oil or fat. If the fish is lean, fasten a couple of strips of bacon from the tail end to furnish some basting. Support the bark with sticks and stones, propping it upright, tail-end up, in front of a good campfire. Baste the fish occasionally with oil or fat as it cooks. When the fish is golden brown and the flesh flakes to a prod, lift out the bones, add salt, pepper, and lemon juice, and eat right from the bark.

With this method, one needn't wait for a bed of coals. It's done facing the campfire and not directly exposed to the flames. The plank may be moved around to avoid smoke. (See "Broiling" in Chapter 8.)

Birds, split-dressed, may be planked as described for fish; flattened, the birds are fastened to the plank skin-side out.

Baking over the Coals

Big Fish over the Coals: Be it dolphin off Key West, or lake trout from Great Bear Lake, Wayne Andrew of Port Credit, Ontario, cooks the big ones by baking them in foil over the coals. Ingredients are no problem wherever he is—he carries everything he needs as part of his fishing tackle. This is his method:

Fillet a lake trout or dolphin of around 10 pounds or less. Skin the fillets and wipe them clean. Tear off two pieces of heavy-duty aluminum foil, each big enough to completely wrap the fillets laid

side by side, and place one on top of the other to make a double thickness. Grease the top side of the foil with bacon fat or oil, and then lay the fillets on the foil. Spread slices of green pepper, slices of lemon (Andrew uses 2 lemons), and about 2 cups of chopped, canned or fresh tomatoes over the fish. Add salt and pepper to taste.

Double fold the edges of the foil around the fish (in drugstore style) to seal the package. Place it on a grill over a deep bed of coals—not too close—letting everything cook in the contained juices. The fish should be done in 30 to 40 minutes, depending on the heat of the coals.

Breast of Grouse over the Coals

Allow 1 bird per serving, or 1 large bird for 2 servings. Pluck or skin, and remove the breasts from the bird. Wash and wipe them clean. (Partridge, duck, and wild goose may be used instead of grouse.)

Tear off aluminum foil, to use double ply, large enough to wrap the breasts and everything that goes into the package. Oil the top side of the foil well or grease it with bacon fat. Place a slice of bacon, cut in two, in the center. Place the meat on the bacon, and sprinkle about ½ teaspoon of onion soup mix over the top. Cover with slices of potato and carrot and a slice of onion. Dab with margarine, or lay a couple of slices of bacon over the top. Seal the package drugstore style and place it on the rack 4 to 6 inches above the glowing coals. Turn the package over from time to time. Lower the rack as the coals burn down.

After about an hour, open and tear back the foil with tongs. Season to taste and eat from the foil.

Rabbit, Squirrel: Dress and cut in serving portions. Cook as for Breast of Grouse.

Fish: Cook pan-size dressed fish whole; fillet, split, or cut larger fish into individual portions. Wrap oiled vegetables separately in foil, and give them a head start in the fire. A 1- to 2-pound fish should cook in 30 to 40 minutes, depending on the heat of the coals and the thickness of the fish.

Baking in the Coals

The principle behind the ancient practice of wrapping fish and game in mud, clay, or foliage and baking it in the coals (see Chapter 2) has various applications on the open hearth. One is the wrap of flour-and-water dough encased in aluminum foil described in the recipe for Campfire Venison which follows. Fish, fowl, rabbits, squirrels, and similar game may be cooked in this way. Dressed small game or fish also may be packed or wrapped in damp green foliage, grasses, seaweed, grape leaves, or corn husks, depending on where you're cooking and on what's available; dampened newspaper is commonly used in northern Ontario in the same way as the flour-and-water dough, all wrapped in foil. The meat comes out clean and moist, with all the natural flavors locked in. Skin and scales peel away from a fish.

Small game and fish should be dressed "oven ready." Fish need not be scaled. Pluck or skin birds, and skin small animals. Wash each well and wipe dry. Rub all over with fat, including the cavity. Tuck in sprigs of herbs and seasoning—whatever is available—and a few chunks of fat bacon. Wrap the fish or game in one of the materials just described.

With the variables involved in wood-fire cooking, timing is a matter of judgment and good guessing. Once the fire is hot, venison, small game, and fowl take about 30 minutes per pound (total package); fish about 20 minutes (a 3- to 4-pound pike wrapped cooks in 1½ to 2 hours) as long as an adequate bed of coals in maintained.

Campfire Venison

2- to 3-pound roast of venison
  (properly aged)
4 cups flour
Margarine or bacon fat
8 strips fat bacon (approximately)
Seasonings as available

Make a stiff, manageable dough of the flour and 1½ to 2 cups of water. Roll dough into a circle about ½-inch thick. Spread the dough with margarine or bacon fat, or whatever shortening you have. Lay 3 or 4 strips of fat bacon on the dough and sprinkle with available seasonings.

Put the meat on the bacon. Put the remaining bacon strips on top of the meat. Bring up the dough and seal. Wrap in foil. Place in hot coals at the edge of a wood fire. Rake some coals onto the top of the foil package. Arrange a reflector to windward. Turn the package occasionally, raking fresh coals over the top. Cook for 1 to 1½ hours.

Gold Pan Salmon

Dress the salmon to fit the pan—whole, pan-dressed, or filleted. Put a layer of clean, damp grasses in the bottom of a gold pan. Rub the cavity of the fish with fat and sprinkle it with seasonings as desired or available. Cover with more damp grass and top with another gold pan, inverted. Seal the edge of the pans with mud or clay. Push away the coals from the center of a campfire and put in the pan of salmon. Rake coals back over the top and let the fish bake for an hour.

Barbecuing

Laying their fish vppon this hurdle, they make a fyre vnderneathe to broile the same.
—John White
Artist with Raleigh
Roanoke Island, 1585

The primitive barbecue may be a rack of green poles supported by stones or logs across a bed of wood-fire coals in a shallow pit dug in the ground. Or it may be a fireplace built up of stones, supporting a rack across the top. The size and sturdiness are in proportion to the size or amount of meats to be cooked, and apparently the early barbecue was used chiefly for fish and small game.

Barbecuing, like all outdoor cooking, is a matter of method rather than recipe. Durable sheet iron and gratings have replaced wood poles and logs and extended the usefulness of the barbecue. Open pits are built above ground with cement blocks, some pits virtually amounting to outdoor cookstoves. All pot and kettle recipes can be used on the open-pit barbecue.

NATIVE-STYLE OPEN-PIT BARBECUE

For small-scale open-pit barbecuing, dig a shallow pit about a foot longer and a foot wider than needed to accommodate the meats without crowding. The depth of the pit depends on the thickness of the meat—the coals must last until the meat is cooked. A haunch of young deer should have a good 6 to 8 inches of coals under it, while fish cooks very quickly and requires a relatively shallower bed of coals.

Build up a bed of hardwood coals in the pit. Lay green logs or poles along each side of the pit. Place green poles or iron rods parallel across the pit from log to log, close enough together to support the meat. Over this framework place a sheet of strong wire mesh, such as chicken wire. Arrange reflectors to windward if necessary to protect the fire and retain the heat.

Place the dressed meat or fish on the mesh, and cook until tender turning frequently and basting at the same time with a heated barbecue sauce.

All broiling and barbecue recipes in the cookery chapters can be used on the open-pit barbecue.

The grand-scale barbecues, the famous "Pig Pickin'" of North Carolina, and the mammoth salmon barbecues by the Indians at Kiana ("happy place") on Sandy Hook across Puget Sound from Seattle, Washington, are simply an extension of the open-pit barbecue—iron grating across a pit built of cement blocks above ground. The long, narrow pits at Kiana can be fired to any extent required and have served as many as 2,400 people at one barbecue.

DEEP-PIT BARBECUES

Just when and how the barbecue went underground is vague, but somewhere along the line, rack and pit met to give us that culinary spectacular of the North American West—the full-scale pit barbecue.

Oklahoma-Style Pit-Barbecued Venison: Pit-barbecued venison was a specialty of the late H. Clay Potts. The instructions were written by Potts when he was with the Cooperative Extension of Oklahoma State University at Stillwater and appear here through the courtesy of that body.

When selecting venison to be barbecued, keep in mind that the better the quality, the more delicious the product will be after cooking. If a generous serving is desired, ½ pound of boned, uncooked meat should be allowed per person. Cut, bone, and roll the meat with plenty of larding into chunks of about 10 pounds each. Wrap the chunks in parchment crinkle paper and then in burlap and tie them with butcher's twine. Since the chunks of wrapped meat are to be thrown on live coals, wet the burlap wrapping, just before the meat is placed in the pit, to prevent it from catching fire. This may be done by dipping the wrapped chunks in a tub of water.

The length of the trench will depend on the number of pounds of meat to be barbecued. A trench 10 feet long, 3½ feet deep, and 3 feet wide will be sufficient for barbecuing 400 pounds of meat. Be sure the dirt is thrown back far enough from the trench to leave room to walk around it.

Cover the trench and seal it as quickly as possible after the meat has been placed in it so there will be no loss of steam. The most convenient covering is a piece of sheet iron. Boards cleated together may be used. Be sure that the top of the trench is level and that the covering is properly measured to cover the top of the pit. Seal the cracks by placing wet sand over the edges of the covering, and put a tarpaulin or something waterproof over the lid to keep out rain.

Place the meat in the pit about 7 hours before serving time. No harm will be done if it is put in earlier, for after 7 hours the fire will have died down sufficiently that there will be no danger of overcooking. Remove the venison from the pit and serve immediately. Barbecue sauce and salt can be added when served.

Prairie-Style Barbecue: On the prairies, westerners cope with a dearth of hardwood by bringing the Plainsmen's hot stones back into service for their deep-pit barbecue.

Alongside a pit (6 feet long by 4 feet wide by 6 feet deep for 400 pounds of meat), enough good-sized rocks to fill half the pit are loaded on a heavy framework of scrap metal such as old plow beams or mower wheels. A fire of old fence posts or other scrap wood, helped along by coal, is built underneath the framework and is kept up until the stones are red hot. The stones are then dumped into the pit. Sheet iron is placed over the coals. The meat is dressed and wrapped as described for Oklahoma-style pit-barbecued venison except that it is wrapped in a flour-and-water paste instead of parchment. After the wrapped meat is placed in the pit, the pit is closed with sheet iron and covered with a foot of earth. The meat (400 pounds) cooks in 10 to 12 hours.

Woodfire Ovens

Reflector Oven: Biscuits, bannocks, and corn breads can be baked over the coals in a reflector oven. A fish, even a stuffed one, also can be baked in such an arrangement.

A reflector oven for baking can be improvised from forked poles and aluminum foil. It is simply a miniature lean-to tent or canopy of heavy-duty aluminum foil arranged shiny side in, over the grill or rack, over the coals or toward the edge, depending on the fire—flap-side facing the fire and back to windward. Handled with care, the whole thing may be collapsed and reused. (Simpler still is a portable, collapsible campstove oven.)

Mud Oven: Although a mud oven is more troublesome to prepare than a reflector oven, it is more permanent and serviceable. The following procedure for constructing a mud oven is taken from *Buckskin Cookery*, by Gwen Lewis:

Build a strong, dome-shaped canopy of twigs and willows, about 2 by 3 feet. Cover this with a layer of mud 6 inches to 1 foot thick. Leave a large square opening at one end for an oven door, and opposite, in the roof, insert a large tin can (open at both ends) for a chimney. Let the mud dry out completely, then build a fire inside and burn out all the framework. When cool, scrape the inside clean.

To prepare for baking, build a fire inside and heat the mud until red hot. Rake out the fire and ashes, and slide in the sourdough, bannocks, stew, or roast, and block the opening with a rock slab. A correctly made oven bakes beautifully.

Hot-Stone Boiling

Kept in a campfire, round, smooth stones without cracks can attain intense heat. With them, you can boil water (red-hot stones), keep food warm (hot stones), or warm your sleeping bag (medium hot and wrapped).

Two or three red- to white-hot stones, 2 to 3 inches in diameter, dropped into a pot or pail of water will bring it to a boil quickly and replacement of the stones will keep it boiling. The stones will also keep a kettle of soup or stew cooking. The immersion boiling technique of the Indians is the principle behind the modern electric kettle. In camp, the use of hot stones frees precious space on the fire.

Kettles may be improvised. A simple camp arrangement is a pit dug in the ground and lined with heavy aluminum foil or wet canvas. For a small operation, fashion a kettle from aluminum foil, or line a box with it. Or use empty cans.

and a handful of damp chips or sawdust can convert a charcoal barbecue into a minismoker to cook a few fillets of fish or to finish parboiled sausages to a smoky delicacy.

Fuels: Smoking methods are the same all over the continent, although the temperature of the smoke may vary. Apart from the type of game or fish indigenous to a locale, fuels rather than recipes account for regional distinctions in smoked fish and game meats. Different woods lend different flavors and color to the meats. (This applies to broiling and barbecuing as well.) Hardwoods are best for smoking.

On a broad scale, the regional distribution of fuels used in smoking fish and game is along the following lines:

Area	*Woods*
Eastern Canada through New England	Maple, fruitwoods
Eastern states	Fruitwoods, nutwoods
Deep South (Florida)	Florida oak (blackjack oak)
Southwest	Mesquite
West Coast	Fruitwoods, oak, roots of berry bushes
Midwest	Alder, willow, oak
North	Alder, cottonwood

Many of these woods are available in sawdust or chip form from local builders' supply outlets and furniture factories.

The rules for smoking are not hard and fast. Corncobs make a good smoke. Aromatic seaweeds are used on the coasts. On the northern tundra, successful smoking has been done with peat moss over black spruce coals. However, for actual smoking fuels, softwoods and conifers such as pine, spruce, and cedar are best avoided, as the resins impart a pungent flavor to the meat.

It's important to refuel the smoke supply without undue interruption of the heat. Live coals can be fired in advance in a separate barbecue and introduced to the fuel box. Red-hot stones and metal scrap can be used in the same way.

Modern electric smokers like this make smoking fish and game a very simple procedure.

Charcoal briquets hold a much more intense heat than wood coals. Their use is best confined to heat smoking, and they must be introduced cautiously to the fire box. The fire should never be more than smoldering. If it bursts into flame, the fire should be sprinkled immediately with a little water.

Smoking Fish

Next to milk, nature's most perfect food. Made with a magic formula which includes judicious portions of the Puritan work ethic and God's gift from the sea, blended by hand with tender, loving care. Step one: Interrupt one portion rich, energy-laden coho salmon early on her way to the hills to spawn. Before the coup de grâce, ask her forgiveness and dedicate her to a larger service. Step two: Split and ice to firm the flesh and cleanse. Step three: Cut into hand-size portions. Step four: Brine with salt and sugar, then apply generous portions of alder wood for heat and smoke.

—Lucy Crow's Smoked Salmon
Courtesy of *Kuskokwim Kronicle*
Bethel, Alaska

If the origin of smoking fish is obscure, so is the introduction of salting into the process. It's even unclear which came first, although it seems likely that salting predated smoking in coastal lands. However the combination came about, it was fortuitous for fish lovers: Salt and smoke impart the delectable flavor and texture that boosted the coarse, unmarketable Winnipeg goldeye to epicurean fame and fortune and transformed the lake sturgeon of North America into a viand in demand worldwide.

Oddly enough, it is often the coarser, fatter fishes, some low on the flavor scale, that become fare of distinction on any table when heat-smoked. The coarse grain of the flesh takes up the moisture-drawing salt and permits the aromatic smoke to permeate and gently cook the fish.

As the salt-smoke is a drying combination, the oily or fatty fishes retain a more palatable texture than the very lean ones. Nevertheless, most lean fishes take well to the salt-smoke treatment, but those of fragile flesh such as the soles are too delicate and tend to disintegrate.

Oversize fat trouts, salmons, and chars are famous smokers. The lake whitefish, cisco, sea lamprey, eel, carp, ling, shad, and catfish are all excellent smokers, as are suckers and drums. The saltwater mullet, swordfish, sablefish, bluefish, butterfish, dolphin, yellowtail, and drumfish—fishes from pan-size to too big for conventional kitchen cooking methods—are all candidates for the smokehouse.

PREPARATION AND HANDLING OF FISH IN THE SMOKER

The basic procedure for preparing fish for the smoker and its handling in the smoker are the same for cold smoking and hot smoking. These basics are given here, followed by a few special recipes.

As a rule, fish is dressed according to size and given a salt-cure treatment before it goes into the smoker. Whole fish of up to 2 to 3 pounds handle well in the smokehouse. Larger fish should be

Trout and mackerel ready for smoking in an electric smoker. Note that pieces of fish do not touch each other.

steaked, split, or filleted. Scale the fish if necessary, but don't skin it—the skin helps to hold the flesh together in the smoker. When cutting out the gills from a whole fish that is to hang in the smokehouse, take care not to cut through the collar or backbone.

Wash the dressed fish well, scrubbing the cavity until it is glistening clean, and wipe it dry. Apply a salt cure (see recipes in next section), then put the fish into the smoker. Salt-cured fish, described in Chapter 10, also may be smoked; already well cured, they require only a quick flavor-aid treatment in the smokehouse.

In the smoker, any device that will hold the fish intact and allow maximum exposure to the smoke is the one to use. The racks in the refrigerator-type smoker offer a handy arrangement for pan-size fish, small fillets, steaks, and split fish. However, all cuts get better smoke exposure by hanging. A convenient method for hanging small items is to put them in wire toasters or hinged grills and hang them from the rack on steel S-hooks, which are handy gadgets for use in both refrigerator and drum or barrel-type smokers.

For steaks, fillets, and split fish, lace butcher twine (or tough vine) through the flesh, leaving loops for hanging. Tie thick steaks or cross-cuts by running butcher twine through the thick solid part, drawing the flesh together and tying securely, leaving loops by which to hang them. Spread the cavities of individual fish with twigs or spacers, and hang on S-hooks. String small fish such as smelts on a firm wire and hang by hooks from the rack, or place them across the rack as suitable.

The fish, whole or in pieces, must not touch each other in the smoker.

SALT CURES FOR SMOKING FISH

There are two basic types of cures used to prepare fish for smoking: *dry salt*, which draws fluid from the fish to form its own brine; and *brine*, a salt-and-water solution in which the fish is immersed.

The proportions given in the following cures are for about 10 pounds of fish. Metal should not contact the cure. Use a wood, plastic, or ceramic bowl or crock, and wood or plastic spoons.

Dry Salt Cure
1 cup coarse pickling salt
½ cup brown or raw sugar
1 teaspoon black pepper, coarsely ground

Spices and herbs, singly or in combination, may be added to taste to lend variety or to develop a specialty of the house: cayenne (in pinches) or chili powder, ground cloves, curry, cardamom, sesame, caraway and cumin seeds, dill and fennel weeds, tarragon, and numerous savory seasonings of the mint family. Use fresh herbs whenever possible.

Spread a layer of plain salt over the bottom of a bowl or crock. Combine the salt, sugar, and seasonings and rub the mixture well into all exposed surfaces of the fish. Tuck fresh herbs into cavities and between layers of whole fish and between flesh sides of fillets.

Overnight curing is sufficient for small fish and fillets; bigger fish take longer. The general rule is 12 hours per pound of whole fish, or 2 days for a 4-pound fish.

Remove the fish from the cure. Rinse it well under cold water. If it's too salty, soak the fish in clear water for an hour. Hang it outside to drain in a cool, shady, breezy place, protected from insects, for about 3 hours or until a thin, shiny skin (pellicle) has formed on the surface. The fish is now ready for hot or cold smoking.

Brine Cure
1 gallon water, boiled and cooled, or demineralized
1 cup coarse pickling salt (approximately)
¼ cup brown or raw sugar, or molasses
1 tablespoon peppercorns, cracked
1 bay leaf
Dill weed or fennel

Dissolve enough salt in water to float an egg. Dissolve sugar in a small amount of brine, then stir it back into the brine. Add herbs and spices as desired to the brine (see Dry Salt Cure above). Tuck dill weed into the cavities of the fish and between the layers. Place fish in the brine. For timing and further handling, see the preceding recipe for Dry Salt Cure.

Beer and Molasses Smoker
1 cup coarse pickling salt
12 ounces beer or ale
½ cup dark molasses
1 teaspoon peppercorns, cracked
½ teaspoon whole cloves
Pinch cayenne or chili powder

Make a brine of 4 cups of water and ½ cup of the salt and set it aside. Combine the beer, molasses, remaining salt, pepper, cloves, and cayenne or chili powder and mix well. Smear this mixture over all surfaces of the fish. Put in a deep earthen bowl or crock and refrigerate for an hour or more, depending on the size of the fish—about an hour per inch of thickness.

Stir any remaining beer-molasses mixture into the prepared brine and pour over the fish. Refrigerate for 3 to 4 hours for small fish (up to 1 pound), overnight for thick cuts. Drain as directed above under Dry Salt Cure, and heat-smoke.

This cure is good for drums, sheepshead, suckers, catfish, carp, and fat, coarse-fleshed fish.

HEAT SMOKING

For heat smoking, the smoke is made in the smoker. Prepare a dense smoke, bringing the temperature up to 110° to 120° F (43° to 50° C). Put the prepared fish in the smoker. Since heat smoking is actually a cooking process, the timing varies with the size and density of the fish, the length of time in the brine, and the strength of the brine. Taste-testing will ultimately determine the degree of doneness.

A heat-smoked fish is ready when it takes on a gold-tinged gloss, is hot all the way through, and gives off an irresistible aroma. A few trial runs should put a chef at ease with the smoker. Generally, fast-cooking small fishes like smelts are ready to eat after about 30 to 40 minutes of smoking; meaty fillets may take up to 2 hours. Thick, bound sections and whole fish of 5 or 6 pounds can smoke for the better part of a long evening.

Serve the fish hot from the smoker. Heat-smoked fish may be refrigerated for a day or two and eaten cold or rewarmed. Don't freeze heat-smoked fish—it loses much of its unique quality in the freezer. Instead, freeze the fresh fish until you're ready to smoke it. Fish that has been frozen takes up the salt and smoke more readily than fresh fish and actually gives a superior product.

A pair of mackerel fillets and small trout right out of the smoker.

Barbecue-Smoked Fillets of Fish

No elaborate apparatus is required to heat-smoke a few fillets of fish. Any arrangement that directs smoke and heat to the fish will do the job—whether it's a tepee of green brush over a smudge pot or an elaborate smokehouse built for the purpose. A backyard hibachi or barbecue can be used to smoke 2 or 3 pounds of fish.

If the barbecue has a hooded cover, so much the better. If not, a deep, roomy hood can be fashioned out of a double thickness of heavy-duty aluminum foil, pinched to the edges of the barbecue to contain the smoke. A fairly shallow bed of charcoal, fired to an even glow and then covered with a layer of damp hardwood chips or sawdust, creates a hot smoke, trapped under the canopy, and will last long enough to cook the fish.

Treat the fillets with the Dry Salt Cure or Brine Cure described above. An hour or so before smoking the fish, remove it from the cure and let it drain on the oiled barbecue rack. Fire the barbecue, letting the charcoal burn down to coals and cover with damp sawdust. Place the rack and fish at the highest level, cover with a foil canopy if the barbecue does not have a hood, and let it smoke. The fish should be ready in 30 to 45 minutes, depending on the heat and on the thickness of the fillets. Don't let the fish overcook. As soon as the fish takes on a golden glaze and flakes to a prod with a fork, serve it with wedges of lime or lemon.

COLD SMOKING

For cold smoking fish on a domestic scale, the smoke is usually generated from outside the smoker and ducted into it. Put live coals in the smoke box and smother with damp hardwood sawdust or chips. Make a light-to-moderate smoke for the first 8 hours or so; then build it up to a dense, cool smoke. It should read 90° F (32° C) by thermometer or feel cool to the bare hand. If it feels warm, it's too hot.

Put the prepared fish in the smoker. Maintain this dense smoke and temperature for 1 to 2 days, during which time the fish will take on a glossy brown or gold tinge. When smoked to your liking, and it will take some experimenting, the fish is ready to eat.

Cold-smoked fish is neither cooked nor preserved. It may be temporarily refrigerated or frozen, or canned. It is excellent basted with butter and lightly broiled, or oven-poached in milk (after a soaking in water) and served with a cream sauce.

Cold-Smoked Salmon

This recipe combines salting with cold smoking to produce translucent fish with a robust smoky flavor, similar to smoked salmon available in grocery stores.

> Salmon, cleaned and filleted
> 2 cups salt
> 1 cup brown sugar
> 2 tablespoons white pepper
> 1 tablespoon each crushed bay leaves, allspice,
>   crushed whole cloves, and mace

Combine the salt, brown sugar, and other spices. Dredge salmon fillets in the salt mixture to collect as much as will adhere to the flesh. Leave for 6 to 8 hours. Rinse and scrub the fillets under running water to remove all traces of salt, then soak in running, or frequently changed, water for 4 to 6 hours. Dry in fresh air for 6 hours. If the day is damp, dry for 8 to 10 hours.

Start a fire and let it burn down to coals; the temperature of the smoke should not be over 90° F (32° C). Smoke the fish for 8 hours, then build up a dense smoke, keeping the temperature below 100° F (38° C) (using a spray of water when necessary), and continue smoking for 16 hours. It is best to keep the fire going continuously for the 24 hours, but if you must let the fire die at night, start it again in the morning. When finished, the fish is almost tender enough to spread with a knife.

— The Fisherman Returns
Cooperative Extension Service
University of Alaska, Fairbanks

Smoking Game

The combination of salt cure and smoke transforms the toughest cuts of game, old animals, and birds long past their table prime into viands of distinction. Preparation of the smokehouse and smoke, cold or hot, is the same as for fish. Use only fresh, expertly field-dressed and cared-for game meats. Frozen meats (considered fresh as opposed to cured) smoke well.

Meat should be kept under the brine by means of a weighted plate. The weight must be non-metallic—a clean brick, a pet rock, or a plastic jug filled with water or sand all make serviceable weights. Use wooden spoons to handle the meat in the brine.

Always hang salt- or pickle-cured meats by strong twine from the smokehouse hoods. Do not spear the meat on metal hooks. The twine may be run through the meat or tied securely around it, leaving a loop for hanging. Meats may be crowded in the smokehouse but must not touch each other or the sides of the smoker.

Pickle-Cured Smoked Venison,
Buffalo, Antelope, Mountain Sheep, or Goat

Use haunch or roasting cuts from the hind or shoulder, trimmed to shape, leaving only a thin layer of fat. The proportions below are sufficient to cure 10 pounds of meat.

> 1 pound salt (approximately)
> 1 pound brown sugar or maple sugar
> Saltpeter, size of a pea
> ½ teaspoon cayenne
> 8 to 10 juniper berries, crushed,
>   or 4 to 5 coriander seeds, crushed
> 2 quarts water, or enough to cover the meat

Rub half the salt well into the meat and lay it in an earthen crock, wooden or plastic tub, or a carton lined with a tough, leakproof, plastic garbage bag.

In a kettle, dissolve the remaining salt in the water. Add the rest of the ingredients and heat to boiling. Remove all scum. Boil for 10 minutes and cool. Test the strength of the brine with a fresh egg, adding more salt as necessary to float the egg. Pour the brine over the meat. Make more brine with salt and boiled water if necessary to cover the meat. Place a weighted plate or board on the meat. Cover with cheesecloth.

The meat may stay in the brine for 5 to 6 weeks or more, but since this is not a preservative curing process, the meat may go into the smoker after a day or two, according to preference.

Cold Smoke: Remove the meat from the brine the day before smoking, let it drain, then scrub it with a brush in tepid water to remove all traces of salt. If it's still too salty, freshen by soaking for a few hours in cold water, changing the water frequently. Hang the meat up to drain overnight in a cool, dry place. If insects are around, dust the meat with pepper and protect it with netting. Leave the meat in the prepared cold smoke for at least 8 hours; the longer the meat is smoked, the more distinctive its flavor will be.

To use the meat immediately after smoking, just slice thinly and serve. Brush thicker slices with a barbecue sauce and broil quickly, or sauté in butter. Leftovers can be refrigerated for several days or frozen for future use in stews or hash.

The meat also may be baked after cold smoking. Wipe the meat with a damp cloth and lay it on a large piece of foil. Glaze with a mixture of honey or maple syrup, mustard, soy sauce, and melted butter. Wrap it closely in the foil and bake it in a moderate oven to about 140° F (60° C) internal temperature. Don't overcook.

If you want to freeze the smoked meat, pack it in a plastic freezer bag, or wrap it in foil drugstore style. Fast-freeze and store in the freezer.

Hot Smoke: Remove the meat from the brine about 8 hours before smoking, drain it, and scrub it well in tepid water. Freshen the meat by soaking it in cold water for about 8 hours, changing the water frequently. Drain it well and wipe it dry with towels. Hang it in prepared hot smoke at 110° to 120° F (43° to 50° C), allowing about an hour per pound, or until the meat is tender. The time may be cut in half by raising the temperature of the smoke to 180° F (82° C) or more; the meat is then more smoke-cooked than heat-smoked—a matter of preference.

Serve hot from the smoker, or chilled, thinly sliced, and piled on French bread with lots of tart relishes. Leftover heat-smoked venison makes great hash (see Corned Venison Hash). Refrigerate leftover meat as you would freshly cooked meat.

Smoked Duck, Goose, Turkey, or Pheasant

Old, tough wildfowl may be prepared using the brine and smoking methods described for Pickle-Cured Smoked Venison. The birds should be freshly killed and dressed, skin intact. When you take the birds from the brine, be sure the cavities are well scrubbed out and that no pockets of cure remain. Hang the birds breast-down in the smoker.

Cold-smoke the birds for 16 to 24 hours. Cook them at once, or freeze them. For a cold delicacy, boil the birds gently until tender, chill them, and serve them sliced, or strip the meat from the bones, press into a bowl, and let set until firm.

Heat-smoke the birds until they're tender and the thighs move easily. Serve hot or cold.

Pickle-Cured Smoked Wild Goose or Turkey

Hang the dressed bird in a cold place for 24 hours before cutting. Remove the legs and breasts; remove the bone from the legs. Trim the meat, removing any bone splinters and shot. The proportions below are sufficient to cure 10 pounds of meat.

> 1 pound salt
> Saltpeter, size of a pea
> ⅛ teaspoon baking soda
> ½ pound brown sugar or granulated maple sugar
> ½ teaspoon mace
> ½ teaspoon ground cloves
> 1 gallon boiled water, cold

In an earthen bowl or crock, layer the salt and meat, starting and finishing with a layer of salt. Dissolve the saltpeter and baking soda in a little warm water and add the sugar and spices. Spread the mixture over top of the salted meat. Add the cold boiled water to cover the meat. Cover the meat with a large plate, weighted with a sealed jar of water so the meat is kept well under the brine. Cover with a clean cloth and leave for 2 weeks. Rinse the meat under cold water, drain it, and wipe each piece dry.

Heat-smoke the meat for several hours, or until it's tender (the time depends on the thickness of the meat and the heat of the smoke), or follow the instructions given for fowl with your smoker appliance.

Use the meat immediately, without further cooking. Serve cold, sliced thinly.

Large wild birds such as wild turkey, grouse, pheasant, and sandhill crane may be pickle-smoked by this procedure.

Smoked Small Game and Wildfowl

Oven-dress the birds or small game. Disjoint large animals such as beaver and raccoon. Bind with string, leaving loops for hanging.

Prepare the Brine Cure described earlier. Put the birds or game into an earthen crock or plastic pail and pour the brine over them. If necessary, make more brine to cover the meat. Place a plate on the meat, weighting it to keep the meat well under the brine. Leave for 16 to 20 hours. Rinse off the brine in cold water, scrubbing the cavities clean. Drain the meats and dry with paper towels. Cold-smoke for 6 to 8 hours.

Preheat the oven to 350° F (175° C). Rub the smoked meats well, all over, with a mixture of soy sauce and melted butter, then put them in a baking pan. Cover lightly with aluminum foil. Bake until tender, removing the foil and basting after about 20 minutes. Serve at once.

JERKY AND PEMMICAN

The long muscles from inside the legs and the flank are best for making jerky. Traditionally the muscle is cut into long, thin, narrow strips and dried completely. It is eaten uncooked, made into pemmican, or boiled and creamed like chipped beef. In the course of jerky's long history of service, it has picked up embellishments along the way.

Cold-Brined Jerky

Cut muscle meat lengthwise of the grain into strips 1 inch thick, about 1½ inches wide, and as long as you can make them. Put the strips into a wooden barrel or nonmetallic container and cover with a sweet pickle or corning solution for 3 days. Hang the meat over a cord line or string to drip for 24 hours, and continue to hang it in a room or other dry place. Keep the strips from touching each other, and protect them from dirt and insects with a light cloth covering, if necessary. The jerky will continue to dry as long as it is exposed to air, so it should be taken down and stored in an airtight container as soon as it is thoroughly dry. A light smoke will add to the flavor and help preserve the meat.

— The Hunter Returns
Cooperative Extension Service
University of Alaska, Fairbanks

Drying jerky over a warm radiator.

Backpack Jerky

4 pounds venison flank or long leg muscle
1 cup soy sauce
½ teaspoon pepper
2 tablespoons salt
1 teaspoon onion powder
2 teaspoons garlic powder
¼ teaspoon cayenne
2 ounces rum or gin

Slice the meat along the grain, not more than ¼ inch thick and 1½ inches wide. Place in a crock or large mixing bowl. Heat the soy sauce and add all other ingredients. Cool and pour over the meat, turning the meat over a few times to coat all surfaces. Cover and refrigerate overnight, then drain and spread the strips of meat, well separated, over an oven rack.

Turn the oven to its lowest heat setting and keep the door ajar. Leave the meat in the oven for 8 to 10 hours. The resulting jerky will not be hard dry, but rather chewy in texture. If it is crisp, the oven was too hot. Pack the jerky in clean plastic bags and store in a cool, dark, dry place. Properly packed and stored, the jerky should keep for weeks.

Venison Jerky

Cut boned meat into thin strips [about ¼ inch thick and 1½ inches wide]. Heat to boiling a large container of salted water. Blanch the meat, a little at a time, using a wire basket if available, until the meat loses its red color. Drain over water, then season with salt and pepper (some people like a little garlic salt). Hang the strips on a drying rack and leave until quite dry and brittle. Hanging time depends on weather conditions. The drier the weather is, the less time needed and the better the jerky will be.

The drying rack consists of either smooth wire or chicken mesh, strung in an out-of-the-way area.

— *What's Cooking in Our National Parks*
Recipe by Barbara Monroe
Montezuma Castle, New Mexico

Highbush Cranberry Pemmican

Cranberries
Dried moose meat or caribou meat (jerky)
1 tablespoon lard per pint meat
¼ teaspoon dried sage per pint meat

Dry cranberries in sunshine or in oven set on low heat. Use 1 part meat to 3 parts berries and grind together. Melt lard and pour over the mixture. Stir well. Add sage and stir. Place in plastic bags and freeze.

— Homer Homemakers
Cooking up a Storm in Homer, Alaska

PART TWO

Big Game

Plentie of Beares everywhere . . . of otters we may take like
store. . . . There are Sea Gulls, murres, ducks, wild geese, and many
other kinds of bordes—numberous. . . . Hares and foxes so
plentiful they stole meat from under men's noses. . . . Great and
mighty beasts like to camels in greatness, with cloven feet.

Antoine Parckhurst
A Report of Newfoundland, 1578

4

The Deer Family and Other Ruminants

... a goodly country, and fruitful soyle, shored with many blessings fit for the use of man: infinite was the company of very large and fat Deere which there we sawe by thousands.
—Sir Francis Drake
On landing on the California Coast, 1579

The big game hunted in North America, grouped here for cooking purposes, includes both ruminant and nonruminant animals. The ruminants, considered in this chapter, comprise the deer family—deer, moose, caribou, and wapiti (elk)—of general distribution, as well as members of the bovine family—bison (buffalo), mountain goat, wild sheep, and antelope—of the West. In addition to their digestive habits, a characteristic that links these ruminant animals in the kitchen is the inherent leanness of their meats. Other, nonruminant, big game is considered in the next chapter.

The deer family, or venison animals, accounts for 90 percent of the big game hunted. The treatment and cooking of venison and the meats of the other ruminants are virtually the same. Recipes for one may be applied to others of comparable size, quality, and cut of the meat.

VENISON

By derivation, the word *venison* means "fruits of the chase." In French and old English cookery the word might mean just that. In North America it has come to refer to the meat of the deer family, only. In this group deer are the most important, occupying virtually the entire continent south of the subarctic regions.

In colonial and frontier North America, deer were recklessly killed by skin hunters. In a money-short market, hides were a medium of exchange. Venison was a cheap staple, and frequently it was the only red meat for sale. From this availability at the meat market, as much as from the fruits of the sporting chase, there sprang a venison cuisine on a continental scale.

The introduction of game laws cut off the market source of the meat, but left us with the know-how to cook venison and assured that there would be game to cook. Deer, the most commonly hunted and cooked big game in North America, is still synonymous with venison in many regions.

The quality of any game meat depends first and foremost on its care from the moment the game is shot all the way to the kitchen. Because of the extreme diversity of conditions on the continent of North America, the variables involved in getting big-game meat from field-dressing to butchering to the cook in maximum quantity and quality can't be presented here. Nonetheless, all methods and recipes in this book are for properly dressed game meats. No recipe can correct or overcome the effects of inadequate field care.

Information on the field care, dressing, and butchering of big game in a particular area usually may be obtained from state and provincial agencies. For detailed, authoritative instructions, see *The Whitetail Deer from Field to Table* (1979) and *The Moose* (1970), both by Ovila and Roger Fortier (National Meat Institute Inc., Montreal, Canada); *Butchering, Processing and Preservation of Meat*, by Frank G. Ashbrook (1955, Van Nostrand Reinhold), which covers meats, including game, in general; and *Care & Cooking of Fish & Game*, by John Weiss (1982, Winchester Press).

Quality and General Preparation

The age, size, cut, and the inherent flavor and texture of any game animal all bear on its cookery.

In general, meat from a big-game animal 1½ to 2½ years old, properly killed, dressed, and aged, is at its tender best, and only the tougher cuts need special attention. However, the hunter cannot always pick and choose, and a tenderizing process such as marinating is recommended for all cuts of venison over 3 years of age.

The coarse-grained meat from older and tougher game lends itself admirably to curing. Cured game—pickled (corned) and/or smoked—is a delicacy and well worth considering as an alternative to fresh meat. (See "Corned Venison" in this chapter, and "Smoking" in Chapter 3.)

The cuts of meat vary in size with the size of the animal, and many methods of preparation are tailored accordingly. As with meat from other animals, cuts from different parts of the carcass of big game vary in structure and tenderness.

The flavor of meat is influenced by the animal's feeding habits. The ruminants (cud-chewers) browse on fresh foliage and twigs, or graze on grains, grasses, and low-growing vegetation in their environment, usually resulting in a fine flavor. Meat from mule deer and antelope of the West may carry a pronounced natural seasoning, imparted by the sage on which they feed. The nomadic caribou, long the dietary mainstay of Indians and Eskimos of the far North, browses on lichens, fungi, mosses, herbs, and other tender plant life; its tender meat may be more delicate of flavor than other venison meats and sweeter than domestic meats. (Caribou should be seasoned lightly, something to keep in mind when adapting other venison recipes.) The recipes included in this chapter have been developed to enhance these natural flavors with seasonings that complement rather than overwhelm them.

The inherent texture of meat from the wild ruminants is lean and relatively coarse—a combination that can mean dry meat. The fat of the deer carries the natural flavor of the meat and should be retained as much as possible. On the other hand, off-flavors also settle in the fat, leading to the common practice of trimming what little fat there is. This simply compounds the problem; so, unless the meat is naturally overseasoned by the animal's diet, it should not be necessary to trim away the fat from big game that has received expert handling from field to kitchen.

The coarseness of the meat increases with the size of the species, as well as with the age of the animal. The flesh of the male is somewhat coarser than that of the female. Coarse-grained meat takes up salt readily, and salt draws juices from the meat. Thus it is best to avoid the direct application of salt during cooking, especially in dry heat. As mentioned, the coarse grain of the meat does, however, permit successful marinating and corning (pickling) of the tougher cuts.

The general methods for cooking various cuts of venison are summarized in the chart, Venison Cooking Methods, which applies to the meat from other big game ruminants as well. (See also Iroquois cookery table in Chapter 2).

VENISON COOKING METHODS

Cut	Method
Young Venison (From animal under 3 years)	
Tender	
Standing Ribs	Cook roasts covered in moderate oven.
Floating Ribs	Pan-fry or broil steaks and chops.
Loin (Saddle)	
Roasts	
Steaks	
Chops	
Whole Haunch (small animal)	
Medium Tender	
Haunch (large animal)	Marinate. Cook by moist heat—pot
Rump Roast	roast, braise.
Round Roast	
Round Steak	

Cut	Method
Less Tender	
Shoulder	Marinate. Cook by moist heat—pot
Round Shoulder	roast, braise, stew, boil.
Short Rib	Cube for collops or mince for sauces,
Blade	sausages, burgers, etc.
Neck	Make soup from bones.
Brisket	Pickle-cure (corn)
Flank	
Shank	
Old/Tough Venison	
(From animal over 3 years or	
under 3 years but tough)	
All Cuts	Tenderize and cook in moist heat.
	Cube or mince.
	Pickle-cure (corn).

TENDERIZING (MARINATING)

Marinating, like pickling, originally meant "to preserve in brine." The term *marinade*, however, has come to be applied broadly to any flavor-enhancing or tenderizing bath. The formula is a matter of choice; any of the marinades given in this chapter may be tailored to size for steaks, roasts, stew meat, etc. The marination time may be anywhere from a few hours to several days, depending on the size and shape of the cut and the degree of toughness.

A buttermilk bath tenderizes without affecting the meat's flavor; the lactic acid breaks down fibers. Commercial tenderizer, used as directed, does not affect flavor either. Extended freezing has a tenderizing effect, so the marinating period for frozen meat is shortened—by how long depends on the size and shape of the cut and the length of time in the freezer. (Meat should be frozen for at least 1 to 2 weeks.)

Cured game meats need no marinating or tenderizing. "High" venison (that is, meat hung to the point of near decomposition) is well tenderized by the long hanging period. Prime cuts require no further tenderizing; other cuts of high venison may be marinated for a short period.

Note that the toughness due to a hard chase of wounded game, or incomplete bleeding, is not the same as the toughness due to the meat's inherent texture. When marinating hard-run game meat, adding salt to the marinade will help to dissolve and draw coagulated blood from the tissues. The meat may then be freshened in cold water; it should be cooked in moist heat.

A FEW COOKING TIPS

Cook only the very tender cuts of venison in dry heat, and then not past medium-rare. Overcooking is drying.

The many variables in venison or any big-game meat make a tabulation of precise cooking times impractical. To roast a tender haunch or loin of young doe to medium-rare in a moderate oven allow 20 to 25 minutes per pound; for buck, allow a little longer, about 25 to 30 minutes per pound.

Frozen or chilled steaks and chops should be brought to room temperature first for fast, even cooking. Thaw frozen roasts only enough to permit larding. Put semifrozen roasts into a hot oven for a quick all-over searing to seal in the juices, then reduce the heat to moderate. Allow extra cooking time, depending on the shape and thickness of the roast. A meat thermometer is the surest way to determine the degree of doneness. (Follow the readings for beef.)

Follow the cooking schedule for beef when using pressure cookers, slow cookers, and microwave ovens, unless otherwise directed.

Roasts should be removed from the oven to a hot platter and allowed to rest for several minutes before carving. They should be served hot on preheated dishes. See Chapter 11 for sauces and condiments to accompany big-game meats.

Cooking Venison

Under the ministrations of a skillful cook, however, game undergoes a great number of scientific modifications and transformations, furnishing the majority of the highly flavored dishes on which a transcendental art is based.

—A Handbook of Gastronomy
Jean Anthelme Brillat-Savarin
1884

Roasts and Pot Roasts

Roast Haunch of Venison
(Paste Method)

The *paste method* is a consistently successful way to cook a haunch of deer or caribou, or a roasting cut of any venison. Described by Mrs. Beeton in 1859 in her famed bible of household management, the method involves simply wrapping the roast in a flour-and-water paste, usually sandwiched between oiled paper or parchment, and cooking it in an oven.

Although now internationally recognized, the paste method is little more than a refinement of the Indian method of wrapping a piece of meat, small game, or fish in clay (or mud) and/or leaves and burying it in the coals to cook in its own juices, thus locking in the natural flavors and protecting the flesh from ashes and cinders. The paste method is still used in this way and is good for baking skinned lean small game like rabbits, as well as venison roasts.

Thaw the haunch of deer or caribou slowly until it's manageable. Preheat the oven to 350° F (175° C).

Wash the meat in tepid water, and wipe it thoroughly with a clean, dry towel. If the meat has a good layer of natural fat, do not lard it. If the fat has been trimmed, lard the meat generously (see *larding* in Glossary).

Starting with 3 cups of flour, make a cohesive, rollable paste of flour and water. Roll it out to about a ½-inch thickness. Prepare enough paste to completely wrap the haunch—make more if necessary.

You'll need three sheets of brown paper large enough to wrap around the meat, and four or five pieces of string long enough to tie around the roast when wrapped. First arrange the strings on the table, and lay two sheets of the paper on top of them. Spread the rolled paste over the paper. Oil the remaining piece of paper well with fat or cooking oil and lay it on the paste. Place the roast, topside down, in the middle and wrap the whole paper-and-paste sandwich around it, overlapping the

Haunch of venison and materials needed to prepare it by the paste method.

Rolled-out paste on top of wrapping paper. Larded haunch is in background.

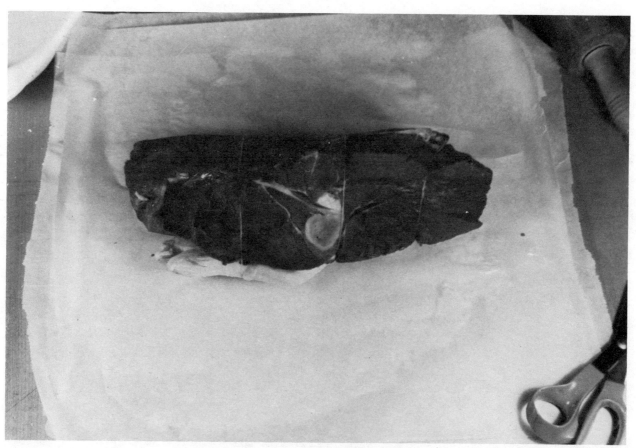

Haunch of venison ready to wrap in paper-and-paste sandwich.

Wrapped haunch of venison ready for the oven. The outside is brushed liberally with cooking oil.

Roast haunch of venison cooked by the paste method ready for serving with pan gravy on the side.

edges to close completely. Tie securely. Brush the outside with fat. Flip the package over and brush the rest of the outer layer of paper with fat until it is thoroughly saturated. Place the package in a roasting pan, and add a little water to the bottom of the pan. Put into the oven. Based on the weight of the whole package, allow 20 minutes per pound for doe, 25 minutes for buck.

About 20 minutes before the roast is done, crack the casing and remove and discard it. Prick the meat in a few places to allow the juices to run into the pan. Baste generously with melted butter, and dust lightly with flour. Return the roast to the oven and bake until golden. Transfer to a warm platter. Keep warm while the meat rests for about 20 minutes. Meanwhile make a brown pan gravy from the roast's own drippings. Season to taste. Traditionally this English-style haunch is served with green string beans and red currant jelly.

A haunch of antelope, mountain sheep or goat, a sirloin or sirloin tip roast of young moose or elk, and a cut of buffalo hump may also be cooked by the paste method.

Blue Mountain Venison

This recipe may be used to cook a haunch or loin of young deer or caribou, loin roast, or top round of elk or moose.

Preheat the oven to 425° F (220° C).

Wipe the meat with a damp cloth. Lard well by the needle or pique method (see *larding* in Glossary). Put the meat in a roasting pan. Rub the top of the roast with prepared mustard. Coat lightly with brown sugar and dust with pepper. Top with thick slices of onion and generous dabs of

butter. Add ½ cup of water to the pan. Cover completely with aluminum foil, pinching the foil to the edge of the pan. Place in the hot oven and turn the heat down to 350° F (175° C). After ½ hour, baste with the pan drippings, adding a little water to the pan if necessary. Continue basting from time to time.

Allow about 25 minutes per pound for rare meat. Half an hour before the meat is done, remove the foil. Baste completely with melted butter or pan drippings. Dust lightly with flour and brown to a crusty gold. Then transfer the roast to a hot platter and let it rest while you make brown pan gravy from the drippings.

—Mrs. Alice Slauson
King's County, Nova Scotia

Braised Rump of Moose
5-pound cut of moose rump
Marinade
Salt and pepper
Oil
2 pints beef gravy
1 tablespoon tomato paste
Buerre manié (see Glossary)
3 shallots
½ pound mushrooms, preferably fresh
½ cup white wine

Marinade:
1 medium onion
1 stalk celery
1 medium carrot
1 cup wine vinegar
2 cups red wine
2 bay leaves
3 cloves
1 tablespoon juniper berries, crushed

To prepare the marinade, slice the onion and cut the celery and carrot into 1-inch pieces. Mix the vinegar, 2 cups of water, and the red wine together with the vegetables, bay leaves, cloves, and juniper berries. Bring to a boil, and then cool completely.

Wipe the meat with a damp cloth. Put the marinade in a deep bowl just big enough to contain the roast. Immerse the meat in the marinade and keep at room temperature for about 48 hours. The meat should be covered by the marinade. If not, turn it over occasionally to keep all surfaces well moistened.

Remove the meat from the marinade, dry it off well with a towel, and season with salt and pepper. Strain and reserve the marinade. Pick out the vegetables and reserve them separately.

Using a Dutch oven, brown the meat in hot oil on all sides. Add the vegetables from the marinade and continue browning everything for 20 minutes, turning frequently. Blend the strained marinade, beef gravy, and tomato paste and pour the mixture in. Cover and keep at a slow boil on top of the stove until the meat is done (2½ to 3 hours). Transfer the meat to a deep, heated platter.

Thicken the sauce with *buerre manié*, and strain through a sieve. In another saucepan, sauté finely chopped shallots in butter, add mushrooms, white wine, and the sauce. Stir and cook for a few minutes. Slice the meat and pour the sauce over it. Serve with red cabbage and potato dumplings. *10 to 12 servings.*

—Gunter Gugelmeier
Executive Chef, Loews Westbury Hotel
Toronto, Ontario

Western-Style Elk Pot Roast

4- to 5-pound roast of elk
1 cup navy beans
Fat
Pepper
12 ounces beer
1 medium onion, sliced
2 or 3 carrots, sliced
2 or 3 stalks celery, diced
Salt and pepper
Seasonings to taste

Trim the meat, leaving a layer of fat, and wipe with a damp cloth. Pour boiling water over the beans and let stand for 2 hours.

In a large Dutch oven, heat fat to about a ⅛-inch depth. Brown the roast well on all sides. Pepper the meat lightly while browning. Pour off the excess fat and add water to the pot to a depth of about ½ inch. Cover and simmer for ½ hour. Then slowly pour half the beer over the meat. Drain and add the beans, along with the sliced onion. Add more water if necessary to just cover the beans. Cover and simmer for 2 hours. Slowly pour the remaining beer over the meat, then add the sliced carrots and celery. Add salt and pepper to taste, along with any other seasonings (such as garlic powder and/or herbs) desired. Cover and simmer for another hour or until the meat is tender and the beans are cooked.

Transfer the meat to a heated platter and keep warm. Lightly thicken the remaining vegetable-bean sauce by stirring a thin paste of flour and water into it. Adjust seasonings to taste. Slice the meat and serve with the sauce on hot cooked rice.

−Mrs. Ed McKenzie
Rocky Mountain House, Alberta

Caribou Pot Roast

Caribou meat should be eaten with relish or the caribou will be offended and the herds will not return.

−Old Chipewyan Lore

4- to 5-pound rump or shoulder roast of caribou
Seasoned flour
Bacon fat
2 to 4 carrots, sliced
1 large onion, slivered
2 green peppers, cut in squares
½ pound mushrooms, sliced or whole

Lard the meat by the needle or pique method (see *larding* in Glossary). Sprinkle the meat all over with seasoned flour and rub in. Over medium heat, melt bacon fat to a ¼-inch depth in a Dutch oven. Brown the roast well on all sides. Slip a rack under the meat and scatter the carrots, onion, and green peppers around it. Add enough water to just show through the vegetables. Bring to a boil, cover, and turn the heat down to low. Cook until tender, about 2½ to 3 hours. Turn the meat over once or twice during cooking. Replace liquid as necessary to keep the bottom of the pot covered.

When the meat is almost done, check the vegetables. If they look limp and cooked out, remove them with a slotted spoon and discard. Otherwise leave them. Add the mushrooms−shaggy manes are preferred in season. Cover and cook another 10 minutes, or until the meat is tender.

Transfer the meat to a warm platter. Remove the vegetables with a slotted spoon and keep warm. Thicken the remaining gravy. Slice the meat and serve, topped with mushrooms and gravy; serve the vegetables on the side.

−Rita Foucher
Fairbanks, Alaska

Cranberry Deer Pot Roast

Applying tart red cranberries to venison makes a dish that is the deer hunter's version of a traditional New England pot roast. The result is a finely flavored tender meat with a piquant gravy.

3- to 4-pound haunch or shoulder cut of deer
½ teaspoon black pepper, freshly ground
⅓ cup flour
¼ pound salt pork
2 cups cranberries
2 tablespoons sugar
1 onion, stuck with 2 cloves

Trim the meat, then scrape and wipe it with a damp cloth. Mix the pepper and flour. Dredge the meat in the mixture, rubbing it in well all over. Dice the salt pork and sear it in a Dutch oven over medium heat, stirring until it turns a crisp gold. Remove the pork with a slotted spoon. In the hot fat, still over medium heat, slowly brown the venison on all sides.

Meanwhile, cook the cranberries in a cup of water until they pop—about 5 minutes. Pour the hot berries and juice over the browned meat. Scatter the bits of salt pork over the top and sprinkle 1 tablespoon of the sugar over that. Add the cloved onion. Cover tightly and simmer for about 3 hours, or until the meat is tender. The time will depend on the size and thickness of the cut. Check the pot roast from time to time during cooking. The liquid surrounding the meat should be simmering, never boiling, and it should not be allowed to cook dry. Add a little water if necessary.

Transfer the meat to a warm serving platter and keep it hot. Remove the onion. The remaining sauce may be strained or not. Either way, add the remaining sugar, bring to a low boil, and thicken slightly. Combine 2 tablespoons of flour with ½ cup of warm water, and mix thoroughly. Add slowly to the boiling sauce, stirring constantly until the sauce is thickened to the desired consistency. Serve the gravy with the roast. *About 6 servings.*

Stews

When the venison in the freezer gets down to odds and ends of unidentifiable cut, they may be trimmed and made into a glorious, savory stew. Provided the game received proper field care and dressing in the first place, stewing—sometimes combined with marinating—will transform tough meat into a tender, succulent dish.

Marinated Moosemeat Stew

2 to 3 pounds moosemeat, cut in stewing cubes
Marinade
Olive oil
Flour

Marinade:

1 cup red wine
¼ cup cider vinegar or white vinegar
1 large carrot, sliced
1 large onion, sliced
1 or 2 stalks celery with tops, broken
1 teaspoon sugar
Few peppercorns, crushed
Few juniper berries or pine nuts, crushed
1 bay leaf, broken
½ teaspoon mustard seed

Combine all the marinade ingredients in a saucepan and add enough water, plus a little sweet pickle juice if handy, to make a quart of marinade. Bring to a bubble, remove from the heat, and let steep while you trim the meat and cut it into chunks. Put the meat into an earthen bowl, and pour the hot marinade over it. Turn the meat over with a spoon several times. Cover and refrigerate it for 1 to 2 days, turning the meat over twice daily.

Drain the meat, and strain the marinade. Pat the meat dry between towels, flicking off any bay leaf, peppercorns, etc., sticking to it. Dust the meat lightly with flour. In a large Dutch oven, heat olive oil, ¼ inch deep, and brown the meat lightly on all sides. Use plenty of oil, as the meat is very lean. If the Dutch oven won't take all the meat with room to spare, brown the excess in another pan before adding it to the Dutch oven. To the browned meat add enough strained marinade to cover. Bring to a bubble, reduce heat, and cover. Let simmer for a couple of hours, adding marinade as necessary to keep the meat well moistened.

Refrigerate the stew, covered, until about 2 hours before serving. An overnight rest improves the flavor; freezing will do no harm.

To finish the stew, put it in a 325° F (165° C) oven. After an hour, add the following vegetables:

> 1 green pepper, cut in squares
> 1 cup sliced carrots
> 1 cup sliced mushrooms
> Few pearl onions

Add hot stock, water, or the remaining marinade, according to taste—just enough to barely show through the vegetables. Don't stir. Just let the vegetables steam on top of the meat for about ½ hour; then use wooden spoons to gently turn the vegetables into the meat, which by this time will have a nice thick, dark brown sauce. Don't let the vegetables overcook; they should have a little bite left in them. Serve with fluffy white rice or, better still, wild rice. *6 to 8 servings.*

Pappas' Stifado
(Venison Stew with Onions)

> 2 pounds stewing venison
> 2 tablespoons olive oil
> 2 tablespoons butter
> 1 pound small onions, whole
> ¼ cup olive oil
> 2 tablespoons claret wine
> 2 tablespoons white or cider vinegar
> 4 tablespoons tomato paste
> 2 teaspoons salt
> ¼ teaspoon pepper
> 2 cups hot water
> 4 cloves garlic, unpeeled
> 2 tablespoons pickling spices, tied in cheesecloth

Trim and cut the venison into 1-inch cubes. Heat the oil and butter in a skillet and add the meat, turning and browning it on all sides for about 10 minutes. Remove the meat to a heavy saucepan or Dutch oven. Add the onions to the skillet and brown in the hot oil. Add to the meat.

In a bowl, combine all the remaining ingredients except the pickling spices. Stir the mixture well and pour it over the meat and onions. Place the spice bag in the middle of the stew. Bring to a boil. Cover and reduce the heat. Simmer for about 2 hours, or until the meat is tender. Remove the spice bag when the stew is seasoned to taste.

Thicken the gravy with a small amount of flour and water mixed to a thin paste. For additional color, add ½ teaspoon of paprika. *6 servings.*

—Louis Pappas
Pappas' Restaurant
Tarpon Springs, Florida

Venison à la Bourguignonne

Whether you call it Burgundian Ragout, Annie Oakley Stew, or something else, the dark, winy stew that originated in the French province of Burgundy and made its way to the American West is one of France's greatest contributions to North American game cookery. With typical French economy, the process transforms a lesser cut of meat (be it venison, buffalo, antelope, sheep, bear, or beaver) into a culinary masterpiece.

The following recipe is party-sized, serving 16 to 20 people. It can be made ahead, as its flavor improves after a day in the refrigerator or a stint in the freezer.

> 4 pounds trimmed, boneless well-hung venison
>   (round, rump, or shoulder of deer, caribou,
>   young moose, or elk)
> ¼ cup fine olive oil or rendered venison kidney suet
> 4 teaspoons sugar
> Flour
> 4 medium tomatoes, quartered
> 4 green peppers, cut into 1-inch squares
> 2 cups beef stock
> ¼ teaspoon thyme
> 12 ounces red table wine
> Salt and freshly ground pepper to taste
> 1 teaspoon chili powder or other spice to taste

Wipe the meat with a damp cloth. Cut it into 1½-inch cubes and pat between towels. Heat the olive oil in a large iron skillet, and brown the meat well on all sides. Sprinkle with the sugar and continue to cook for 2 or 3 minutes. Transfer the meat and oil to a large casserole or Dutch oven. Sprinkle enough flour over the top of the meat to absorb the fat. Put the meat into a 375° F (190° C) oven and let the flour brown. Reduce the heat to 325° F (160° C). Add the rest of the ingredients listed above. Cover and bake until the meat is almost done, 2 to 2½ hours.

(Note: Up to this point the dish may be prepared a day in advance, cooled, refrigerated, and reheated, or it may be prepared a week ahead and frozen. Reheat slowly in the oven to a bubble, and then carry on.)

To the bubbling casserole add:

> 2 cups small young carrots (or new carrots, sliced)
> 2 cups small white onions
> 2 cups button mushroom heads
> 32 ounces burgundy or other good red wine

Cover the casserole and continue cooking until the vegetables are tender but not soft, about

½ hour. Serve with slices of crusty French garlic bread and small, steamed potatoes, preferably new, garnished with parsley. Serve with burgundy or dry red wine.

Yukon Moose Stew

Moose round steak, about 2 pounds
Flour, garlic powder, onion salt, salt, and pepper
Bacon fat
1 tablespoon Worcestershire sauce
2 medium onions
20-ounce can of tomatoes
Chopped vegetables as available

Cut the meat into 1-inch cubes. Mix together about ½ cup of flour, a bit of garlic powder and onion salt, and salt and pepper to taste. Roll the meat in the flour mixture to coat completely. Heat enough bacon fat to coat the bottom of a frying pan, and brown the meat lightly on all sides.

Bring about 2 cups of water to a boil in a medium-sized pot, adding the Worcestershire sauce, onions, and tomatoes. Add the browned meat, and enough boiling water to cover the meat, if necessary. Cook uncovered over low heat until tender—about 2 hours.

During the last 45 to 60 minutes of simmering, add chopped carrots, celery, potatoes, green peppers, and any other vegetables you have handy—diced turnip is especially good. Mushrooms may be added during the last ½ hour of cooking. Serve with hot bannock. *6 to 8 servings*.

—Don Sawatsky
Whitehorse, Yukon

Ground Venison

The neck, shanks, flank, brisket, and the trimmings that remain after tidying up the choicer cuts of the animal contain a lot of good meat. It can represent a respectable percentage of the carcass's available meat if the animal has been properly butchered. With the bone removed (reserved for soup stock) and sinew trimmed, much of this scrap meat can be chunked for stewing and braising recipes—but all of it is meat for the food grinder.

A variety of recipes that use ground venison follows. Variations in each are limited only by the cook's imagination and larder.

Venison Tourtière

A meat pie of Christmas Eve fame in Quebec, the *tourtière* is traditional fare at *reveillon*, the post-midnight Mass festivities. In its early days in New France, the *tourtière* usually was made from pork, or from venison, hare, or grouse with pork or salt pork added to provide the necessary fat. Seasoned according to preference and the ingredients at hand, each version was unique.

A classic make-ahead dish, the *tourtière* is best kept chilled for several days, as it improves with time. *Tourtière*s may be stored in the freezer for up to 6 weeks, so make several at one time and use them as needed.

The following recipe makes three 9-inch pies. The seasonings and spices may be varied, or their amounts adjusted, to taste.

[67]

2 pounds venison
1 pound fat pork
2 medium onions, minced
Dash each ground bay leaf, allspice, mace,
  and powdered garlic
1 teaspoon salt
1 teaspoon freshly ground black pepper
Pastry for 3 double-crust pies

Using a medium disc, grind the venison and pork together. In a deep saucepan combine the meat, onion, and seasonings and add just enough water to barely cover the mixture. Bring to a boil, turn down the heat, skim off the fat, and then cover. Let simmer for 1½ to 2 hours, or until the liquid is reduced to a thick sauce. Stir up from the bottom of the kettle occasionally. Skim fat from the surface.

Meanwhile, prepare pastry for three double-crust pies. Line three 9-inch plates with pastry. Fill each with a third of the meat mixture. Cover with top crusts, pinching the edges together to seal. Do not score the tops. Bake in a preheated 375° F (190° C) oven for about 45 minutes, or until nicely browned.

Let the *tourtière* cool in the pie plate, then turn it out upside down on a cake rack. Pierce the bottom crust with the tip of a knife to allow the vapor to escape, and let the pie cool thoroughly. Double-wrap it in heavy-duty aluminum foil and refrigerate for 3 or 4 days, or freeze.

To reheat a frozen *tourtière*, place the wrapped frozen pie in a low-to-moderate oven for 1 hour, removing the foil for the last 15 minutes. Unfrozen pies may be unwrapped and eaten cold, although they're really better warm.

This recipe makes a rather dry *tourtière*, which goes well with a tossed green salad or green tomato pickle.

Picadillo
1 pound ground venison
2 tablespoons olive oil
½ bell pepper, chopped
4 medium tomatoes, peeled and chopped
6 tablespoons tomato paste
½ cup tomato sauce
1 tablespoon minced onion flakes
⅔ cup water
¼ teaspoon oregano
½ cup dark raisins, rinsed and drained
½ cup white raisins, rinsed and drained
Salt and pepper
Slivered almonds or split pecans

In a large, heavy frying pan, heat the oil and brown the meat. Drain off the oil. Add all the remaining ingredients except the nuts. Mix well and simmer slowly, stirring frequently, for about 30 minutes. If the meat mixture is too thick to use as a dip, stir in a little hot water. Serve in a chafing dish with nuts sprinkled on top.

Picadillo is an excellent dip for tostados (quartered and deep-fried tortillas). This recipe serves about 20, but any leftovers can be frozen.

Venison Burgers with Herbs

The difference between beef burgers and deer, moose, caribou, or elk burgers is in their fat content. For a succulent burger, venison needs added fat, which may come from beef or pork—about 1 part fat to 2 parts venison. Sausage meat does the job well and provides a tasty accent. If any form of pork is added, the burger must be cooked through, no pink showing. Otherwise, prepare and cook as you would beef burgers.

> 1 pound ground venison
> ½ pound pork sausage meat
> 1 slice stale (but not completely dry) white bread
> 1 egg, beaten
> 1 medium onion, minced
> 1 tablespoon butter or margarine
> Salt and freshly ground pepper to taste
> 1 tablespoon dry sweet basil or marjoram
> Red wine or cold water
> Vegetable oil

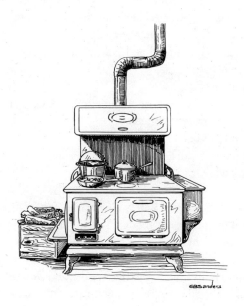

Combine the venison and the sausage meat. Soak the bread in the beaten egg. Sauté the onion in the butter, let it cool and add it to meat. Add the bread-egg mixture, the seasonings, and 2 tablespoons of wine (or water) to the meat. Mix with your hands until thoroughly blended. Form into 8 patties about 1 inch thick.

Heat oil in a large iron skillet until a flick of water spits back. Brown the patties well on both sides, turning once. Turn the heat down to low. Sprinkle ¼ cup of wine over the meat, cover tightly, and cook slowly until no pink shows in the middle of a burger, about 15 minutes. Transfer to a hot platter and serve with buns and relishes or your favorite tomato sauce.

Judy's Mom's Venison Mincemeat

"We always had venison mincemeat for Christmas. The house was full of the aroma of fruits and spices while it simmered at the back of the stove." That's how Judy Eberspaecher remembers her childhood Christmases in Nova Scotia.

> 4 pounds venison stewing meat, trimmed
> 1 cup suet or ¾ pound fat pork
> 12 medium-size sour apples (if apples aren't sour,
>   add 2 cups cranberry sauce to the apples)
> 2 pounds raisins, washed
> 2 cups frozen strawberries
>   or strawberry preserves with juice
> 2 cups orange marmalade, fruit jam, or citron preserves,
>   or a combination (other fruit preserves may be
>   included to make up the 2 cups)
> 2 oranges, rind grated and pulp chopped
> 4 cups brown sugar
> 1 cup molasses
> 2 tablespoons each ground cinnamon, cloves, and allspice
> 2 whole nutmegs, grated
> 1 teaspoon salt
> 4 cups apple cider or apple juice
> 2 cups wine, or 1 cup rum or brandy

Put the venison and suet into a saucepan. Barely cover with water. Bring to a boil, turn down heat, skim, and cook slowly until the venison is tender. While the meat is cooking, core the apples (skin can be peeled or left on, as you wish) and cook separately until soft, using only enough water to keep from boiling dry.

When the meat is tender, lift it with a slotted spoon, and let it drain over the pan. Reserve the stock. Put the meat through a food chopper, using a medium disc.

In a large kettle or stock pot, combine the meat, cooked apples and any juice, raisins, and remaining fruits with their juices. Stir in the sugar, molasses, spices, and salt. Add the cider and the reserved stock from the meat. If using wine, pour it in now (rum should be added later). Mix thoroughly. If necessary, add enough water or fruit juice to barely cover the mixture. Slowly bring to a bubble, reduce the heat, and simmer uncovered, stirring frequently and replacing lost moisture with water as required, until the raisins have swelled and the spices are well blended. Now add the rum or brandy, stir, and continue simmering.

In the old days, the mincemeat used to simmer all evening on the wood stove. Then, after we all went to bed, it was left at the back of the stove until the fire went out. Cooked with electricity or gas, it still takes close to 8 hours to cook.

—Mrs. Alex Eberspaecher
Oakville, Ontario

The McTees' Two-Alarm Venison Chili

Chili is synonymous with Tex-Mex cookery. Despite the controversy that flourishes in Texas over its origin and content, there seems little doubt that the fiery dish originated at San Antonio when abundant venison provided the staple meat for the indigenous Mexicans.

Chili powder, the basic seasoning, is a combination of spices indigenous to the southern region: various peppers, cumin, garlic, etc. Chili powder is not particularly pungent, and chili is not necessarily mouth-searingly hot. "Hotness" is varied by the judicious addition of various dried peppers. Whether it's rated one-alarm, two-alarm, or three-alarm, a great chili is a sensation more than a taste. It fills the head with a blend of aromatic fumes and a tingling flavor, followed by an all-over warm glow from within.

This remarkably fine chili recipe is the production of Charly and Pat McTee of San Antonio. Though rated two-alarm, it may be adjusted for more or less hotness.

Have the venison chili-ground (a Texas butcher's term for a very coarse grind) or cut into small cubes, and add a little beef fat. For each pound of meat, you will need:

> 1 clove garlic, chopped
> 1 dried chili pod (large black)
> 3 to 5 chili petines
> 2 to 4 Jap chilis
> Salt
> Pinch cumin
> ⅛ cup chili powder

Heat enough oil to cover the bottom of a large pot or Dutch oven; add the garlic, stir-fry a moment, then add the meat and lightly brown it. With scissors cut the chilis into the pot, seeds and all (removal of seeds will make the chili milder). Add water to more than cover the meat and chilis. Add the cumin and chili powder, and salt to taste. Simmer, stirring in more water as needed, for hours, all day, very slowly. When ready, the meat will be very tender and all the chilis will have cooked into the sauce. Skim off any surface fat, thicken it with a little flour, and return it to the simmering sauce, stirring until thick and smooth.

You may use additional seasonings, such as oregano, onions, or other kinds of chilis to adapt the recipe to your own taste. Keep in mind that chili is better on the second or third day.

Cook pinto beans separately and mix them into the finished chili before serving, if you wish.

Venison Spaghetti Sauce

This party-size recipe requires long, slow cooking. For a smooth, well-blended sauce, it is best started the day before the party and finished after an overnight rest. If you're not having a party, use as much as you need and freeze the rest in meal-size quantities.

3 pounds venison
½ pound pork or beef fat
3 tablespoons olive oil
3 onions, chopped
2 green peppers, chopped
1 sweet red pepper (pimento)
Top half of a bunch of celery, with leaves, all chopped
3 cloves garlic, minced and crushed
1 teaspoon salt
½ teaspoon black pepper
1 teaspoon fresh oregano (more if dried)
½ teaspoon fresh sage (more if dried)
½ teaspoon cumin
½ teaspoon Tabasco sauce
2 tablespoons Worcestershire sauce
7-ounce can tomato paste
2 10-ounce cans cream of tomato soup
1 cup tomato juice
6 large fresh (or canned) tomatoes
10-ounce can beef bouillon, or venison stock

Grind the venison and fat together. Heat the oil in a large Dutch oven. Stir in the chopped vegetables, including the garlic, one batch at a time so as not to reduce the heat. Sauté over medium heat until vegetables are limp. Remove vegetables with a slotted spoon and set them aside. Turn up the heat, and brown the meat—half in the Dutch oven and half in a hot greased skillet. When evenly browned, drain off the excess fat and combine all the meat in the Dutch oven.

Return the vegetables to the meat and mix. Add the seasonings and stir in the remaining ingredients, one at a time. Pour in enough hot water to completely cover. Bring to a boil, and then reduce the heat. Keep at a low simmer, with a few bubbles barely breaking the surface, for 4 to 6 hours. Stir up from the bottom from time to time. Replace water to just keep the mixture from sticking. Remove from the heat, cover with a towel and plate, and store overnight in a cold place.

The next day, remove most hardened fat, leaving only a bit. About 3 hours before serving, reheat slowly, stirring up from the bottom. Taste-test and adjust the seasonings. Add water only if necessary, and continue simmering until serving time, stirring frequently to prevent sticking. The sauce should have cooked down to a very thick, rich, dark sauce.

Serve over spaghetti, and top with a sprinkling of grated Parmesan cheese. *12 servings.*

SAUSAGE

The word *sausage* derives from the Latin *salsicium*, meaning "salted," and probably once meant "salted meat." Just when the term came to mean *any* seasoned forcemeat stuffed into a casing is not known; but by the time sausages were included in a ban on festive orgies in early Rome (and consequently bootlegged along with the booze), they were evidently a national addiction. The seductive delicacy has continued to flourish internationally in infinite variety. The North American hunter's choice is fresh (i.e., uncured) venison sausage, country style. It is relatively simple to make.

All venison is lean, and sausage requires a good proportion of fat to yield a moist, succulent product. The fat, usually in the form of pork, is combined with the venison in the ratio of one part pork fat to two parts venison; or equal parts pork shoulder and venison.

The work area should be clean and cool, the utensils scrupulously clean. The meat must be kept cold: If you work slowly, keep a plastic bag of ice cubes on the meat while working.

Country-Style Venison Sausage

The intensity of seasoning of this basic sausage is medium. Whether store-bought or homegrown, the seasonings should be fresh. Don't forget that fresh, homegrown or wild seasonings can be strong. The seasonings given here are in starter amounts and may be adjusted along the way. CAUTION: *Don't taste-test the raw meat mixture.* Instead, make a thin patty, fry it in a little oil, and taste it. Adjust the seasonings and repeat this process until you've got just what you want.

> 5 pounds venison, trimmings and/or any coarse cut
> 3 pounds fat pork, chilled hard
> 1 clove garlic, minced
> ½ teaspoon cayenne pepper
> 1 teaspoon powdered bay leaf
> 1 teaspoon thyme
> 1 teaspoon sage or savory
> 1 tablespoon onion salt
> 2 teaspoons freshly ground black pepper
> 1 tablespoon salt
> ⅓ cup water or red wine
> Pork casings (optional)

Cut the meat in chunks or thick strips, trimming away sinew. Using the coarse disc, put the meat through the grinder. Mix in the garlic and seasonings and blend thoroughly. Mixing by hand gives the best blend. (If you hesitate to use your bare hands, wear clean throwaway plastic gloves.) For a finer texture, put the seasoned meat through the grinder again. Taste-test as described, then mix in the wine or water and refrigerate until well chilled.

To make the sausage hotter or milder, substitute the following seasonings:

For Hot Sausage: Use 1½ tablespoons salt, 1 teaspoon freshly ground black pepper, ½ teaspoon cayenne pepper or Tabasco sauce, 1 tablespoon chili powder, 2 cloves garlic (peeled and minced), 1 tablespoon savory or oregano, and ¼ teaspoon cloves.

For Mild Sausage: Use 1 tablespoon salt, 2 teaspoons freshly ground black pepper, 1 tablespoon poultry seasoning, and ½ cup water.

After the seasoned meat has chilled, finish preparing the sausage by one of the following methods:

Stuffed Sausage: Stuff the mixture into pork casings loosely but evenly, gently pulling the casing as it fills to avoid too tight a pack. Twist into links about every 5 inches. Prick any air bubbles with a pin.

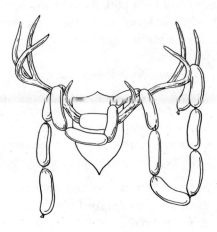

The sausage may be cooked at once or packed in meal-size quantities and stored in the freezer for up to 6 weeks. Two or three days in a cold smoke before cooking or freezing will add zest to the sausage.

Unstuffed Sausage: Put the meat in pudding bowls or clean plastic containers, packing it down well. Cover completely with melted fat and store in the freezer for up to 6 weeks. To use, remove the fat. Form the meat into rolls about 2 inches thick, and slice into patties. Dust lightly with flour and pan-fry. These are delicious with fried apples.

Breakfast-Style Sausage: Follow the basic recipe for Country-Style Sausage, but grind the seasoned sausage meat a second time, using the medium-fine disc. Stuff into *lamb* casings and twist into 3- or 4-inch links, or pack in pudding bowls and freeze as directed for Unstuffed Sausage. This fine grind may be hand-rolled into finger sausages or made into patties.

Italian-Style Venison Sausage
4 pounds venison, trimmed and chunked
4 pounds pork shoulder, strips or chunks
4 tablespoons salt
Fennel seed
Black peppercorns, cracked
Hot red pepper flakes
Dry red wine (optional)
Pork casings

Use a coarse disc to grind the meat, alternating venison with pork. Spread the meat over a large platter and add the salt. Sprinkle fennel seed over the meat, starting with about 3 tablespoons. Next add about 1 tablespoon of cracked peppercorns, then sprinkle on 1 teaspoon of crushed hot pepper flakes. Mix with the hands until well blended. Test the seasonings by making a small patty of the mixture and frying it in a little hot olive oil. Taste it, and add more fennel and black or red pepper as desired. Repeat the test, adjusting until the desired seasoning is attained. Then sprinkle the red wine over the meat, cover lightly, and refrigerate until well chilled.

Loosely fill the casings, twisting them into 5-inch links; prick any air bubbles with a needle. Cook immediately or freeze.

—Mrs. E. Bev Sanders
Mississauga, Ontario

Steaks and Chops

Steaks and chops from the well-aged loin section of the young venison are pan-fried or broiled. At their best, steaks and chops are lean cuts and tend to dry out in cooking. They should be cooked quickly, no more than medium-rare, and served sizzling on hot plates.

The loin steaks and chops from an older animal are usually less tender. When well aged, they may respond to a tenderizing treatment and may then be pan-fried or broiled. Such cuts, however, are best braised or cut into collops for a superb marinated game dish. Generally, steaks cut from the shoulder should also be given a tenderizing treatment before pan-frying or broiling them.

Broiled Venison Steaks and Chops

Bring the meat to room temperature, scrape with the back of a knife, and wipe clean with a damp cloth. Gash the fatty edges, and follow one of the cooking variations below.

Open-Fire Broiled: Prepare steaks or chops as described, and brush both sides with melted butter or oil. Place the meat on a greased, heated rack, and broil close, but not too close, to deep live coals of charcoal or hardwood. (If you don't have a rack, an old-fashioned hinged wire toaster will serve admirably.)

The area of the coals should be greater than that of the meat so that the heat under the meat is uniform for even cooking. The meat should never be in contact with the flame. Use a water gun to put out the flame from burning drippings.

Cook the meat on one side until the juice begins to break through the top; turn and brown the other side to taste—rare, medium, or well done. Turn only once.

Oven-Broiled: Prepare steaks or chops as described earlier, brushing both sides with melted butter or oil. Preheat the oven broiler to "broil" (very hot). Oil the broiler rack and place meat on it. Leave the oven door ajar while cooking.

Meat 1 inch thick should be placed about 3 inches from the source of heat. For rare steaks or chops allow approximately 7 minutes on the first side and 5 minutes on the other. For medium, allow about 9 minutes on one side and 7 on the other. Thinner steaks should be broiled a little closer to the heat and will, of course, require less cooking time.

Pepper-Broiled: Rub freshly ground pepper into the steaks or chops on both sides. Dip the meat in melted butter and broil over an open fire or in the oven, as described above. Melt 2 tablespoons tart currant jelly in 1 tablespoon butter. Put the broiled steaks on heated plates. Season them with salt and pepper and pour the melted jelly over them.

Brandy-Seared: Brush the steaks or chops with brandy or gin and sear both sides in a clean flame or by a quick flip over the coals. Brush the meat with melted butter or oil, and broil over an open fire. Season with salt and pepper. Serve with a wedge of lemon.

Pan-Fried Venison Steaks and Chops

Wipe or scrape the steaks or chops. Gash the fatty edges, and rub the meat with oil or melted butter. Place a heavy iron frying pan or skillet over a high flame. Coat the bottom of the pan well with venison or beef fat, and heat until it just starts to smoke. Lay the pieces of meat in the pan without crowding them. Reduce heat to moderate. When the juice begins to break through the top, turn immediately and cook to rare or medium as desired. Season with salt and pepper.

Marinated Venison Steaks

Various preparations may be used to tenderize venison steaks. These include French- and Italian-type salad dressings, as well as various commercial barbecue sauces. The following marinade is simple and effective, and adds an extra zest to any game.

Lay the steaks on a deep platter, and pour a mixture of equal parts of lemon juice and salad oil over them. Turn the meat over 2 or 3 times to coat well. Cover the meat with waxed paper and refrigerate from a few hours to overnight, depending on the age and cut of the meat. Turn the meat over occasionally to keep it coated with marinade. Drain the meat, and then broil or pan-fry as desired.

For another variation, pour buttermilk over the meat to cover. Turn the meat over and treat as for marinade. Drain, then scrape the meat with a table knife and pat it dry with paper towels. Brush the meat with oil and broil or pan-fry.

Country-Style Deer or Moose Steak

If the steak is large, lard it with small pockets of fat by the pique method (see Glossary). Rub both sides of the steak with crushed juniper berries or crushed cranberries. Sandwich the steak between thick branches of juniper or spruce, then wrap in brown paper or newspaper and age in a woodshed or other cold place for 2 or 3 days. A number of steaks may be thus sandwiched in one package.

Scrape the surfaces of the steaks, brush them with oil, and broil or pan-fry them without further treatment. Salt and pepper to taste, and serve with a sharp meat sauce.

Venison Tenderloin

The tenderloin, fillet, or backstrap is a cone-shaped mass of muscle located in the lumbar region of the animal. In deer and caribou it is relatively small and is probably best left in the steaks or roasts. But in moose and elk, it is considerable, and as in beef, it is a select cut. Well-larded venison tenderloin can be roasted in the same way as beef tenderloin, or it can be cut into steaks.

There are three classic tenderloin cuts: Tournedos are thick, round, small steaks sliced from the tapering end (tip trimmed off and reserved for fine stews or for steak à la tartare); the center cut is chateaubriand, left whole for roasting or steaked; the thick, fleshy end is the filet mignon, although the whole fillet steaked may be called filet mignon. All cuts from the tenderloin should be cooked no more than rare, as the delicate meat dries out easily. The steaks are broiled or grilled.

Broiled Filet Mignon of Moose or Elk

Cut the tenderloin, at a slight angle across the grain, into slices about 1½ inch thick. Preheat the broiler to "Broil" (very hot). Preheat the rack and then brush it with oil.

Mix soft butter with finely chopped fresh parsley and salt and let it firm up. With a spoon, mold the mixture into little balls about ½ inch in diameter. Refrigerate until needed. The balls need not be uniform—the main thing is that they be ready when needed.

Place the slices of meat on the preheated and oiled broiling rack. With the oven door ajar, broil the slices 5 minutes on the first side and 3 minutes on the other (they should be served rare). Place a butterball on each sizzling steak and put under the broiler just long enough to start the butter melting. Serve immediately on hot plates with a wedge of lemon.

Braised Round or Shoulder Steak of Moose or Elk

> 1½ to 2 pounds round or shoulder steak
>   of moose or elk, about 1½ inches thick
> Buttermilk
> Flour, seasoned with black pepper
> ¼ pound salt pork, in small dices
> 1 large onion, sliced
> 1 green pepper, cut in rings
> 2 or 3 carrots, cut in sticks
> 1 bay leaf
> ½ teaspoon thyme, pounded
> 1 clove garlic, minced
> 1 teaspoon sugar
> ½ cup beef bouillon or beef stock
> ½ cup dry red wine
> 1 cup diced mushrooms

Scrape the steak with the back of a knife and wipe it with a damp cloth. Cut it into serving portions. Put it in a deep platter and cover the meat with buttermilk. Turn the meat over to coat it well. Refrigerate the meat for 8 to 24 hours. Drain well and pat between towels to absorb excess moisture. Dredge the meat in the seasoned flour.

In a large, heavy skillet, sear the salt pork until it's crisp and golden. Use a slotted spoon to transfer the salt pork to a paper-lined dish. Add the steak to the remaining hot fat and brown well on both sides. Stir in the vegetables, and cook until limp. Add seasonings, garlic, and sugar. Blend in the hot bouillon and wine. Taste-test and adjust seasonings, adding a little salt to taste. Scatter the salt pork over the top. Bring to a boil, then turn down the heat, cover tightly, and simmer until tender, about 1½ hours. After 30 minutes, check occasionally, stirring lightly for even cooking. Add a small amount of hot stock or wine as necessary. (Note: Instead of stove-top simmering, you may put the meat into a slow oven and forget it for 2½ to 3 hours.)

Transfer the meat to a warm serving platter. While the sauce is simmering down to the desired thickness, sauté the mushrooms and pile them on top of the meat. Strain the sauce and pour it over the meat. If the vegetables don't look too cooked out, put them on the meat as well. *4 to 6 servings.*

Chicken-Fried Venison Steak

1½ to 2 pounds venison, haunch or shoulder
¼ cup seasoned flour
Shortening or oil
1 cup milk
½ cup mushrooms (optional)

Slice the meat across the grain into serving-size portions roughly 3 by 5 inches and ½ inch thick. Season the flour well with salt, pepper, and your favorite herbs or spices, and spread it on a plate. Dredge both sides of the steaks in the mixture; use a mallet to pound in as much flour as the meat will hold. Shake off loose flour.

In a heavy frying pan, heat the shortening to a depth of ¼ inch. Fry the meat to a nice brown on the outside and no more than rare in the middle, turning once. Put on a heated platter and keep warm in the oven.

Pour off the excess fat from the frying pan. Scrape up the "trash" (Southerners' word for the rich brown bits on the bottom of the pan). Whip the remaining seasoned flour (there should be about 2 tablespoons) into 1 cup of milk until evenly mixed and frothy. Stir into the hot frying pan. Cook and stir until smoothly thickened. If too thick, stir in more milk. Add fresh or canned mushrooms if desired. Simmer, stirring frequently, for 5 minutes. Pour over the meat and serve. *4 to 6 servings.*

—Mrs. Charly McTee
Schertz, Texas

Venison Shish Kabob

The current popularity of shish kabob in North American cookery is a revival rather than a novelty. In the Middle East, where the method originated, kabobs (small pieces of meat) were traditionally lamb and were cooked over hot coals, usually on a skewer. Nowadays this ancient method is applied to a variety of meats and firm-fleshed fish.

2 pounds venison
½ cup salt
Freshly ground black pepper
3 or 4 cloves garlic, slivered
1 tablespoon dill seed
Handful chopped parsley
Boiled white cider vinegar, cooled
Boiled water, cooled
Onions, bacon, cherry tomatoes, mushrooms,
   cucumber chunks
Butter or olive oil

Trim the venison and cut it into 1½-inch cubes. Place in an earthen bowl and sprinkle the salt over the meat. Add a generous amount of pepper, then scatter the garlic on top. Add a tablespoon or more of dill seed, and scatter a handful of chopped parsley over all. Add enough vinegar and water to completely cover the meat. Cover with a plate, using a nonmetallic weight on the plate to keep the meat submerged. Let the meat marinate for 6 to 10 hours. Drain and pat the meat dry with paper towels.

Spear the meat on long skewers, 4 or 5 chunks on each, interspersed with onions, bacon, cherry tomatoes, mushrooms, and/or chunks of cucumber. Brush with butter or olive oil and broil quickly over a low charcoal fire, until rare. Shish kabobs make a spectacular patio presentation when flamed with brandy. Serve one skewer per person, or let guests cook their own. *8 to 10 servings.*

Caribou Stroganoff

Russian dishes in Alaska are a legacy from the days when the Russian American Fur Trading Company held sway on the northwest coast.

> 1½ pounds sirloin steak
> ¼ cup flour
> 1 teaspoon salt
> 2 small onions, minced
> ½ pound mushrooms
> 1 clove garlic, minced
> 3 tablespoons fat
> 2 tablespoons flour
> 1 cup beef bouillon
> 1 tablespoon Worcestershire sauce
> 1 cup sour cream
> Steamed rice

Dredge the steak in combined flour and salt. Over medium heat sauté onions, mushrooms, and garlic in fat for 5 minutes. Add the steak. Brown evenly all over. Remove meat, mushrooms, and onions from the pan. Combine 2 tablespoons flour with drippings in pan, stirring until evenly blended. Add bouillon and Worcestershire sauce. Cook and stir until thickened. Blend in sour cream; heat slowly just until gravy simmers. Add the meat and vegetables and heat for a few minutes.

Serve hot over steamed rice. *4 to 6 servings.*

—Reindeer and Caribou Recipes
Cooperative Extension Service
University of Alaska, Fairbanks

Corned Venison

An ancient preservative process, corning simply involves pickling meat in brine. Over the years, the crude brine has been refined by the addition of spices and sugars, which increase the meat's flavor and keeping qualities. The addition of saltpeter (sodium or potassium nitrate) inhibits the growth of botulism spores and enhances the color of the meat.

Nitrates and nitrites have recently come under scrutiny as food preservatives and are no longer used in the quantities once common. The brine recipe that follows uses only ¼ teaspoon of saltpeter for 10 pounds of meat.

Tough, coarse-grained meat takes up salt readily and corns well. Thus corning is a remarkably satisfactory treatment for those cuts of venison too often relegated to the grinder or ignored altogether.

Corned Venison

Choose fairly large cuts (2 to 3 pounds) of flank, brisket, neck, or shoulder. From an animal past its youthful tenderness, use the rump, round, or haunch as well. Remove all bone and trim off the fat.

The ingredient proportions given below are enough to corn 10 pounds of meat. They may be increased or decreased as needed. This is a fall recipe. If the weather is warm, increase the salt.

> 1 to 1¼ pounds pickling salt
> ¼ teaspoon saltpeter
> ⅛ teaspoon baking soda
> ½ cup dark molasses or brown sugar
> ⅛ teaspoon each ground mace and allspice
> ½ teaspoon each cracked peppercorns and whole cloves
> Distilled or cooled, boiled water

Use an earthen crock big enough for the quantity of meat, allowing a good 6 inches of head room. Scatter some of the salt over the bottom of the crock, add a few pieces of meat, sprinkle with salt; add meat and salt alternately until all the meat is in the crock. Sprinkle remaining salt over the meat. Leave overnight covered with cheesecloth or a clean towel.

The next day, dissolve the saltpeter and baking soda in a cup of warm water and add to the molasses or brown sugar. Mix in the spices and pour the mixture over the meat. Add distilled or cooled, boiled water, enough to completely cover everything. Put a large weighted plate or clean board on top of the meat to keep it submerged in the brine. (Note: Do not let metal or stone come in contact with the meat or brine.) Cover the crock with a doubled cheesecloth and keep in a cold, clean, dark place.

Once a day for the first week, turn the meat over with wooden spoons. From then on, turn it every few days. The meat may be used after 10 days. Submerged in the brine, the venison should keep through the winter months. Always use clean wooden spoons when removing pieces.

Freshen the venison by soaking it in clear, cold water for several hours before cooking. To cook corned venison, see the next recipe, Corned Venison with Cabbage.

Corned Venison with Cabbage

> 3 to 4 pounds corned venison
> ½-pound piece salt pork
> 1 firm cabbage, quartered and cored

Soak the corned venison in cold water overnight to freshen. Drain and rinse in cold water. Put the meat into a deep kettle, just wide enough to accommodate it, along with the salt pork. Add cold water to cover the meat. Place over high heat and bring to a boil; skim carefully. Turn down the heat, cover, and simmer until the meat is tender. Remove the salt pork. Let the meat cool in the stock until about ½ hour before serving time. Skim off all the fat from the surface. Pour 2 cups of the stock into another kettle and bring to a boil. To this add the cabbage and cook until tender. Meanwhile, heat the meat in the broth that remains in the kettle. Drain and place the meat in a heated deep platter. Drain and add the cabbage to the meat, and serve with a mustard or horseradish sauce. *6 to 8 servings.*

New England Variation: Prepare as above, but while cooking the cabbage, remove the meat from the stock and add 12 small peeled potatoes, 1 cup of diced turnip, 3 or 4 sliced carrots, and 3 or 4 sliced parsnips to the kettle. Cook until all the vegetables are tender. Return the meat to the stock long enough to reheat it. Put the venison on a warm platter and arrange the drained vegetables, including the cabbage, around it. Serve piping hot with mustard sauce, and pickled beets for color and pique.

Corned Venison Hash

1 cup cooked corned venison, cold
2 or 3 large cold boiled potatoes
Butter
1 onion, chopped
2 or 3 slices bacon or salt pork, diced
Salt and pepper to taste
Venison stock, gravy, or boiling water

Chop together, finely, the venison and potatoes. Grease a large frying pan with butter, and brown the onion with the diced bacon or salt pork. Add the meat and potatoes, season to taste with salt and pepper, and mix well.

Add enough stock to just moisten the hash. Cover and let steam and heat through thoroughly. Stir occasionally, turning the hash over from the bottom of the pan. When done, the hash should be neither dry nor watery. *2 to 4 servings.*

Leftover venison roast or steak may also be prepared in this way. Use curry or savory seasonings to taste.

Western-Style Spiced Venison or Buffalo

18 to 25 pounds boned and trimmed lean venison
    or buffalo—round, shoulder, or rump—in cuts
    to fit size of crock (a 10-gallon crock takes two
    10-pound roasts)
½ to 1 teaspoon saltpeter
2 cups coarse salt
1 cup coarsely cracked pepper
1 cup brown sugar
2 tablespoons ground allspice

Bind each cut of meat with string. Rub the saltpeter all over meat and let it stand overnight in stone crock.

On the following day, thoroughly mix the remaining ingredients and rub well into the meat, covering the entire surface. Place the meat in a tightly covered crock, and turn it once a day for 21 days so that each side of the meat is kept moist. Use wooden spoons to turn the meat.

Before cooking, make sure the meat is still tied tightly. Wrap the roast in at least 3 layers of heavy aluminum foil, pouring all of the juice from the crock into the foil. If there is more than one piece of meat, divide the juice proportionately among the pieces.

Place the wrapped meat in a roasting pan and bake in a 275° to 300° F oven (135° to 150° C) until a meat thermometer reaches the rare beef reading. Chill the meat, clean off the cooked juices with a knife or spatula, and slice razor-thin. Pile the meat on hot French bread or buns and serve with green salad and wine. The meat may be kept frozen indefinitely.

—Mrs. J. D. Ironside
Swift Current, Saskatchewan

Offal

Heart, kidneys, brain, cheeks, tongue, tripe—all the edible inner and outer organs of the freshly killed game—went into the big pot. With a pint of rum to moisten and a handful of chilis to season, it was all simmered long and slowly over a pit of coals. This fortifying dish, invented on the range by cowhands, became known in the West as Son-of-a-Bitch Stew.

—Legend

Hunters who do not retrieve the offal from big-game animals leave some nutritious delicacies behind. Furthermore, in most states and provinces they fail, through carelessness or ignorance, to comply with regulations that clearly state that no edible flesh from a kill should be destroyed or allowed to spoil.

The word *offal* (in supermarket terms, *variety meats*) covers the edible organs of the visceral system—liver, kidneys, heart, and tongue, to name those dealt with here—along with such delicacies as moose muffle and caribou hoofs, also discussed here. In deer and caribou, some of these organs may be too small to be worth the trouble of retrieving, but in moose and elk, all are of a size well worth attention.

Offal are extremely perishable. However, given prompt and careful attention in the field the wholesome organs from a healthy big game animal, unless shot-damaged beyond repair, can provide memorable feasts in the hunt camp. The organs require no aging. In fact, all offal, except perhaps the tongue (which may be salt-cured), should be used fresh (or be quickly frozen)—and you'll never get any fresher offal than those resulting from your own successful hunt.

The following recipes are given in proportions for specific animal organs. They may be applied to offal from any big game ruminants; it's just a matter of scale.

HEART

To protect the heart during transport do not remove the pericardium, or sheath, until cooking time. To prepare heart for cooking, first pull off the sheath. With a sharp boning knife, square off the top of the heart. Open it up slightly and clean out all the cardiac machinery—arteries, veins, etc.—and any blood clots, making a clean pocket. Take care not to puncture the muscle. Cover the cleaned heart with salted water and let stand for 2 or 3 hours to draw out blood. Rinse well, and wipe dry. The heart is now ready to cook.

The heart is a lean, firm muscle and tends to dry out during cooking. It should be cooked with plenty of fat and by a moist-heat method such as braising.

Braised Stuffed Heart of Moose or Elk

Prepare your favorite moist, savory bread stuffing (see "Stuffings" in Chapter 11), adding a little extra butter or margarine. Loosely stuff the heart from a moose or elk and close it with string and skewers or sew it up, leaving some slack to allow the stuffing to swell.

Melt about 2 tablespoons of fat in a Dutch oven. Brown the heart on all sides. Cover completely with strips of bacon. Add a cup of stock or a mixture of water and red wine. Put into a preheated 325° F (165° C) oven and bake covered until tender, about 3 hours. It also may be cooked over a low heat on top of the stove. Check the moisture from time to time; don't let it cook dry. Transfer the meat to a warm platter.

Thicken the gravy by mixing flour into 1 tablespoon of cooking oil or soft butter until it is mealy in texture. Sprinkle over the gravy and stir until smoothly thickened. Remove the bacon, slice the heart, and serve it with the gravy on the side. *4 to 6 servings.*

Braised stuffed heart is an excellent candidate for the slow-cooking appliance; it also may be browned and cooked in a pressure cooker. Prepare as directed above, and cook according to the instructions for beef in the appliance manual.

Leftover heart with stuffing makes a fine hash (see Corned Venison Hash).

Camp-Style Braised Heart
1 moose or elk heart, or 2 deer or caribou hearts
½ pound bacon squares or salt pork
½ cup flour, seasoned with salt and pepper
Red wine (optional)
Dash sugar
½ package cream of onion soup mix

Trim and soak the heart as directed earlier, and cut it into cubes. Dice the bacon and brown it in a frying pan. Remove the bacon with a slotted spoon and reserve.

Place the heart cubes in a bag with the seasoned flour and shake until the meat is well coated. Add the meat to the hot bacon fat and brown well but quickly. Add 1 cup of water or wine and the sugar. Cover and simmer for 30 minutes or until the meat is almost tender.

Mix the onion soup mix with 1 cup water and stir into the meat; continue to stir until smoothly thickened. Let simmer uncovered at the back of the stove for 10 minutes, stirring occasionally. Serve with mashed potatoes, corn bread, or bannock. *4 to 6 servings.*

TONGUE

Moose, elk, and buffalo tongue are cooked in the same manner as beef tongue. Tongue takes well to a couple of days' salt cure, so the hunter can transport it in the cure and have an extra-delectable viand when he arrives home.

Spiced Jellied Tongue
1 moose, elk, or buffalo tongue
½ cup coarse pickling salt
Scant pinch saltpeter
1 tablespoon sugar
½ teaspoon ground cloves or allspice

Scrub the tongue in plenty of cold water, and pat dry. Trim off the ragged ends at the base. (Note: 2 or more smaller tongues of venison, antelope, mountain goat, or mountain sheep also may be prepared at one time by this recipe.)

Combine the remaining ingredients and rub well into the entire surface of the tongue. Place the tongue in a small bowl, cover with a plate, and store in a cold place. Turn the tongue each day, for up to a week, to keep it well moistened in the fluid, or pickle, that forms.

To take it home from camp, line a covered can or plastic container with a strong, new plastic bag. Put the tongue and all the pickle into the bag and seal it tightly; cover the container. Kept cold, the tongue may be left in the cure for a total of about a week. Should it be in transit for more than 12 hours, turn the plastic bag over in the pail occasionally, so that all meat surfaces stay in contact with the cure.

When ready to use, remove the tongue from the cure and cover it with water for a couple of hours to freshen. Rinse it well, put into a deep, close-fitting saucepan, and cover with cold water. Add a bay leaf. If the tongue is not already sufficiently spiced, add ½ teaspoon of whole cloves or whole allspice and ½ teaspoon of peppercorns. Do not add any salt.

Bring to a boil, then reduce heat, cover lightly, and cook the tongue gently for 3 to 4 hours, depending on the size, until it is fork-tender and the skin has loosened. Turn the tongue over occasionally as it cooks. Do not replenish water while cooking unless absolutely necessary.

Place the tongue on a chopping board. Let the stock continue to boil down until it's reduced to about a cupful. Slit the skin on the underside of the tongue and peel it off. Remove the small bones and fatty matter at the base. When the tongue is neatly trimmed, curl it into a pudding bowl, pressing it down. Strain and pour the reduced stock over the tongue, just enough to cover. Press down firmly with a saucer. Pour off excess stock, leaving the tongue barely covered. Place a heavy weight on the saucer, and refrigerate until cold and jelled.

Turn out on a plate and garnish for the table, or slice the tongue, cutting across the grain, and serve in sandwiches or as cold cuts with horseradish or a sharp mustard sauce.

Variations: The fresh tongue may be cooked and jelled as described, skipping the salt cure (add the bay leaf and spices to the cooking water). The cooked, skinned tongue may also be served hot with a mustard or wine sauce.

LIVER

To be edible, the liver must not have any nodules, lesions, or other abnormal swellings; otherwise, it should be discarded. Even if the liver has been examined in the field, check it over again before cooking. Cut into the liver in two or three places—this helps to drain the fluids and should also disclose any inner flaws. If the shot has gone through relatively cleanly, the affected area may be trimmed away. If the liver has been badly damaged by an abdominal shot, it will probably be beyond rescue.

Wipe the liver with a clean, damp cloth. Remove the outer casing and cut the liver into slices about ½ inch thick. Unless it can be fast-frozen, cook it right away or at least within the next several hours. Fresh venison liver is tender and cooks quickly by the same methods used for beef liver.

Venison Liver and Bacon
6 slices venison liver, ½ inch thick
Salt
½ cup flour
½ teaspoon pepper
1 tablespoon dry mustard
Sliced bacon (2 to 3 slices per person)
2 tablespoons butter
½ cup hot water or red wine

Cover the liver slices with cold water; add 1 tablespoon of salt to draw the blood and soak for ½ hour or so. When ready to cook, drain and wash each slice in clear, cold water. Pat dry between towels.

Mix the flour with 1 teaspoon salt and the pepper and dry mustard. Spread the mixture on a plate and dredge each liver slice, both sides, in it. Fry the bacon in a large frying pan until medium crisp. Remove the bacon and let it drain on paper; keep it warm.

Pour off excess bacon fat, and add the butter to the pan. Quickly sear both sides of the liver, then cook for 2 or 3 minutes on each side, just until no more red shows in the meat. Overcooking toughens liver. Transfer the liver to a warm platter, add the bacon, and serve at once.

A pan sauce may be made by stirring ½ cup of hot water or red wine into the drippings and pouring it over the fried liver.

Spiced Venison Liver

Prepare the salt cure previously given for Spiced Jellied Tongue. Sprinkle some over the bottom of a bowl. Add slices of liver in layers, sprinkling more cure between slices, and topping with a layer of the salt mixture. Make more if necessary.

Cover and refrigerate overnight, up to 2 days, turning the liver occasionally. Drain the liver and freshen it by soaking in cold water for ½ hour. Pat it between towels. Cook as for Venison Liver and Bacon. This dish is a favorite of those not usually fond of liver.

KIDNEY

To prepare kidneys from moose, elk, or buffalo for cooking, remove the outer membrane, then trim the fat and reserve it. Remove *all* of the white spongy mass in the center (this is a filter system, and it can contribute a nasty taste). Kidneys may be sliced, floured, and fried, or cubed and braised for kidney pie.

Kidney Pie

2 moose or elk kidneys
Flour, seasoned with salt and pepper
Butter
Salt
1 onion, stuck with 2 cloves
Vegetable flakes or ½ package onion soup mix
  (optional)
½ cup red wine
Pastry mix for 2 crusts

Trim the kidneys as directed earlier. Soak them in salted water for 2 to 3 hours (see below for keeping overnight). Cut the kidneys into chunks, and dredge these in the seasoned flour by shaking all together in a bag.

Render some of the suet from the kidneys in an iron frying pan, adding bacon fat or vegetable oil if there isn't enough suet. Brown the kidney in the hot fat, turning it as it browns. Pour in enough water to barely cover. Add 2 tablespoons butter, salt to taste, and the cloved onion. Vegetable flakes or onion soup mix may be added. Lace with the red wine. Bring to a boil, reduce the heat, and simmer until the meat is tender and the sauce thick.

Meanwhile, prepare the pastry from a mix. Line a 9-inch frying pan or a deep pie dish with the pastry. Fill with meat and sauce. Add dabs of butter. Cover with pastry, score, and bake at 400° F (205° C) until nicely browned—about an hour.

[85]

Instead of making the kidney into a pie, the braised meat may be served on hot corn bread, biscuits, or bannock.

Note: To hold fresh kidney overnight, marinate it in 1 cup each of red wine and water; add a dash of sugar, a few crushed juniper berries, 2 or 3 cloves, and any other spices desired. The next day, drain the kidney and dry between towels. Strain and reserve the marinade. Proceed as described for Kidney Pie, using the marinade, instead of water and wine, for moistening. Remove the extra cloves or stick them into the onion.

MOOSE MUFFLE

It's called moose muffle in British Columbia, moose muzzle in Quebec, and moose nose (which is what it is) in Alaska. But no matter what it's called, this great delicacy is well worth the effort required to prepare it.

The cartilaginous member of the moose's facial anatomy jells firmly. The stock may be used to make soup or with any soup recipe that calls for water or stock.

Alaska-Style Jellied Moose Nose

Cut away the upper jawbone of the moose just below the eyes. (Note: In Quebec the practice is to remove the nose, or "muzzle," by cutting across the skin just back of the lip crease and freeing the flesh from the upper jaw, leaving the skull intact.) Put the jawbone in a large kettle of scalding water and boil it for 45 minutes. Remove it and put into cold water to cool. Pluck the hairs from the nose as you would the feathers from duck (the boiling loosens them), and wash it thoroughly.

Put the nose in a kettle and cover it with fresh water. Add a sliced onion, a little garlic, and pickling spices. Boil it gently until the meat is tender. Let it cool overnight in its stock.

In the morning, take the meat out of the broth, and remove the bones and cartilage. You will have two kinds of meat: The bulb of the nose is white, and the thin strips along the bone and jowls are dark. Cut the meat into thin slices, pack it into a loaf-type pan, and add strained juice to cover. Salt, pepper, or other spices may be added if needed; some people add vinegar to suit their own taste. The mixture will jell and, when firm, can be sliced for serving cold.

What is left may be saved by freezing in waxed or plastic containers. Save the stock for soup.

—After the Kill
Cooperative Extension Service
University of Alaska, Fairbanks

Yukon-Style Moose Nose

Saw the entire top part of the nose away from the skull, teeth and all, in the same manner as for Alaska-Style Jellied Moose Nose. Build a fire and tie the nose to a piece of wire and roll it through the flames to singe off the hair. Scrape with a knife and singe again, making sure that every hair, including those up in the nostrils, is completely cleaned off and that all that remains is the bare skin.

Carefully remove the nose portion—the meaty section from the upper jawbone; this can be done before or after the hair is singed off; but it's easier to handle if done after. Wash well in clean water. Put into a stock pot and cover with cold water. Add ¼ cup of vinegar, and season with chopped onions, salt, pepper, and sage to taste. Bring to a boil, skim, and boil for 3 to 4 hours, until the meat is tender.

Eat it either hot or cold, or jelly the meat (see Alaska-Style Jellied Moose Nose).

—Don Sawatsky
Whitehorse, Yukon

HOOFS AND HEAD

Caribou Hoofs

Indians and Eskimos of the Northwest Territories use the hoofs of the caribou. When the hoofs are covered with hot water and boiled for a couple of hours, the skin peels off easily, revealing tender, sweet meat.

Venison Head Cheese

Place the cleaned head of a deer or caribou, split if necessary, in a large kettle with enough water to cover. Add ¼ pound of fat, fresh pork chunks. Bring to a boil and cook uncovered until the meat falls from the bones. Transfer the meat from the pot to a large wooden bowl or cutting board, leaving the stock in the kettle to boil down.

Remove every trace of bone and cartilage from the meat. Chop the meat, along with the pork, into very small pieces, and place it in a mixing bowl. Add a small amount of stock and the following seasonings to the meat:

> 1 tablespoon salt
> 1 teaspoon black pepper
> 1 tablespoon fine herbs
> Dash allspice

Mix the meat and seasonings well. Blend in enough soft butter to make a heavy paste. Lay a square of clean white cloth—large enough to wrap the meat—in a colander, and place the meat mixture in the middle. Fold the cloth closely over the meat, and put a small, lightly weighted plate on top of it. Leave in refrigerator for 24 hours to set and chill. Slice thinly for salad or sandwich, and serve with hot mustard sauce.

The reduced liquor may be clarified for consommé or stock.

OTHER RUMINANTS

As happened with so much of the wildlife of North America, the animals of the West were named by the settlers for Old World species they resembled. Hence the antelope, or pronghorn, is not in fact an antelope but an animal of an entirely different family; and the North American mountain goat is actually a peculiar mountain antelope, more closely related to the Alpine chamois. Wild Rocky Mountain sheep really are sheep but of their own distinct species, *Ovis canadensis*. Buffalo is bison, and the elk is wapiti, a big deer.

As mentioned earlier, these are all ruminant animals, inherently lean, and their meat can be treated basically the same way as venison. Field and home care are similar and equally important. Kitchen treatment is a matter of scale rather than species. Recipes for venison of comparable size, age, and cut may be used for these other ruminants, and vice versa. Recipes for antelope, mountain goat, and mountain sheep are interchangeable.

Antelope

The antelope's liking for a sagebrush diet may give the meat a robust natural seasoning with a noticeable aroma. If this natural seasoning is very strong, trim off the fat (where the sagebrush flavor concentrates) and increase the larding. When cooking antelope according to recipes for other species, omit savory herbs in the marinade and other strong seasonings.

Marinated Roast of Antelope

4- to 5-pound haunch or loin roast of mature antelope

Marinade:
1 cup dry red wine
½ cup lemon juice
1 drop oil of *natural* juniper (berries) from the drugstore,
    or 4 or 5 crushed juniper berries
2 carrots, sliced
2 tablespoons raw or brown sugar
2 tablespoons vegetable oil

Combine the marinade ingredients in a saucepan and heat to a simmer. Lard the roast well, then put it into a ceramic bowl and pour the hot marinade over it; turn the meat several times to coat well. Cover the bowl and refrigerate 2 to 3 days, turning the meat occasionally.

Remove the meat from the marinade, drain, and towel-dry. Roast, using any of the deer recipes given for the same cut. *8 to 10 servings.*

Prairie-Style Haunch of Antelope

Thaw the haunch of antelope if frozen, and bring to room temperature. Wash in tepid water and towel-dry. Preheat oven to 300° F (150° C).

Make a stiff biscuit dough, about 1½ times the standard recipe. Lace it generously with poultry seasoning. Knead well. Roll the dough out until it's about ½ inch thick. Spread it lavishly with softened butter, then add a layer of thinly sliced onion. Place the haunch, topside down, on the dough in a roasting pan, and wrap completely, overlapping the edges of the dough. Trim the dough and save the trimmings for patching. Place the package in the roasting pan, seamed-side down. Bake uncovered for 4 to 5 hours, or about 40 minutes per pound. (Check after ½ hour; if the dough has cracked open, patch it.)

Remove the roasting pan and turn up the oven to 425° F (220° C). Lift out the meat and discard the crust. Return the haunch to the roasting pan. Brush with butter, dust lightly with flour, and put it back into the hot oven to brown for a minute or two. Serve with Pepper Sauce (see Chapter 11). Creamed cauliflower, sweet potatoes, and fresh or frozen peas go well with this dish.

—Mrs. J. D. Ironside
Swift Current, Saskatchewan

Wild Mountain Sheep and Mountain Goat

Although nonresident hunters may be attracted by trophy-quality mountain sheep and goat, the natives of the northwest Rockies tend to prefer the more tender meat of younger animals. The tougher cuts of the trophy sheep or goat, just as those of venison, should respond to a meat tenderizer, a marinade, or a pickle cure; they also may be ground and made into burgers.

The wild mountain sheep is a fastidious eater, and thus has a fine pure flavor. The young sheep is tender. If tenderizing marinades are needed for older or trophy animals, they should be delicately seasoned.

The trophy goat, like the trophy sheep, is a mature, lean animal. Although excellent in flavor (unless it's an old billy in rutting season), the meat may be somewhat tougher than sheep meat. It should be hung for 10 to 12 days in a dry place, just above freezing, with good air circulation. Trimmed of fat, the lean goat is cooked the same way as sheep or venison, without salt and with plenty of larding. Unless the goat is young, a tenderizing marinade should be used.

Mountain sheep and mountain goat may be cooked by recipes for venison of comparable size, age, and cut.

Sweet and Sour Rocky Mountain Sheep
3 to 4 pounds lean mountain sheep or goat
Marinade
Flour
¼ cup fat or cooking oil
½ pound bacon, cubed
1 tablespoon sugar
3 carrots, sliced
2 onions, sliced
1 stalk celery, diced
1 cup sour cream
2 tablespoons raisins,
    washed and soaked to plump
2 tablespoons pine nuts or capers

Marinade:
1 cup vinegar
1 cup dry red wine
1 tablespoon honey
2 bay leaves
6 to 8 peppercorns, cracked
1 onion
1 large carrot, sliced
1 stalk celery with leaves, broken

Cut the meat in 1½-inch cubes and place in a ceramic bowl. Combine the marinade ingredients and heat to a boil. Simmer for a couple of minutes, and pour over the meat. Cover and refrigerate for 2 to 3 days, stirring the meat occasionally. Drain the meat and pat dry between towels. Strain and reserve the marinade.

Dredge the meat in flour, coating it well on all surfaces. Heat the fat in a large Dutch oven or casserole over high heat. Add the bacon and sheep, and brown well on all sides. Sprinkle the sugar on top of the meat, and continue to brown for 2 or 3 minutes. Blend in 3 tablespoons of flour, and then the reserved marinade. Add the carrots, onions, and celery. Bring to a boil and cover tightly. Reduce the heat and simmer for about 3 hours, or until the meat is tender. Blend in the sour cream, the raisins, and capers or pine nuts. Simmer gently and stir lightly for 2 to 3 minutes. Add salt to taste. Serve with hot bannock or fluffy cooked rice. *10 to 12 servings.*

Buffalo

Historically, the hump and tongue were the prized parts of the buffalo, or bison, and stories abound of the wanton waste of the rest of the carcass during the opening of the West. The tongue, roasted in hot ashes, was considered a delicacy.

Buffalo is comparable to lean range-fed beef and, if well larded, may be cooked according to beef recipes. Recipes for elk, moose, or comparably sized cuts of any venison may also be used. (The recipe for Venison à la Bourguigonne yields a winy buffalo stew of unsurpassed succulence.)

Buffalo Brandy Braise

In applying an exotic and involved *flambé* recipe to buffalo for my earlier book, *Canadian Game Cookery*, an error was made in the experimental cooking procedure. The outcome was so satisfying that this wayward method has since been applied to venison, beef, and even fish.

2 pounds buffalo round steak, 1½ inches thick
4 ounces brandy
4 tablespoons fat
Pepper
2 onions
3 faggots (see Glossary)

Wipe the steak as dry as possible. Cut it into cubes, wiping each piece again. Heat the fat in a heavy iron frying pan. Spear the meat, two pieces at a time, on a long-handled fork, and brush each piece with brandy. Sear the meat in a clean flame.

Brown the meat quickly on all sides in the sizzling fat. Add water and any remaining brandy to just cover. Season the meat with pepper, and slice the onions over the top. Place the faggots in with the meat. Cover and simmer until the liquid is reduced to a thick brown sauce. Remove the faggots. Season the buffalo with salt and serve in its own sauce. *6 servings.*

Buffalo Steak à la Tartare

1 pound lean buffalo steak, round, hump, or loin
½ teaspoon salt
½ teaspoon freshly ground black pepper
1 ounce brandy

Put the meat through a food grinder using a fine disc. Add the salt, pepper, and brandy and mix thoroughly. Adjust seasonings to taste. Shape into a mound on a serving plate. Chill until ready to serve. Serve garnished with parsley, and place a small bowl of chopped chives and capers soaked in lemon juice or tartar sauce on the side.

Variation: Steak à la tartare may also be served in individual portions with a raw egg nested on top. This has a reputation for easing a hangover.

5

Other Big Game

Your best plan is to stand out on the sea ice till you catch a bear, then keep right on talking till you make him see your point of view. If he refuses, you may never get off the ice, so what you say is important.

—Arctic Recipes
Indian and Northern Affairs, Canada

Other big game hunted in North America include bears from all over, sea mammals of the North, and wild pigs of the South. These are nonruminant animals with omniverous or carniverous habits. Fall bears* and sea mammals are extremely fat; the pigs relatively lean. All require preparation and cooking methods that dispose of excess fat and cook the meat thoroughly.

BEARS

Fattened on wild berries, blossoms, nuts, and such, the young fall bear can provide the hunter with a succulent bit of meat. There are, however, two main problems to consider when cooking bear.

First, the fall bear before hibernation is extremely fat—both outside and in. Outside fat can be trimmed, but unless the meat is treated to render out the intermuscular fat, the texture is too oily for many palates. The rich, sweet fat of the fall bear needn't be wasted; it is prized as a pastry shortening, and its cosmetic value to skin care and use in soap making are legendary.

A second, and far more serious, problem in cooking bear is that it is a notorious carrier of trichinosis. In the 1960s, it was considered advisable to treat bear like pork, and prolonged freezing was recommended as a means of killing the trichinosis-causing parasite. The procedure applied to bear meat came into question after an outbreak of the disease in 1968 and again in 1978—both attrib-

*The spring bear is too thin to be palatable. The spring hunt is primarily for pelts.

[91]

uted to eating bear taken in Alaska. In each case, the meat had been held for lengthy periods in the freezer—at 0° F (−18° C) and 5° F (−15° C), respectively. Laboratory tests on the meat showed no loss of activity in the trichinal larvae. All this has led to the speculation that the trichinae in bears of the far North have built up a massive resistance to cold, or have even evolved into a separate strain; possibly, the strain of the parasite in bears in general is a different one from that in pork. In any case, it's now considered advisable to discount the prolonged freezing of bear meat as a trichinosis-prevention measure, and to cook the meat thoroughly. (The same advice applies to marine mammals and claw-footed small game animals.)

Roast Bear

4- to 5-pound rump or shoulder roast of bear
Garlic
Vinegar
Brown sugar

Basting Sauce:
1 cup skimmed hot stock
2 tablespoons brown sugar
½ teaspoon ground ginger
½ teaspoon black pepper
1 tablespoon prepared hot mustard
1 teaspoon salt

Trim as much fat as possible from the roast. Randomly pierce the meat and insert slivers of garlic (more or less to taste). Cover with cold water, adding about 2 tablespoons of vinegar and 1 tablespoon of brown sugar to the gallon, or use the juice from a bottle of sweet pickles. Bring to a boil, skim, reduce heat, and cook very gently for about 1 hour.

Meanwhile, preheat the oven to 425° F (220° C). Remove the meat and rinse under hot water. Put the meat into a roasting pan.

Combine the basting sauce ingredients and baste the meat well. Put the roast into the oven. Reduce the heat to 350° F (175° C) and cook, uncovered, applying the basting mixture frequently, until the meat is well done. Allow 35 to 40 minutes per pound, or follow the pork reading on a meat thermometer. Serve with red applesauce or cranberry sauce. *8 to 10 servings.*

A brown pan gravy can be made from the drippings. Let the drippings cool, lift off the excess fat, and save the gravy for a leftover casserole dish.

McQuarrie's Roast Bear

4- to 5-pound roast of bear, fat trimmed

Marinade:
2 cups dry red wine
½ cup vegetable oil
1 bay leaf
1 teaspoon rosemary
1 teaspoon sweet basil
1 teaspoon dry mustard
½ cup apple juice

Combine the marinade ingredients and pour over the roast. Refrigerate for 6 to 8 hours, turning the meat over occasionally.

Preheat the oven to 325° F (165° C). Drain the roast, reserving the marinade. Place the meat in a roasting pan, and lay a strip of bacon over the top. Cover and put the roast into the oven for about 3 hours. Remove the roast from the oven, and turn the heat up to 400° F (205° C).

Remove the cover and pour ¼ cup of reserved marinade over the roast. Dust with 1 tablespoon of ground cinnamon. Return the roast to the oven for 30 minutes, basting 2 or 3 more times with the marinade or the pan drippings. Serve with apple fritters. *8 to 10 servings.*

—George McQuarrie
Chairman, Zone 5
Ontario Federation of Anglers and Hunters

Great Smoky Mountain Bear Pot Roast

3- to 4-pound haunch, loin, or shoulder
  cut of fall bear, frozen
Salt and pepper
Fat
1 clove garlic, crushed
1 medium onion, chopped
2 stalks celery, broken
1 small pod dried red pepper
¼ teaspoon rosemary needles
½ bay leaf
2 tablespoons catsup
2 teaspoons Worcestershire sauce
½ teaspoon celery salt
½ teaspoon dry mustard

Trim the excess fat from the bear roast, leaving only a thin layer. Place the frozen meat in tepid water until completely thawed, then drain well and pat dry with a towel.

Rub the meat generously all over with salt and pepper. Melt enough fat to cover the bottom of a heavy Dutch oven and sear the meat well on all sides. Add boiling water, about a quarter of the way up the roast, then add all the remaining ingredients. Cover tightly and let simmer, turning the roast occasionally and adding water as necessary to keep well moistened. When very tender (about 3 hours), transfer the roast to a hot platter and keep it warm.

Skim excess fat from the surface of the gravy and bring to a boil. To thicken the gravy combine about 1 tablespoon of flour and ½ cup of warm water and stir the mixture into the boiling liquid. Stir until it reaches the desired consistency. Strain the gravy.

Slice the bear meat thinly and top with gravy. (The meat and gravy should be served as hot as possible.) Serve with wild rice or long-grained rice. *6 to 8 servings.*

Braised Bear Steak

2- to 3-pound bear steak (top round of the leg),
  1 to 1½ inches thick
Marinade
2 tablespoons olive oil
2 tablespoons chicken fat or butter
1 cup mild consommé or beef stock
1 tablespoon tomato paste

Marinade:
1 medium carrot
1 medium onion
A few celery leaves
½ teaspoon black pepper, cracked
½ clove garlic, crushed
2 teaspoons Worcestershire sauce
Pinch ground cloves
2 teaspoons dry mustard
½ to ¾ cup dill pickle juice,
   or half juice and half dry red wine

Trim the fat off the steak to a ¼-inch thickness. Scrape the surface of the meat lightly with a knife to remove any hairs and splintered bone. Wipe the steak with a vinegar-moistened cloth. Place the steak in a shallow oblong baking dish or on a deep platter. Finely chop or grate the carrot, onion, and celery leaves, and combine with the other marinade ingredients. Spread the mixture over the meat and cover. Refrigerate for 12 to 14 hours. Turn the steak 2 or 3 times, spooning a little of the marinade over the top after each turn.

Drain the steak; strain and reserve the marinade. Gash the fat edge. Heat the olive oil and chicken fat (or butter) in a large, heavy skillet. When it's hot but not smoking, add the steak. Brown the steak slowly on both sides, about 15 minutes. Pour off the fat and add a mixture of the consommé and tomato paste. Cover the skillet tightly and simmer the steak until tender, 1½ to 2 hours. Put the steak on a heated platter and keep hot.

Combine 3 tablespoons of soft butter and 3 tablespoons of flour, and stir the mixture into the pan juices. When the gravy is thick and smooth, add half the strained marinade and enough boiling water to thin the gravy to the consistency desired. Test and adjust the seasoning.

Cover the steak with fried onions or mushrooms mixed with a third of the gravy. Serve the remaining gravy separately.

—Elaine Collett
Director, L'Ecole des Arts Culinaires
Mississauga, Ontario

Polar Bear Steaks

Polar bear steaks can be quite delicious when properly prepared. In the young fall bear the meat may be overly sweet—remove all excess fat and cook by the preceding recipe for Braised Bear Steak.

It should be noted that the liver of the polar bear is inedible due to an overconcentration of vitamin A. Eskimos, when dressing out a polar bear have been observed to push the liver through a hole in the ice to prevent their dogs from eating it.

SEA MAMMALS

Since time immemorial, sea mammals have been a valuable and in some cases vital food source in the coastal regions across the top of North America, from Newfoundland to Alaska. Today the important food sources are whale, seal, and walrus. Just how valuable they are as a source of nutrients, in comparison with beef and moose meat, is dramatically evident in the accompanying table, Selected Food Values of Various Meats.

SELECTED FOOD VALUES OF VARIOUS MEATS*

	Beef (66% lean/ 34% fat)	Moose	Beluga Whale	Seal	Walrus
Protein (g)	16.500	25.100	24.500	28.300	19.200
Fat (g)	28.000	2.500	.500	33.000	13.600
Ca (mg)	10.000	10.000	7.000	17.000	18.000
Phosphorous (mg)	152.000	219.000	270.000	245.000	122.000
Iron (mg)	2.500	2.700	26.600	19.800	9.400
Vitamin A (IU)	60.000	155.000	335.000	1,050.000	550.000
Thiamine (mg)	.070	.074	.070	.135	.180
Riboflavin (mg)	.150	.027	.400	.452	.346
Niacin (mg)	4.000	5.000	6.800	7.000	3.200

*All food values given per 100 grams (about 3½ ounces) of meat. Figures taken from Composition of and Nutritive Value of Alaskan Game Meats, table in *Alaska's Game is Good Food*, Cooperative Extension Service, University of Alaska, Fairbanks.

Whale

Whale meat is lean and dark. Some devotees describe its flavor as a cross between fresh salmon and turkey; others compare it with beef. Whale meat is usually cut into steaks, which may be fried in a hot, lightly greased pan. Trim any fat, and brush with bacon fat or oil on both sides. Whale steaks are equally good braised or cut up into stews (see recipes for venison stews in Chapter 4). Cook well, but with care—it toughens if overcooked.

Whale Steak Ragout

Cut a 1½- to 2-pound whale steak into cubes and dredge lightly in flour. Dice ¼ pound of fat bacon. In a hot frying pan, sear the bacon to a crisp light gold. Remove and drain on paper. Add the whale meat to the remaining hot fat and stir-fry until well browned. Pour off the excess fat. Pour in enough water to show through the meat. Add freshly ground pepper and a bundle of fresh herbs according to taste or availability. Cover and simmer over low heat until the whale meat is just tender and the sauce is reduced to a bare presence.

Spread a layer of sliced mushrooms over the top of the meat, and smother everything in a good commercial or homemade (meatless) tomato sauce. Let simmer uncovered for about 20 minutes, or until the whale meat is tender. *4 servings.*

Muktuk

Muktuk is a thin layer of highly nutritious meat between the skin and blubber of a whale. Its smooth, firm texture somewhat resembles overcooked mushrooms, and it tastes much like fried eggs.

The Innuit and Eskimos hang sheets of muktuk to dry for a couple of days. It is then cut into pieces about 6 inches square, dropped into boiling water, and cooked until tender. Cooked muktuk is kept in large drums of oil and stored in a cold place for future use. It is prepared in various ways, usually heated in a tomato, mustard, or curry sauce, or served in a salad.

Canned muktuk is marketed.

The less choice cuts of venison can be used in various recipes calling for ground meat. These
VENISON BURGERS WITH HERBS may look like beef burgers, but their taste sets them apart.

Tart red cranberries give CRANBERRY DEER POT ROAST a traditional New England flavor. After the meat is done, the pan sauce is thickened into a piquant gravy to accompany the finely flavored tender meat.

In BLUE MOUNTAIN VENISON, a simple but tasty method for roasting a haunch or loin of young deer or caribou, the roast is spread with prepared mustard, coated lightly with brown sugar, and topped with thick slices of onion and generous dabs of butter. Serve with brown pan gravy, roasted potatoes, and carrots.

COUNTRY-STYLE VENISON SAUSAGE is relatively simple to make and can be seasoned—hot, medium, or mild—to taste. Because venison is so lean, sausage preparations require the addition of considerable fat (usually pork) to achieve a moist, succulent texture.

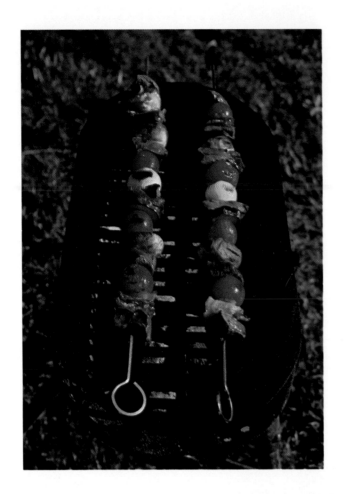

Combining different varieties of small game into POACHER'S POTAGE makes a delicious, unusual stew. Combinations of hare, grouse, partridge, pheasant, and/or squirrel are all suitable.

An adaptation of the ancient Middle Eastern recipe that traditionally uses lamb, VENISON SHISH KABOB is cooked on skewers, preferably over an outdoor barbecue. Shish kabobs are a colorful summertime favorite.

In ROAST HAUNCH OF VENISON cooked by the paste method, the natural juices are sealed in by wrapping the roast in a flour-and-water paste, then sandwiching it in an oiled paper wrap. When the roast is nearly done, the casing is removed and the meat is basted and returned to the oven until golden. This method is a refinement of the Indian technique of wrapping meat in clay and/or leaves and burying it in the coals. Similar techniques were evolved in several parts of Europe.

Topped with a few sliced mushrooms and onions, and served with a green salad, Small-Game Fricassee is another "mixed bag" that may contain various gamebirds, rabbit, and/or squirrel. Before cooking, the meat is marinated in a mixture of wine, pickling spices, sugar and garlic.

Like many recipes for rabbit or hare, JUGGED RABBIT calls for marinating the meat before cooking. Traditionally, this savory stew was cooked in an earthen jug placed in a deep pan of boiling water on the stovetop; nowadays, it's usually cooked in a Dutch oven in the oven or in an electric slow-cooking appliance.

Moravians who settled in North Carolina are credited with originating BRUNSWICK STEW. Today it's often made with chicken, but the traditional dish uses squirrel. Simmered on the stovetop, this stew also contains beans, corn, potatoes, and tomatoes.

Wild rice is not rice but a tall, grain-bearing aquatic grass. Because of its delicate, nutlike flavor, wild rice goes well with game, and many stuffings for game are prepared with it. In EMPRESS-STYLE WILD RICE, diced bacon, green onions, mushrooms, and cooked wild rice are combined, topped with Parmesan cheese and baked in a casserole dish.

Other Big Game

Walrus

In a quest for alternatives to boiled walrus, a number of beef recipes were adapted to the longer cooking times required for this large sea mammal and to the available supply of seasoning. Prepared in an Alaskan home kitchen, each walrus preparation was presented to a taste panel of Eskimos and rated as "very good," "pretty good," or "not good." The recipe given here, Walrus Kyusolik, was among those rated "very good." (*Kyusolik* means "meat with little gravy.")

Walrus Kyusolik

1 pound walrus meat
1 tablespoon vinegar
¼ teaspoon salt
¼ teaspoon pepper
1 teaspoon dry mustard
½ teaspoon meat tenderizer (optional)
2 tablespoons fat
1 tablespoon onion flakes
1 cup water plus ½ cup dry milk powder,
   or ½ cup canned milk
2 tablespoons catsup

Cut the walrus meat into small chunks. Add the vinegar to 4 cups of water in a bowl. Soak the meat chunks in this mixture for 10 minutes, then pour off the liquid. Sprinkle the salt, pepper, mustard, and tenderizer over the meat. Let the seasoned meat stand for 2 hours, then roll the chunks in flour.

Heat the fat in a frying pan. Add the meat and onion flakes, and cook until the meat is browned on both sides. Remove the chunks from the pan. Add a little more flour to the fat, and stir. Then pour in the water and milk powder, or canned milk. Stir until the gravy is smooth.

Put the meat back in the gravy, and add the catsup. Cover the pan and cook very slowly until the meat is tender. Check it occasionally, and add a little more water if it begins to get dry. Serve over cooked rice.

—Cooperative Extension Service
University of Alaska, Fairbanks

Seal

Seals play a vital role in the economy of the natives of Alaska and northern Canada. Seal skins are used for clothing, boots, and boats; their flesh is used for food; and their copious fat is fuel for heat and light.

Young seal is very tender. To call seal meat flavorful is something of an understatement: It is strong and somewhat fishy. To modify the flavor, remove as much fat as possible from the carcass and hang it in the fresh, frosty air for a few days before cooking. The meat may then be further rid of flavor-laden oils by parboiling. Seal should be gently cooked and liberally seasoned.

High Arctic Seal Casserole

2½ pounds young seal steak

Flour, seasoned with salt and pepper

3 tablespoons bacon fat or cooking oil

½ cup dried onion flakes

3 whole cloves

1 teaspoon thyme

1½ cups water

1 cup dried carrots

1 cup dried turnips

2 bouillon cubes

2 tablespoons butter

2 tablespoons flour (approximately)

To parboil: Cover the meat with cold water. Bring to a boil. Turn down heat and barely simmer for about 10 minutes. Remove and let steep until cooled off. Skim, then pour off the water. Wipe or scrape the meat.

Preheat oven to 300° F (150° C).

Cut the seal steak into 2-inch chunks. Dredge in seasoned flour and brown on all sides in hot fat. Transfer the meat to a 2-quart casserole. Add the onion flakes, cloves, thyme, and water. Bake covered for 1½ hours.

Meanwhile, simmer the carrots and turnips in water until almost tender. Drain the liquid into a saucepan and add the vegetables to the casserole. Heat the liquid in the saucepan, dissolve bouillon cubes in it, and simmer for 10 minutes. Knead the butter in flour until mealy. Sprinkle over the simmering liquid; stir until smooth and thickened. Pour over the meat in the casserole. Cover and return to oven until vegetables are tender.

—Arctic Recipes
Indian and Northern Affairs, Canada

Newfoundland Seal Flippers

4 seal flippers, skinned

1 tablespoon baking soda

2 tablespoons rendered pork fat

Seasoned flour

2 large sliced onions (optional)

1 tablespoon flour

Worcestershire sauce

Seal flippers are not parboiled. Instead, soak them in cold water, adding the baking soda, for about ½ hour. The soda makes the fat show white. With a sharp knife, remove all traces of fat.

Heat pork fat in a frying pan. Coat the flippers with seasoned flour and brown well on both sides in the hot fat. Brown the onions along with the flippers. Remove the flippers to an oven casserole and put the onions on top.

Brown the flour in the hot fat, stirring until smooth and bubbly. Stir in hot water, about a cupful, and stir until smoothly thickened. Season with Worcestershire sauce to taste. Pour the gravy over the flippers and bake in a preheated oven at 350° F (175° C), until tender.

The flippers may be served as they are, or finished under a pastry (see Seal Flipper Pie below). Garnish with parsley and wedges of lemon.

— The Treasury of Newfoundland Dishes
Maple Leaf Mills Limited

Seal Flipper Pie: After removing the baked flippers from the oven, turn the heat up to 400° F (205° C). Cover meat with a rich pastry. Score the pastry, and bake for 25 minutes, or until crust is nicely browned.

Seal Liver*

Sauté seal liver in clear butter until light brown, then cut into 2-inch cubes. Add thinly sliced Arctic puffballs to about equal weight of liver. Place in buttered casserole, cover with whole milk (powdered or tinned). Bake 15 minutes in preheated oven (375° F, 190° C) or until milk is thick.

— Arctic Recipes
Indian and Northern Affairs, Canada

WILD PIGS

Wild pigs in North America fall into three groups: peccary, wild pig, and European wild boar. All three should be well cooked.

The young peccary, or javelina, sometimes called muskhog, has fine-grained, tender meat. When properly field-dressed, it can be quite palatable. Javelina is commonly used by Mexicans in making tamales.

The javelina has a musk sac in the middle of the back, forward of the hips, which must be removed as soon as the pig is killed. The animal should be immediately gutted and the carcass chilled. It is skinned, fat-trimmed, soaked in a vinegar solution, and then frozen or prepared for cooking. Javelina is not aged, but further marinating helps subdue its characteristic strong flavor. Jim Mosley, Texas expert in game cookery, says bay leaf and garlic cure a lot of ills; he suggests using plenty in the following recipe.

Javelina and Sauerkraut

2 to 3 pounds dressed javelina meat
   (see instructions above)
1 medium onion, sliced
1 bell pepper, sliced
2 bay leaves
3 or 4 cloves garlic, crushed
1 teaspoon paprika
½ cup lemon juice
½ teaspoon salt
2 cups drained sauerkraut

---

*The liver of bearded seal (whose meat in any case is rated low as food) may be toxic due to a high concentration of vitamin A.

Cut the meat into stewing chunks and put into a heavy pot with the rest of the ingredients, except the sauerkraut. Add water to cover, and bring to a boil. Skim, and continue boiling gently until a film starts to form. Pour off liquid and all.

Rinse the meat under hot water and start over with fresh ingredients; this time chop the onion and pepper, and add chopped garlic to taste. Cook until the meat is very tender and the liquid is reduced to about half. Add the drained sauerkraut. Heat through and serve.

—Jim Mosley
G & M Catering Services
Austin, Texas

Braised Cutlets of Wild Pig

1½ pounds boneless fresh ham of young pig
Flour
1 teaspoon salt
¼ teaspoon freshly ground black pepper
2 tablespoons bacon fat
½ cup chopped onion
1 clove garlic
⅛ teaspoon dry thyme or fennel
½ cup hot water
½ cup red wine
1 medium onion, sliced
2 ripe tomatoes, sliced
3 green peppers, sliced
½ pound button mushrooms,
 or large mushrooms, sliced

Slice the meat across the grain into 4 cutlets, about 1 inch thick. Pound to flatten. Combine the flour, salt, and pepper and dredge the meat in the mixture. Heat 1 tablespoon of the fat in a heavy skillet. Brown the meat quickly, about 2 minutes on each side.

Heat the remaining fat in a saucepan and sauté the chopped garlic and onion until translucent. Add the thyme or fennel and hot water. Cover and cook gently for a couple of minutes, then pour over the meat in the skillet and add the wine. Bring to a boil, and cover tightly. Reduce the heat to low and simmer until almost tender, about 45 minutes. Replenish lost moisture with hot water as needed.

Scatter the vegetables and mushrooms over the cutlets. Cover and cook until the meat is well done and the peppers are just tender. Serve with fluffy mashed potatoes or rice. *4 servings.*

Variation: A haunch of wild boar may be prepared by this recipe.

Pit-Barbecued Shoat

In sandy soil dig a pit about 2 feet by 3 feet, and about 1½ feet deep, big enough to contain the young pig when wrapped. Line the bottom with stones or bricks. Fire the pit with hardwood or charcoal until the walls of sand spit back to water and there is a good bed of coals in the bottom.

Meanwhile, scrub the carcass of a young pig, and stuff the cavity with apples and halved oranges and lemons. Close the eyes and curl the tail. Brush the pig all over with a mixture of melted butter and lemon juice. Wrap in a heavy paste of flour and water (see Bad River Beaver). Double-wrap the pig in aluminum foil, folding the edges to seal. Place on the coals, and cover with about 6 inches of soil. Build a fire on top. Leave for 8 to 12 hours, replenishing the fuel as it burns down.

Pull the pig from the pit, and take off the wrapping and paste. Remove the rind and serve with applesauce.

Wild Boar Stew with Celery Root
2 pounds wild boar, diced
½ teaspoon salt
½ teaspoon coarse black pepper
2 tablespoons vegetable oil
1 cup diced onion
1 cup peeled and diced raw celery root
1 heaping teaspoon tomato paste
2 cups beef gravy

Marinade:
2 cups dry red wine
2 bay leaves
1 carrot, diced
1 stalk celery, diced
1 onion, coarsely chopped
3 whole cloves

Combine the marinade ingredients, pour over the meat, and let stand for 24 hours, turning the meat occasionally. Pour off the marinade and reserve. Drain the meat well.

Season the meat with the salt and pepper. Brown the meat in very hot oil for several minutes. Add the onion and celery root and fry for 5 more minutes. Add the tomato paste. After a few minutes, add the strained marinade and beef gravy. Simmer over low heat for 2 to 2½ hours, or until the meat is done. The onion and celery root will mix into the sauce and enhance the flavor of the stew.

—Gunter Gugelmeier
Executive Chef, Loews Westbury Hotel
Toronto, Ontario

PART THREE

Small Game

. . . two Cotton Tail Rabbits stuffed and baked. Oh, the fragrance of the dressing seasoned with her home-grown savories!

Jack Miner
Jack Miner and the Birds

6

Small Game Animals

Roast your squirrel over an open fire. Because squirrel meat is rather sweet in taste, tuck in a few seeds of Shepherd's Purse — these seeds have a peppery taste so don't use too many.
—Joe Van Haagen
Instructor, National Wilderness Survival, Inc.
Campbellford, Ontario

Whether it's possum in a pie or rabbit in a stew, the rest of North America is learning what Southerners have known all along: Some mighty fine wild meats enrich the table of those who pursue small game animals.

From the days of the colonists, small game has traditionally been an important ingredient in southern cooking. The celebrated Kentucky Burgoo, an enormous stew served from huge cauldrons on Derby Day, originally was made from small game meats found in the Kentucky woods. The contemporary recipe* calls for 600 pounds of lean meat, 200 pounds of fat hens, 2,000 pounds of potatoes, and various volumes of vegetables and seasoning fortifiers, along with squirrels in season — a dozen squirrels to each 100 gallons.

Small table game includes the commonly hunted members of the hare and squirrel families, as well as raccoon and opossum. The trap lines also yield some tasty and valuable wild meats — beaver and muskrat.

In fact, most small game animals of good health and wholesome dietary habits are not only edible but palatable when properly prepared. The porcupine filled many a pioneer's kettle in lean days. The armadillo is a delicacy in parts of the Southwest. The meat of woodchuck (groundhog) and prairie dog, members of the squirrel family, can be quite delectable. Gopher stew is listed in the culinary lore of early Florida settlers.

*As given in *The Southern Cookbook*, compiled and edited by Lillie S. Lusting, S. Claire Sondheil, and Sarah Rensel (1939, CULINARY ARTS PRESS).

CAUTION: Hunters should be very cautious about approaching wild animals that appear tame or sluggish; they could be rabid or tularemic. Avoid handling such animals, and report them to the nearest wildlife authorities. *Don't* eat them. *Don't* touch them.

GENERAL PREPARATION

The highlights of caring for small game in the field and kitchen are presented here. For more detailed information on the field care, skinning, and butchering of small game, see *Care & Cooking of Fish & Game*, by John Weiss (1982, Winchester Press).

Field Care

To savor the good flavor of small animals, field care is all-important. It involves a clean shot, skinning and removal of scent glands, gutting, bleeding, cooling, and generally getting the meat home to the cook in good shape.

Trapped animals (beaver or muskrat), to be at their table best, should be taken alive from the traps and killed and dressed out right away like other game. Certainly they should be freshly killed. Drowning is not conducive to good meat. If the animal is found frozen in the trap, it is best not to use the meat.

Removal of musk or scent glands is vital to the flavor of the meat. These glands usually are beady little kernels embedded in a filmlike membrane, and much disagreeable taste in small game is due to their incomplete removal. Various animals lubricate their fur with musk, and a trace of musk left by a few stray hairs can taint the meat. A good skinning job will take care of the offensive glands. Skinning before gutting avoids contact of hair with the meat. For the protection of the meat, however, the skin is often best left on for the trip home.

Kitchen Care

Once home, the skinned small game should be washed well, wiped with a vinegar-dampened cloth to remove any hairs, and refrigerated for about 24 hours before cooking or freezing. (It is not aged in the sense that venison is "hung.") Small game may be cut up before cooling, depending on its size. During the refrigeration period, the meat should be covered loosely, or placed in a vinegar solution or marinade.

The carcass of the small animal is usually cut in the kitchen and then cooked immediately or frozen in recipe-size packages. It also may be cooked or frozen whole. For general packaging instructions, see Freezing under "Home Care" in Chapter 7. Package the meat in meal-size lots. Lean small game may be stored in the freezer for 8 to 10 months; fat game for 3 to 4 months.

CUTTING SMALL GAME

The extent to which small game is cut depends on the size of the animal, the recipe or serving requirements, and the size of the pot.

Hare is used for the cutting directions that follow because it ranges in size from the cottontail rabbit of 2 or 3 pounds to the Arctic hare, which may weigh as much as 12 pounds. But the directions and diagrams can serve as a guide for cutting other small animals as well.

Where fat is excessive, trim off as much of it as possible before cutting the animal. Probe for and remove shot, and trim discolored flesh around wounds. Keep the knife sharp.

Cutting a Small Hare (under 5 pounds): For roasting, the small animal may be used whole, or with the head removed. To prepare serving or stewing pieces, follow the cuts diagrammed:

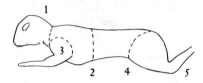

1. Cut off the head;
2. Cut through the body between the saddle and ribs, and split each piece down the back;
3. Cut off the forelegs with the shoulders;
4. Cut off the haunches;
5. Cut each haunch in two (optional).

Cutting a Large Hare (over 5 pounds): Cut in two parts behind the shoulder (see below). The hind section may be roasted without further cutting.

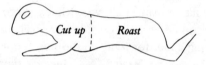

To prepare stewing pieces, from just the front section or from the entire animal, follow the cuts shown:

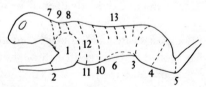

1. Cut off the shoulders;
2. Cut foreleg from the shoulder;
3. Cut off the haunches;
4. Cut each haunch in two;
5. Cut hind leg in two (optional);
6. Cut away flank on each side and cut each in two;
7. Cut off the head and discard;
8. Cut off the neck;
9. Cut the neck in two;
10. Cut the breast from the loin;
11. Cut breast in two pieces, and then
12. Cut each piece in three, lengthwise (two breasts and one back);
13. Cut loin across in pieces about 2 inches thick.

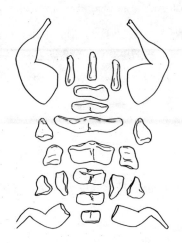

COOKING SMALL GAME

For cooking purposes, small game is divided into two groups: (1) lean animals—hare, rabbit, squirrel, and muskrat; and (2) fat animals—(fall) woodchuck, raccoon, beaver, and opossum.

Fat or lean, small game should be well cooked. The small animal feeds in close contact with the ground, digging and clawing about for food, so thorough cooking is a rule of prudence.

The meat is done at 185° to 190° F (85° to 88° C) by meat thermometer, or when it leaves the bone easily and no pink shows in the juice from a cut. Relatively fine grained and tender as the meat generally is, care should be taken not to overcook it. To ensure even cooking, frozen or refrigerated meat is best brought to room temperature first.

Dietary flavors of game cleanly shot and properly dressed are in the fat, and all healthy animals have some fat. In the small vegetarian animals, these flavors are generally good, though the hare by nature and occasionally by diet is a special case and frequently requires a flavor aid (marinade). No treatment will save meat that has spoiled or been tainted through inadequate field care.

The young animal, of course, provides the best table fare. Only the meat of the older critter requires tenderizing, followed by cooking in moist heat. Skinned animals, especially the lean ones, tend to dry out during dry-heat cooking. Always keep the surface well oiled.

The Iroquois open-hearth cookery table (Chapter 2), which separates the lean from the fat and the young from the old, is a good basic guide to cooking methods for small game. Many healthy small wild animals not included here may be used for food as long as the basics of field dressing and cooking are observed. Lynx, fox, and otter were among the delicacies mentioned by early explorers and skunk has been said to taste like rabbit.

LEAN SMALL GAME

Hare, rabbit, squirrel, and muskrat are inherently lean animals, although the fatter they are, the better. A fat squirrel or hare is a prize.

In cooking the flesh of these lean ones, the addition of fat or larding is required to improve texture and avoid drying (see *larding* in Glossary). It is also advisable to avoid adding moisture-drawing salt directly to lean meats, especially when cooking in dry heat. Properly bled meat should not require salt-soaking. Salt can always be added to the finished dish. Otherwise, these lean small game animals may be cooked much like chicken.

The young small animal may be stuffed, larded, and roasted whole under cover, or cut into serving or stewing pieces and cooked by one of the moist-heat recipes. The middle-aged to old critter should be cut up, marinated, and cooked in moist heat. Partially cooked cuts covered with a barbecue sauce and oven-baked to tenderness are excellent.

Wild Hare and Rabbit

O hare it is good eating,
Thus did old Adam say,
Old Adam was a poacher,
Went out one day at fall
To catch a hare for roasting
And eating bones and all.

—Old English hunting song

The most widely hunted small game in North America, the members of the wild hare family have been collectively known as rabbits through generally accepted usage. Recipes calling for hare or rabbit are applicable to all such animals of comparable quality and cut, or they may be adjusted to fit.

Hares are vegetarians, though they are not as choosy as the squirrels. The cottontail rabbit is generally dependable in flavor. The pungent evergreen plant life that is part of the snowshoe (varying) hare's diet is often noticeable in the flesh, more so in winter. This dietary flavor is best subdued by using a marinade that counteracts rather than overwhelms it.

These marinades may vary from a simple solution of vinegar and water to a concoction well fortified with spices, herbs, and wine. (A familiar example is the traditional *hasenpfeffer*, or "spiced hare," of international fame.) Crushed wintergreen leaves or a few drops of *natural* oil of wintergreen (from the drugstore) also may help the evergreen flavor in the flesh. Wintergreen may be used in any recipe—added to a marinade or put right into the pot (for stews, etc.). Tomatoes, with their astringent flavor-aid effects, give a boost to the old basic recipes for wild hare, rabbit, or any other small game.

Dressed hare should be washed well in several clear, warm-water baths. Soak it in vinegar and water (2 tablespoons of vinegar to 1 quart of water), tomato juice, or seasoned marinade for 2 to 24 hours, depending on the animal's size and age. Then rinse the carcass well and wipe it dry, unless directed otherwise. Be sure the meat is clean of hair. Meat should be at room temperature for thorough, even cooking.

Stuffed Cottontail Baked-In-A-Blanket

    1 young cottontail rabbit
    Lemon wedges
    ⅓ cup olive oil, garlic-flavored
    Larding
    Savory stuffing
    Carrots and onions
    Fat bacon, sliced
    Flour-and-water dough
    Thyme or savory
    Butter, softened

Cut off the legs of the dressed rabbit at the first joint. Wash and towel-dry. Wipe the cavity with a wedge of lemon, and rub inside with olive oil in which a crushed clove of garlic has soaked.

Preheat the oven to 350° F (175° C).

Stuff the rabbit lightly with Basic Stuffing seasoned lightly with fresh thyme or savory. Sew or skewer to close cavity, and truss the legs to the body. Brush all over with the garlic-oil. Lay the rabbit in a roasting pan on a bed of thickly sliced carrots and onions, or on a trivet. Cover with slices of bacon.

Mix a stiff, cohesive dough of flour and water, working in a little crushed thyme or savory. Roll it out about ¼ inch thick and brush generously with soft butter. Flip the dough over onto the rabbit, tucking it in underneath. Add about ¼ cup of water to the bottom of the pan.

Put the rabbit into the oven and bake, allowing 25 to 30 minutes per pound of wrapped stuffed weight. About 20 minutes before the rabbit is done, remove the pastry and bacon. Baste the rabbit well with the garlic-oil, dust with flour, and return to the oven until brown and tender. Place the meat on a warm platter. Make a brown pan gravy from the drippings (vegetables removed), or serve with a tart cranberry sauce.

This recipe may also be used to bake a saddle of hare.

Hasenpfeffer

A literal translation of *hasenpfeffer* is "spiced hare." Webster's defines it, more precisely, as "a stew made of rabbit meat which has been soaked in vinegar and pickling spices, and to which sour cream is added before serving." But versions of the dish are countless, limited only by the cook's imagination and spice rack. This recipe comes from the Pennsylvania Dutch country.

    1 hare or 2 rabbits, dressed for cooking
    Hare giblets, or ¼ pound chicken giblets
    Marinade
    4 to 6 strips bacon
    2 tablespoons butter
    3 tablespoons flour
    1 cup sour cream

Marinade:

1 to 1½ cups vinegar
3 cups water
1½ teaspoons salt
1 teaspoon sugar
1½ teaspoons mixed pickling spices
  (tied in cheesecloth)
1 carrot sliced
1 large onion, sliced

Cut the hare into serving pieces, and place in a deep bowl along with the giblets. In a saucepan combine the marinade ingredients. Heat to a boil, cook 2 to 3 minutes, and let cool. Pour over the meat and place in the refrigerator for a day or two. Turn the meat occasionally.

Transfer the meat to a Dutch oven, casserole, or clay baker. Strain and reserve the marinade. Cover the meat with strips of bacon and dabs of the butter. Add 1 cup of strained marinade (or use wine for a more subdued seasoning). Cover and bake in a 325° F (165° C) oven until the meat is tender, about 1½ to 2 hours.

Remove the hare to a heated platter and keep it warm. Combine the flour and sour cream and blend into the pan liquid. Cook and stir until evenly thickened. Pour the gravy over the meat and serve (or return the meat to the gravy and serve from the pot) with hot biscuits. *6 to 8 servings.*

Winter Hare with Sauerkraut

This recipe uses wintergreen berries to help offset the evergreen flavor sometimes found in winter hare. A few drops of natural oil of wintergreen, bought for the purpose from a pharmacist, may be used if berries are unavailable.

Wash a dressed, skinned, and trimmed hare several times in clear, warm water. Put it into a deep container and cover with a solution of 2 tablespoons of vinegar to 1 quart of water. Add a few crushed wintergreen berries, or a few drops of natural oil of wintergreen. Depending on the age of the hare, let it soak for 2 to 24 hours, turning it occasionally.

Preheat the oven to 375° F (190° C).

Rinse the hare well and wipe it dry. Rub the hare with cooking oil all over, inside and out. Stuff the cavity loosely with washed sauerkraut. Skewer the cavity but don't close it completely. Lay 3 or 4 thick strips of pork fat in the bottom of a roasting pan and place the hare on them. Place 2 or 3 strips of fat bacon on top of the hare, and heap some more sauerkraut on top. Cover the pan tightly, and bake until the meat is well done, about 25 or 30 minutes per pound.

Remove the cover and take the bacon from the top of the meat. Baste well with the pan drippings and dust lightly with flour. Brown for a few minutes until crusty gold, and then serve at once. (This method of cooking hare is superb when done in a clay baker—follow the manufacturer's instructions.)

—Mrs. Shannon Asam
Poplar Dale, Ontario

Seminole-Style Baked Rabbit

Preheat the oven to 350° F (175° C). Cut 1 rabbit, prepared for cooking as described earlier, into serving-size pieces. Wipe the meat with a vinegar-dampened cloth. Season ½ cup of flour with salt and pepper and put it in a paper or plastic bag. Coat a few pieces of meat at a time by adding them to the bag and shaking.

Heat bacon fat in a heavy skillet and brown the meat well on all sides. Transfer the meat to a baking dish and cover with milk. Cover the dish and bake for 1 hour, or until tender. Remove the meat to a warm platter. Thicken the gravy by adding 1 tablespoon of flour blended into ½ cup of milk; stir until thickened, and pour over the rabbit. Serve with hot corn bread. *4 to 6 servings.*

Rabbit Pie

What can compare with a Welsh Rabbit rare, unless it's a pie of rabbit fare.
—Legend on an old English plate

2 cottontails or 1 large hare
Marinade (see *Hasenpfeffer*)
Seasoned flour
Bacon fat
1 large onion, diced
1 medium carrot, thinly sliced
1 parsnip, thinly sliced
Bouquet garni
Pepper to taste
1 tablespoon sugar
Meat stock
1 tablespoon butter
1 tablespoon flour
Rich pastry for 2-crust pie

Cut the rabbits or hare into large pieces—legs, loin, back, breast, and head. Prepare the meat and marinate overnight as for *hasenpfeffer*. Then remove the meat, reserving the marinade. Keep the legs and loin for the pie, and use the remainder of the carcass to make stock (see Glossary). Preheat the oven to 375° F (190° C).

Dust the marinated legs and loin with seasoned flour. Heat bacon fat, about ⅛ inch deep, in a skillet. Brown the meat well on all sides, then place it in an oven casserole. Add the vegetables and *bouquet garni* along with the pepper and sugar. Cover with stock and/or strained marinade (use stock alone for a delicately seasoned pie, or all marinade for stronger seasoning). Cover the casserole and bake until the meat is ready to fall from the bones, 1 to 1½ hours.

Remove the casserole from the oven, and turn the oven up to 425° F (215° C). Remove the bouquet of herbs, and put the meat on a platter. Strip the meat from the bones and return it to the casserole. Rub the flour in the butter until mealy; sprinkle over the meat and rub in. Add salt to taste. Cover the meat with the pastry, pinching it to the edge of the casserole. Score the pastry and return the pie to the oven until the crust is nicely browned. *6 servings.*

Variation: Include a grouse. Put the breast in the pie and use the remainder for the stock.

Jugged Rabbit

Jugged meat in the classical sense means a stew slowly cooked in an earthen jug placed in a deep pan of boiling water. The fame of hare or rabbit so cooked to a savory, melting tenderness is of long standing, although the method has been modified. The traditional jug in water on the stovetop has given way to a Dutch oven or bean crock in the oven. Jugged hare is also a good candidate for the slow-cooking appliance.

1 rabbit or hare
Marinade
1 tablespoon butter
½ pound bacon
3 tablespoons flour
1 onion, finely diced
1 dozen mushrooms

Marinade:
¾ cup cooking oil
1 carrot, finely sliced
1 onion, finely sliced
2 stalks celery, finely sliced
1 clove garlic
2 bay leaves
½ teaspoon peppercorns
Pinch whole thyme
Salt to taste
½ cup vinegar
1 cup red wine

Skin and dress the hare. Check for blemishes on the flesh. Remove badly discolored flesh around shot wounds. Wash the hare in cold water. Cut it into about 10 pieces. Place the meat in a terrine or earthen bowl.

To make the marinade, heat the oil in a saucepan with the carrot, onion, and celery. Crush together the bay leaves, garlic, peppercorns, and thyme, and add to the pan. Stir-fry until the vegetables are partly cooked. Add the vinegar and cook a few minutes longer. Remove the saucepan from the heat and let cool. Add the red wine, and pour the marinade over the hare. Cover the terrine and let stand for 3 to 4 hours, turning the meat over 2 or 3 times. Drain and pat dry between towels, reserving the marinade.

Preheat the oven to 375° F (190° C). Put the butter and coarsely diced bacon into a Dutch oven. Cook the bacon to a golden brown, and then transfer it to a warm platter. Add the flour and diced onion to the remaining hot fat, and stir continuously until light brown. To this roux, add the hare pieces, mixing well. Pour the marinade and vegetables over the meat; add the cooked bacon and mushrooms. The stew must be well covered with liquid. If necessary add some beef stock or more dry red wine. Bring to a boil, cover, and bake for 45 to 60 minutes. *4 to 6 servings.*

Variation: If you're using a bean crock (or a slow-cooking appliance), put the drained marinated hare into the crock. Strain the marinade and reserve. Cook the bacon in a frying pan. Remove the bacon and keep it warm. Brown the flour and diced onions in the hot fat. Add the drained marinade to the roux and stir until the sauce thickens. Pour the sauce over the meat. Add the vegetables from the marinade and the mushrooms. Spread the bacon over the top. Add beef stock or red wine to cover, if necessary. Put the crock into a 365° F (185° C) oven and bake until meat is tender, 1½ to 2 hours. If using a slow cooker, follow manufacturer's instructions for cooking stew.

Conejo Mexicana (Rabbit Mexican Style)

2 1- to 1½-pound rabbits
½ cup peanut oil
2 small chili peppers
2 cloves garlic, crushed
Flour

Sauce:
⅓ stick butter
1 large carrot, finely diced
½ cup finely chopped onions
3 tablespoons chopped green pepper
1 cup chopped mushrooms
2 tablespoons flour
2 cups chicken broth
Juice of 1 small orange
1 heaping tablespoon peanut butter
½ teaspoon cumin seeds
1 tablespoon toasted sesame seeds
3 cloves
3 slices orange peel
Dash nutmeg
Salt and pepper to taste
1 tablespoon chopped parsley

Cut the legs from the rabbits, and cut the backs into 3 pieces. Preheat a heavy kettle, add the oil, and heat. Drop in chili peppers and let them fry until brown, pressing them occasionally with a fork to extract the pepper juice, then discard. Rub each piece of rabbit with the crushed garlic, then flour lightly and sauté pieces in the chili-flavored oil. When golden brown, remove the meat from the kettle and place in a large covered baking dish. Keep warm in oven at very low heat while preparing the sauce.

Pour off the oil in which the rabbit was cooked and heat the butter in the kettle. When hot, add the carrots, onions, green pepper, and mushrooms. Sauté over very low heat, stirring frequently, until tender. Be careful not to let the vegetables brown. Add the flour and mix well with the vegetables, then add the broth and stir until slightly thickened. Add all of the rest of the ingredients except the parsley. Let the mixture simmer for about 10 minutes until thoroughly blended.

Sprinkle salt over the rabbit in the baking dish and pour the cooked sauce over it. Sprinkle with parsley, cover, and bake in a preheated 350° F (175° C) oven for about 1 hour, or until tender. Baked potatoes go well with dish. *6 servings.*

—Victor J. Bergeron
Trader Vic's Book of Mexican Cooking

Squirrel

The squirrel's natural diet of nuts and berries imparts a delicately sweet flavor to the flesh. This is best preserved by simple cooking with low-key seasoning. Because most squirrel meat is tender, only old squirrels need any tenderizing treatment. The tenderizing agent may be a commercial product, a buttermilk bath, or an astringent rather than an aromatic marinade.

To prepare squirrel for cooking, wash the dressed animal well in several waters. Wipe with a damp cloth, removing any trace of hair. Cover and refrigerate overnight.

Squirrel meat is lean and should be cooked—well cooked, but never overdone—with lots of butter. Squirrel may be fried or broiled in the same manner as young chickens, stuffed and roasted, or made into stews.

Chestnut-Stuffed Squirrel

Prepare dressed squirrels for cooking. Oil them well with butter inside and out. Prepare Tom Schirm's Famous Chestnut Stuffing (see Chapter 11). Stuff the squirrel loosely, allowing space for the stuffing to swell, and close the cavity with a skewer. Truss the legs to the body. (Seal the remaining stuffing in buttered aluminum foil and bake separately.)

Preheat the oven to 350° F (175° C). Place the squirrels in a small roasting pan. Lay a double-folded piece of cheesecloth soaked in melted butter over each squirrel. Add ¼ inch of stock (see Glossary) or water to the bottom of the pan. Cover lightly with foil and bake until tender, basting frequently first with melted butter and then with the pan drippings. Remove the foil and the cheese-cloth. Baste again from the pan. Dust very lightly with flour and return to oven for a few minutes until golden brown.

Make a pan gravy and pour it over the squirrel, or serve it on the side with the extra stuffing. *1 squirrel per serving.*

Squirrel Fry

Cut 4 or 5 young squirrels, dressed and prepared for cooking, into serving-size pieces. Wipe each piece of meat with a damp cloth. (Note: Meat from older, less tender squirrels should be parboiled slowly in water containing a little salt and an onion or two, until soft and almost cooked. Drain, pat between towels, and continue with the recipe.)

Dip each piece of squirrel in milk, let it drip a moment, and dredge well in flour seasoned with salt and pepper. In a heavy frying pan, melt a mixture of butter and bacon fat or cooking oil to a depth of about ¼ inch. Heat to sizzling but not smoking. Add the squirrel and fry to a rich brown, turning once, until the meat is tender and no pink shows in the juice. Drain on paper and keep warm.

Pour off most of the fat, and scrape up the browned bits from the pan. Add 2 tablespoons of butter and melt. Stir in 1 tablespoon flour; stir and cook over medium heat until smooth and bubbly. Add 2 cups of warmed milk and stir until thickened. Season with salt and pepper to taste. Pour over the squirrel or serve separately. *4 to 5 servings.*

Brunswick Stew

Brunswick Stew is a traditional dish of the Old South, its invention credited to the Moravians who settled in North Carolina. Often made today with chicken, the classic Brunswick Stew calls for squirrels, with perhaps a rabbit or gamebird thrown in. In the Deep South, venison may be included. The stew always includes beans, corn, and tomatoes, although proportions and seasonings may vary according to local taste and larder. Brunswick Stew freezes well and is often made in large quantities; simply increase the ingredient amounts below as needed.

> 4 small dressed squirrels, or 2 or 3 large ones
> ¼ cup salt pork, diced
> 1 large onion, diced
> ½ teaspoon salt
> ¼ teaspoon black pepper
> 1 teaspoon sugar
> 28-ounce can tomatoes
> 2 cups diced potatoes
> 1 cup small lima beans,
>   or 2 cups cut butter beans
> 1½ cups fresh or frozen corn niblets
> Dash Worcestershire sauce
> 2 tablespoons butter

Cut the dressed squirrels in half. Lightly sear the salt pork in a Dutch oven or heavy kettle. Add the squirrels, cover completely with water, and bring to a boil. Skim. Add the onion, salt, pepper, and sugar and simmer uncovered until the meat falls from the bones. Lift the squirrels from the broth and remove the bones. Dice the meat and return it to the pot.

Mix in the tomatoes, potatoes, beans, and corn, adding water if necessary to barely cover. Continue simmering, stirring up from the bottom of the pot as the stew thickens. Add salt and pepper to taste and a good dash of Worcestershire sauce. Simmer until the stew is reduced to the consistency of thick soup, stirring frequently to prevent scorching. Before serving, blend in the butter. *4 to 6 servings.*

Small Game Animals

Muskrat

Muskrat, marsh hare, or marsh rabbit—whatever you call it, this small animal is delicious and nutritious. In fact, when it comes to protein, minerals, and vitamins, muskrat rates with moose and caribou, and is superior to rabbit, beaver, and beef.

The common muskrat weighs 2 to 3 pounds and has relatively lean, fine-grained, dark-red tender meat. Its rather distinctive flavor reflects its diet, which can vary across the land. Vegetarian by preference, it feeds on roots and stems and aquatic vegetation, although it will feed on clams, mussels, and even fish and turtles if it's hungry enough.

The muskrat's flavor can be improved by removing as much fat as possible and by marinating the meat in an astringent solution of vinegar or wine, more or less spiced, and cooking in moist heat with plenty of fat.

Muskrat tails are consumed with relish in the Northwest Territories, where trapping provides the tails in usable quantity. The tails, which are 8 to 10 inches long, are prepared and eaten much like pigs' tails. They are dipped in scalding water to loosen the skin, which is then pulled off. Boiled tails may be basted with a barbecue sauce and browned over the coals or in a hot oven. Like beaver tails, muskrat tails make an excellent soup stock.

Marinated Muskrat Braise

2 muskrats, dressed
Marinade
1 teaspoon salt
¼ teaspoon black pepper
½ cup flour
Cooking oil
1 large firm tomato

Marinade:
2 cups water
½ cup red wine
1 teaspoon sugar
1 teaspoon cracked peppercorns
1 each green pepper, carrot, and onion, sliced
1 stalk celery, broken
1 clove garlic, crushed
2 tablespoons cooking oil

Wash and dry the muskrat. Wipe it with a vinegar-dampened cloth, then cut into serving pieces and put into a deep bowl.

In a saucepan combine the marinade ingredients. Bring to a boil and pour over the meat. Turn the meat over in the marinade to coat well. Cover and refrigerate overnight.

Remove the meat from the marinade and drain on a towel. Strain and reserve the marinade. Pick out and reserve the carrot, pepper, and onion. Combine the salt, black pepper, and flour in a soup plate. Dredge the pieces of muskrat in the mixture. Let them rest on a rack for 10 to 15 minutes.

Heat the oil in a large skillet. Brown the meat well on all sides. Add enough of the strained marinade to just show through the meat. Scatter the reserved vegetables on top. Chop and add the tomato. Bring to a boil and reduce the heat. Cover tightly and let simmer for about 1 hour, or until the meat is very tender and the liquid is reduced to a thick sauce. Run a spatula under the meat occasionally to keep it from sticking to the pan. Replenish moisture only if it threatens to boil dry.

Serve the muskrat in its own sauce with fluffy white rice, mashed potatoes, or hot biscuits. *4 to 6 servings.*

Muskrat Smothered with Onions
1 muskrat, dressed and disjointed
Vinegar or pickle juice
1 teaspoon salt
¼ teaspoon paprika
¼ teaspoon black pepper
½ cup flour
3 tablespoons fat
3 large onions, sliced
1 cup sour cream

Soak the muskrat overnight in water, adding about 2 tablespoons of vinegar or pickle juice per quart of water. Drain the meat on a towel.

Combine ½ teaspoon of salt and the paprika, pepper, and flour; dredge the meat in the mixture. Heat the fat in a skillet and brown the muskrat pieces on all sides. Spread the onion over the meat, sprinkle with the remaining salt, and spread the sour cream over the top. Cover the skillet tightly and let simmer for 1 hour. From time to time run a spatula under the meat to prevent sticking. *4 servings.*

Variation: Instead of onions and sour cream, cover the meat with about 2 cups of sauerkraut. Add ½ cup of red wine and dab generously with butter. Cover and cook as above.

FAT SMALL GAME

The meat of fat small game animals is generally dark, rich, and moist. In the young, it is very tender, and only the meat of the veteran is likely to be tough.

A good skinning job takes care of scent glands and offensive flavors from that source. However, natural diet flavors are concentrated in the fat and can be overpowering if the fat is excessive. Trimming off and rendering out excess fat makes for a more palatable flavor and texture in the meat. The methods of cooking all fat small animals are basically similar and simple. Recipes and species may be interchanged. See the Iroquois open-hearth cookery table in Chapter 2.

Beaver

A beaver can weigh up to 40 or 50 pounds, but a young animal that dresses out to 8 to 12 pounds is nicest for the table and gives a large quantity of dark, rich, moist, and usually very tender meat. Beaver should be freshly killed and immediately dressed out. Only then should the carcass be frozen; it may be stored in the freezer for up to four months. As much fat as possible should be trimmed from the carcass, and the meat parboiled before final preparation.

If the excessive oiliness and overpowering flavor is eliminated, the result is a succulent meat that earned culinary mention in the history of New France. Indeed, beaver tails were recorded as a delicacy in the days of Champlain's Order of Good Cheer. Later, beaver tails often replaced salt pork in the bean pot. They also make a superior stock of exquisite flavor.

Burgundy-Baked Beaver

For this savory, winy stew, use the hind half of a young dressed beaver (about 5 pounds), trimmed of fat and split into 2 pieces. You will also need

> 1 tablespoon sugar
> Celery tops, tied in a bundle
> 1 carrot, sliced
> 1 onion, sliced
> 2 tablespoons mixed pickling spices,
>   tied in cheesecloth
> ½ teaspoon mint leaves, dried or fresh
> 1 cup dry red wine, or ¼ cup vinegar
> 1 orange
> 2 teaspoons salt
> 2 tablespoons cooking oil
> Flour

Put the beaver into a large stock pot, and cover it with cold water. Add everything down to the orange. Cut the orange in half, remove any pits, squeeze in the juice, and toss in the peels. Bring to a boil, skim, and add the salt. Reduce the heat, cover the pot lightly with foil, and simmer slowly for about 2 hours. Then remove the kettle from the heat and skim. Discard the spice bag, celery tops, and orange peel. Cover the kettle with a towel and let cool. Refrigerate overnight, weighting the beaver with a plate if necessary to keep it under the stock. Lift out the meat, rinse it under boiling water, and place it on a tray to drain. Discard the stock.

Preheat the oven to 375° F (190° C).

Cut the meat into chunks. Heat the cooking oil in a Dutch oven. Add the chunks and sear lightly on all sides. Lightly dust the top with flour. Put the meat into the oven for a few minutes to brown the flour. Remove the Dutch oven and add

> 2 tablespoons tomato paste dissolved
>   in 1½ cups hot beef stock
> 2 green peppers, cut in large dice
> Dash thyme or savory
> 1 cup burgundy wine
> Salt and pepper to taste
> Trace cayenne

Cover the Dutch oven and return it to the oven. Turn the heat down to 325° F (165° C) and bake until the meat is just about done, about an hour or so. Add 2 cups each of baby carrots, button mushrooms, and small white pickling onions. Continue baking until the vegetables are just tender. Serve very hot with wild rice or white rice. *12 to 15 servings.*

Beaver Smothered in Sauerkraut

1 hind quarter of dressed beaver,
  or half a small beaver
2 bay leaves
⅓ teaspoon cracked peppercorns
½ cup vinegar, or 1 cup pickle juice
1 quart sauerkraut
1 teaspoon caraway seeds
½ cup dry white wine
Butter

Trim and scrape off as much fat as possible from the beaver. Cut as necessary to fit into a deep pot. Cover with water, and add the bay leaves, peppercorns, and vinegar. Bring to a boil and skim. Reduce the heat and slowly simmer until the meat is partially cooked (about 40 to 60 minutes). Let cool in the stock, then refrigerate overnight.

Skim off fat. Remove the meat and rinse under boiling water. Remove the meat from the bones and cut into chunks. Spread a bed of sauerkraut over the bottom of a large casserole. Sprinkle half the caraway seeds over it. Add the meat and smother it with the remaining sauerkraut. Dribble the wine over the top. Sprinkle on the remaining caraway seeds. Dab well with butter. Cover and bake at 350° F (175° C) until the meat is very tender, about 1½ to 2 hours. *8 to 10 servings.*

Bad River Beaver

10- to 12-pound dressed beaver,
  castor glands removed
1 teaspoon baking soda
Stuffing
Flour
Red wine
Stuffing:
2 cups bread crumbs
¼ cup butter
½ cup chopped mushrooms
¼ cup chopped green pepper
1 large onion, chopped
Salt and pepper
Sage
2 eggs

Scrape as much fat as possible from the beaver, and trim. Soak overnight in lightly salted water. Rinse the meat, place it in a Dutch oven, and cover with fresh cold water and the baking soda. Bring to a bubble, turn down the heat, and let simmer for about 40 minutes to float off excess oils.

Meanwhile make the stuffing. Put the bread crumbs in a large bowl or plastic bag. Melt the butter and sauté the mushrooms, pepper, and onion until the onion is soft. Add the vegetables to the bread crumbs along with salt, pepper, and sage to taste. Toss to blend. Break the eggs over the mixture and blend well. Let the stuffing rest for at least 1 hour.

Preheat the oven to 325° F (165° C).

Remove the beaver from the Dutch oven, rinse well in clear water, and wipe dry, inside and out. Stuff the cavity loosely, and truss.

Make a flour-and-water dough: Starting with 4 cups of flour, work in enough water to make a cohesive but not too sticky dough. Roll it out to about pie-crust thickness, and wrap the beaver entirely in the pastry (make more if necessary). Put into roasting pan and baste with red wine.

Bake slowly, allowing 35 minutes per pound (as for pork). Crack off the pastry. Baste with red wine. Dust lightly with flour and baste again. Return to the oven until the meat is browned and tender. Serve with a tart jelly.

—Baden Powell
Bad River Lodge
French River, Ontario

Variation: Baste the baked beaver and serve with Sweet and Sour Sauce or one of the other game sauces in Chapter 11.

Potted Beaver

From pemmican to elegant potted meats or pâtés is a small leap, little more than a matter of refinement and fancy. The smooth texture of the rich meat of the fat small game animals is eminently suited to potting. This recipe for potted beaver is a basic one, which may also be used for possum, raccoon, or porcupine.

Trim as much fat as possible from a small beaver and cut into quarters or smaller pieces. Put the meat into a deep stock pot. Pour in enough water to cover and add ¼ cup of vinegar or lemon juice. Bring to a boil and skim. Turn down the heat and let simmer—little more than steep—for about 30 minutes. Remove from the heat and let the meat cool in the stock. Refrigerate overnight, using a weighted plate if necessary to keep the meat well under the stock.

The next day, lift off the surface fat and pour off the stock. Rinse the meat quickly under boiling water, and drain. Put the meat into a shallow baking pan. Add about ¼ cup of water to the bottom of the pan. Brush the surface of the meat with oil. Over the top lay a piece of foil or, better still, a sheet of flour-and-water paste (a stiff, cohesive, rollable mix), but *don't* seal or crimp it to the edge of the pan. Bake in a very slow oven, 250° F (120° C), until very, very well done—the meat should be falling from the bones. If it seems overdone, this is as it should be for potting. Allow about 1 hour per pound for the largest piece of meat.

Remove the covering. Strip the meat from the bones, trim, and cut into chunks. If a hard crust has formed on the surface, trim it off. Process the warm meat in a heavy-duty blender, ½ to 1 cup at a time, adding enough butter to make a smooth, soft paste. (If the mixture is too oily, the butter can be adjusted in the next lot.) Empty into a mixing bowl. Repeat until all the meat is in the bowl. Estimate its weight.

While the meat is still warm and soft (it will firm up when cold), blend in the seasonings using an electric mixer or a mixing spoon. For each pound of meat add ⅛ teaspoon of allspice or cloves, ⅛ teaspoon of mace, and a pinch of cayenne. Freshly ground black pepper is optional. Start sparingly with the spices and adjust to taste. (Keep in mind that the flavor of the spices develops during storage.) Add 2 tablespoons of brandy per pound of meat, mixing well to blend thoroughly. A few slivered almonds, shaved hazelnuts, or whole pine nuts add flavor and bite to the texture of the pâté.

Store at once in clean small bowls or plastic tubs. Pack closely, pressing out all air bubbles and leaving a good ½ inch of head room. Fill the bowls to the top with melted butter. Refrigerate immediately. When the butter hardens, fill any cracks with more melted butter. Let ripen in the refrigerator for 7 to 10 days before using. (The pâté should keep for several weeks undisturbed; but once opened, all should be used. It may be freezer-stored for 3 to 4 months.) Turn the pâté out on a plate, garnish, and serve with crackers at the cocktail hour or on toast for breakfast.

Beaver Tail Soup

4 small or 2 large beaver tails
1 teaspoon sugar
2 tablespoons vinegar
1 tablespoon mixed pickling spices,
   tied in cheesecloth
1 onion
1 stalk celery, broken
1 carrot, sliced
2 ounces sherry
2 tablespoons pine nuts

Scrub the beaver tails. Plunge them into boiling water for a few minutes to loosen the skin. Drain. Slit the tail skin and peel, pull, and cut it off. (The skin may also be loosened by searing it directly on the coals or under the broiler until it blisters, first on one side of the tail, then the other.)

Place the tails in a large stock pot and cover with 4 quarts of water. Bring to a boil, skim, and boil gently for about 10 minutes, skimming as scum forms. Reduce to a low boil. Add all but the last two ingredients. Cook very slowly, uncovered, until the stock is reduced by about half—4 to 5 hours. Test and adjust the seasonings along the way, removing the spice bag when seasoned to taste. Lift the tails, letting them drain over the pot. Reserve a cup of the meat. Strain the stock and let it chill overnight. Lift off the fat the following day.

Such a fine soup stock should be crystal clear. To clarify: Heat the stock over a medium-hot burner. Whip 2 egg whites with 2 half-shellfuls of water until frothy. Stir this into the stock as it heats, and continue stirring until the stock comes to a boil and froths up. Stop stirring and let cook for about 3 minutes. Strain the stock through a sieve lined with doubled cheesecloth or fine muslin. The strained stock should be clear and amber-colored. Store the stock in a suitable container, tightly covered, for up to 3 days, or store it in the freezer indefinitely.

To serve, heat the soup to a bubble, adding the reserved diced meat. Add the sherry and let the soup rest over a low heat for a few minutes, but don't let it boil. Pour into a heated tureen and garnish with the pine nuts. *8 8-ounce servings.*

Opossum

The word *opossum* comes from an Indian dialect and means "little white beast." Unique among North American mammals, possum, as it's affectionately called, is a marsupial—that is, the female carries its young in a pouch. A popular small game animal throughout the eastern half of the United States, its range extends across the border into eastern Canada and southward through Mexico.

Opossum can weigh from 3 to 14 pounds. Its light-colored, fine-grained flesh is tender and well marbled with fat. This fat, along with bear fat, was prized by colonials as a pastry shortening. Rendered into lard, it was stored by them in deerskin bags, as Indians had done for centuries.

When properly dressed, with the scent glands removed, possum has a good flavor. However, the possum's diet is known to include, along with vegetation, any tasty animal morsels, living or dead, that are available; its flesh should be well cooked. Dressed possum should hang in a cold place (about 50° F, 10° C) or be refrigerated for 24 hours. It is then parboiled in salted water or a light court bouillon to float off excessive oils and ensure thorough, even cooking.

A small possum can be stuffed and prepared the same way as suckling pig. It also broils well and makes good sausage. Young raccoon of comparable size is cooked like possum, and recipes for the two animals are interchangeable.

Stuffed Possum with Sweet Potatoes
5- to 7-pound possum (dressed weight)
1 bay leaf
1 large onion
¼ cup vinegar or pickle juice
1 tablespoon salt

Stuffing:
2 tablespoons butter
1 large onion, chopped
1 possum liver, chopped,
   or ¼ cup chopped chicken liver
1 cup fine dry bread crumbs
1 teaspoon savory
1 teaspoon chopped hot red pepper
¼ cup plumped raisins
1 cup chopped tart apple

Remove the head and tail and as much fat as possible from the possum. Wash well inside and out with warm water. Put it into a deep kettle, cover with cold water, and add the bay leaf, onion, vinegar, and salt. Bring to a boil. Turn down the heat and let simmer—little more than steep—for about 1 hour. Remove from heat. Let cool, cover lightly, and refrigerate overnight. The next day, lift off the fat and pour off the water. Rinse with scalding water. Drain and pat dry.

To make the stuffing: Melt the butter and brown the onion until soft; add the liver and sauté until cooked. Remove from the heat. Combine the remaining ingredients in a mixing bowl, then add the liver-onion mixture. Toss to mix thoroughly. Add salt to taste, and a little hot water or stock to moisten.

Preheat the oven to 300° to 325° F (150° to 165° C).

Stuff the possum about ⅔ full. Sew it up or close with skewers and truss as you would a turkey, with the legs against the body. Place the possum on a greased rack in a shallow pan. Brush with melted bacon fat and cover with a cheesecloth dipped in melted fat. Roast slowly, allowing 30 to 35 minutes per-pound stuffed weight (internal temperature 185° to 190° F, 85° to 88° C).

Meanwhile, parboil 3 or 4 sweet potatoes in their skins. Peel and halve the sweet potatoes. Remove the cheesecloth from the meat 30 minutes before it's done, and place the sweet potatoes around the roast. Baste everything several times from the pan, lightly dusting the meat with flour and the potatoes with brown sugar after each basting.

Transfer the opossum to a heated platter, and arrange the sweet potatoes around it. Garnish with fresh parsley. Serve Southern style with buttered peas and turnip cubes, French-fried green pepper rings, orange and onion salad, steamed brown bread, and cranberry relish or quince jelly. *6 to 10 servings.*

Possum or Raccoon Pie

3- to 4-pound possum or young raccoon
  (dressed weight)
¼ cup vinegar
1 onion, chopped
1 teaspoon salt
¼ teaspoon pepper
1 teaspoon pickling spices, 1 bay leaf,
  and 1 crushed clove of garlic, all tied
  together in cheesecloth
½ teaspoon dried thyme or savory
1 medium carrot, diced
½ green pepper, diced
Other vegetables as available
1 tablespoon flour
1 tablespoon butter
Short pastry for 1-crust pie

Quarter the possum and put into a deep kettle. Cover with water and add the vinegar. Bring to a boil, turn down the heat, and simmer gently for about 30 minutes. Remove the kettle from the heat, cool, then refrigerate overnight, lightly covered. Remove the meat and rinse under scalding water.

Put the meat into a saucepan, cover with water, and add the onion, salt, pepper, and other seasonings. Bring to a boil, reduce heat, cover tightly, and simmer until the meat falls from the bone. Remove the spice bag when seasoned to taste. Take the possum from the simmering liquid, strip the meat from the bones, and return it to the stew. Add the carrot, green pepper, and other vegetables as

you wish. (Thinly sliced parsnips are a nice touch.) Simmer until the carrots are cooked and the liquid has been reduced by about half. Test and adjust the seasoning.

Preheat the oven to 400° F (205° C).

To thicken the stew: Mix the flour with ½ cup of water and slowly stir the mixture into the simmering stew until the desired thickness is achieved. It should be neither runny nor stiff.

Pour the stew into a deep pie plate. Dab with the butter and swirl it into the meat mixture. Cover with a short pastry, score, and bake until the pastry is tender and brown. Possum pie is great with green tomato pickle. *6 servings.*

Raccoon

The raccoon is native to the New World. Its name is an Anglicized version of the Powhaten Indians' *aroughcun* or *arocoun*. Although raccoon grow much larger than opossum (adults run 10 to 30 pounds; weights of up to 60 pounds have been reported but are unusual), is much fatter, and has a stronger flavor, it should be dressed and cooked much like opossum.

The flavor of the omnivorous raccoon *au naturel* can be too much for most tastes. Flavors settle in the fat, and a raccoon getting ready for winter is excessively fat. The dark, long-fibered flesh tends to be coarse and tough, especially in older animals. Trimming of fat and parboiling in a tenderizing flavor-aid marinade, which further reduces the fat, is an all-purpose way to prepare the meat for cooking. Raccoon should be well cooked. Many pork recipes are successful with parboiled or marinated raccoon, and recipes for beaver, opossum, and woodchuck may be applied to raccoon, marinated or not. Raccoon meat parboiled in marinade may be ground and made into fine "coonburgers," meat pies, sausages, etc., (see "Ground Venison" in Chapter 4).

The raccoon's coarse flesh takes up salt and smoke readily; after a few hours over a hickory smoke, a marinated young raccoon roasted under a basting of barbecue sauce is a meat of some distinction (see "Smoking" in Chapter 3).

Parboiled, Marinated Raccoon

1 small whole raccoon, or a large one cut
  to fit the kettle
1 tablespoon salt
¼ cup vinegar, or 1 cup pickle juice
1 cup red wine
1 teaspoon mixed pickling spices
2 bay leaves
Handful fresh garden herbs as available
Few slices each of carrot and green pepper
1 stalk celery, broken

Put the raccoon into a deep preserving kettle and cover it with cold water. Add the salt and vinegar to the water. Bring to a boil, and skim. Reduce the heat and simmer slowly until the meat is partly cooked—about 10 minutes per pound of the largest cut.

Add the wine, seasonings, and vegetables to make a marinade, and let it all steep for a few minutes. Remove from heat and let the meat cool in the marinade. The marinade should cover the meat; add water if necessary. A weighted plate will keep the meat under. Refrigerate, lightly covered, overnight. The next day lift off all surface fat. Remove the meat and rinse it well under hot water. It is now ready to cook.

Baked Raccoon

Cut about 2 pounds of raccoon meat, across the grain, into boneless serving pieces—chops or cutlets about 1 inch thick. Trim off the fat and gash the edges. Put the meat into a saucepan and cover with cold water, adding ¼ cup of vinegar and 1 teaspoon of salt per gallon. Bring to a boil, turn down the heat, and simmer slowly for 20 minutes. Let the meat cool in the water, then drain and rinse under hot water. Dry between towels.

Season ½ cup of flour generously with salt, black pepper, and a good pinch of cayenne. Dredge the meat in the flour, pressing it in. In a large, heavy skillet, heat cooking oil, about ⅛ inch deep. Brown the meat well on all sides, as much at a time as the pan will take without crowding. As each lot is browned, transfer it to a greased baking dish. Sprinkle the meat lightly with basil, and smother it all with onion rings.

Pour ½ cup of red wine into the skillet in which the meat was browned, swirl it around, and pour it over the meat. Cover tightly and bake in a preheated 350° F (175° C) oven until the meat is well done, about 1 to 1½ hours, depending on the size and thickness of the pieces. Serve with green tomato pickles and hot corn bread. *6 servings*.

Armadillo

A borderline Texan in pioneer days, the armadillo has migrated more recently through Texas north and east to Oklahoma, Arkansas, and Mississippi. With proper field care and preparation, the meat of the armadillo is quite tasty, and it is often compared with pork.

Armadillo should be dressed out as soon as it is killed. Once the shell (armadillo means "little armored one") is cut away, it can be treated like other small game. Entrails and the anal portion should be removed intact, and care taken to not puncture anything. All fat should be trimmed from the carcass, particularly from under the front and back legs.

The carcass should be washed thoroughly in water containing ½ cup of salt, and refrigerated for 24 hours. Armadillo, like other fat small game animals, is usually parboiled before cooking.

Barbecued Armadillo

Dress an armadillo, soak it in salt water for 24 hours, and then cut it into serving pieces. Put the meat into a saucepan, cover with water, salt lightly, and bring to a boil. Skim. Boil the meat gently until almost tender, 20 to 40 minutes, depending on size.

Remove and drain the meat, then salt and pepper the pieces, using lots of freshly ground black pepper. Put the meat in a shallow pan, baste lightly with a mixture of melted butter, liquid hickory smoke, and steak sauce. Cover the pan with aluminum foil and cook in a 300° F (150° C) oven for about 1 hour, basting with the sauce every 20 minutes.

Woodchuck

Whether you call it woodchuck, marmot, pig whistle, or groundhog, this outsize member of the squirrel family provides a tasty bit of meat after a long summer's living off the fat of the farmer's land. A summer diet of grasses, wild shoots, clover, alfalfa, young corn, and carrots, topped off in the fall with apples and pears, adds up to a fatty meat of remarkably fine flavor by hibernation time.

As with other small game animals, prompt and good field care, including the all-important removal of scent glands, is essential to the quality of woodchuck meat. (See "Field Care" earlier in this chapter.)

The adult woodchuck varies in weight from 5 to 10 pounds but can grow to an extreme of 12 to 15 pounds. Recipes for opossum and beaver of comparable size or cut may be used for woodchuck. Prairie dog, another member of the squirrel family, is also dressed and cooked like woodchuck.

Fricassee of Woodchuck or Prairie Dog
5-pound woodchuck, or 2 prairie dogs
½ cup vinegar
½ teaspoon salt
⅛ teaspoon black pepper
½ teaspoon chili powder
½ cup flour
3 slices bacon, chopped
1 onion, sliced
1 clove garlic, crushed
Pinch thyme or savory
½ lemon, juice and rind
Chicken or veal bouillon
Paprika

Cut the woodchuck into serving pieces, trimming off the fat. Soak the meat overnight in water, adding the vinegar. If the meat is very fat, parboil it gently for ½ hour before soaking. Rinse and drain.

Combine salt, pepper, chili powder, and flour in a bag. Add the meat, a few pieces at a time, and shake to coat well. Let the meat rest on a rack for about 15 minutes.

In a heavy skillet, sear the bacon, add the onion and garlic, and brown lightly. Remove the garlic and add the meat. Cook and turn it until well browned on all sides. Add the thyme and lemon juice, grating in a bit of the rind. Add enough bouillon to barely show through the meat. Cover tightly, reduce the heat, and simmer gently for 1½ to 2 hours, until the meat is tender and the liquid has been reduced to a thick sauce. Adjust the seasoning. Serve from the skillet or transfer to a heated serving dish. *About 6 servings.*

Porcupine

In the North, the porcupine is known as the woodsman's friend. It filled many an early settler's kettle in lean days. The lost-in-the-woodsman can easily catch a porcupine, wrap it in clay, and bake it Indian style (see "Baking in the Coals" in Chapter 3).

The porcupine's flavor, like that of other animals, reflects its recent diet. For best table results, porcupines from the forest's depths are preferred to those living on the outskirts of more inhabited areas since they have a penchant for painted and creosoted docks and boathouses. Porcupine should be field-dressed and cooked like other fat small game.

Sweet and Sour Porcupine
Legs of a porcupine
Fat
1 or 2 onions, sliced
1 cup cider vinegar
½ teaspoon nutmeg
¾ cup brown sugar

In a Dutch oven, brown the porcupine legs in hot fat.

In a saucepan, cook the onions in the vinegar until translucent. Add the nutmeg and sugar. Pour the mixture over the porcupine legs. Bring to a boil, reduce the heat, cover, and let simmer for 3 hours. Remove the porcupine. Strip the meat from the bones and serve with the gravy over hot cooked rice.

The gravy may be thickened with cornstarch.

—Homer Homemakers
Cooking Up a Storm in Homer, Alaska

7

Wildfowl

To return wet with dew, and bearing a feathered prize was and ever will be the highest enjoyment.

—John James Audubon
Ornithological Biography, 1834

The gamebirds of North America are divided here into two major groups, upland game fowl and waterfowl, with some overlapping in between for convenience in the kitchen. General procedures applicable to all wildfowl are discussed in the first section, then specific techniques and recipes for the various species are given.

INITIAL PREPARATION

The dressing and care of gamebirds entail their handling in the field, in camp, in transit, and at home; all steps determine the quality of the bird that eventually reaches the cook's hands. The procedures for preparing wildfowl for cooking are similar to those for domestic poultry, although the circumstances in which they are carried out differ.

Field Care

When to draw a gamebird has long been a subject for debate among game fanciers. Many hunters claim the job may be left for the cook, but most cooks (North Americans, at least) say, "draw it in the field!" And meat inspection authorities say the sooner after killing the better.

When a bird is killed, there is a transition of microorganisms from the gut to the meat. Many birds today, wild and domestic, carry a type of *salmonella*, a culprit in food poisoning, and during evisceration, care should be taken not to cut the gut and thereby contaminate the meat.

In members of the pheasant family and in small wildfowl, such as blackbirds, pigeons, and woodcock, the visceral contents are fairly bland in flavor and *when contained* are unobjectionable as long as the birds have been kept cold and decomposition has not actually set in. In the native grouse family, on the other hand, the visceral contents are characteristically bitter, and postponing their removal does nothing to enhance the flavor of the birds. In field and laboratory tests done by the Iowa State University Extension Service, ducks drawn warm (within an hour of killing) were judged better in flavor than those drawn cold (44 to 48 hours after killing).

According to some reputable old recipes, woodcock and snipe (very small birds) are not eviscerated at all. They are simply plucked or skinned and cooked "in the trail" (intact), as removal of the small twist of gut takes with it a large piece of desirable fat, and cooking the bird intact is considered preferable to losing the fine natural flavor imparted by this fat.

Many Old World methods and recipes recommend hanging the undrawn bird at a low temperature for days or even weeks—"When the belly feathers begin to slip, it's time to cook the bird." Although this decision must be left to the discretion of the hunter/cook, prolonged hanging before evisceration or cooking "in the trail" is not generally compatible with modern scientific findings.

For safety's sake, the bird should never be allowed to remain undrawn for any length of time (i.e., more than a few hours) unless it has been cleanly shot and the weather is cold but not freezing. In all cases, it should be bled immediately and allowed to cool. Any gamebird that has been shot in the body (entrails intact) should be drawn immediately, the shot removed and damaged parts trimmed away. Even if the flesh is badly torn, the bird still need not be a total loss. It may be skinned, split, and the breasts removed and trimmed for a meal in camp. Of course, the bird that is badly shot up is useless to hunter and species.

If the weather is warm, or cold enough to freeze, the gamebird should be field-dressed as soon as it's retrieved. It might also be plucked. The warm bird plucks easily, and in warm weather the plucked carcass cools out more quickly. (Remember to check local regulations for evidence of species requirements before plucking.) Plucked or skinned wildfowl should be cooled out as quickly as possible and kept clean. Birds that have been allowed to freeze before drawing are not recommended for eating.

Home Care

For Immediate Use: Young birds may be used immediately; simply pluck and chill them, then prepare for cooking according to recipe directions.

Older or very large birds that were not sufficiently aged in camp should be hung before using. If a cold enough place is not available for hanging, pluck the birds and chill them in the refrigerator, covered lightly with aluminum foil or a dampened towel. Age for 24 to 48 hours, depending on the size and age of the bird. Longer refrigeration of plucked fowl tends to dry out the meat, but marinating it during aging helps to prevent drying.

For Freezer Storage: By the time the birds get home, they should be aged enough for freezing and require no further hanging. Pluck the birds and prepare them for freezing at once (see Freezing below).

PLUCKING

Most wildfowl should be plucked rather than skinned. In the fine prime bird, the skin encases a thin layer of fat, which in turn flavors the meat. The skin should be preserved whenever possible.

Plucking can be done dry or wet. Dry plucking is considered to be the superior method, but it should be done while the bird is still warm, and done quickly.

Dry Plucking: Hold the bird by its back in one hand, firmly grasping it around the wings and shoulders. A large bird, such as a goose, is more easily held in the lap between the knees. Begin at the breast, about 1 inch below the head, and pluck by grasping feathers between thumb and forefinger close to the skin. A damp thumb helps. With a downward motion, *roll* (rather than pull) the feathers away, taking care not to tear the skin. Turn the bird and continue plucking until it is clean of feathers.

Wet Plucking: Hold the bird by the feet and immerse it in a large kettle of scalding (not boiling) water to which a capful of liquid dishwashing detergent has been added. Dunk upland birds but a moment—the detergent wets quickly and overimmersion will weaken the skin. Waterfowl should be submerged a bit longer to allow the solution to penetrate the birds' natural waterproofing.

Starting on the breast, pluck the feathers away with a downward draw, working quickly, until the bird is clean as far as the head. This method eases the removal of down from the waterfowl—it will just rub off.

Trimming the Plucked Bird: Cut the head from plucked fowl and sever the neck at the body, leaving the skin intact unless the bird is to be cut up for cooking. Remove the wings at the first joint or pinion.

Do not cut off the feet, but pull them away, drawing the leg tendons with them. ("Drawing" the legs removes tendons which otherwise make this part of the bird an inedible piece of meat.) To do this, lightly cut the skin around the hock joints. Crack the scaly lower part of the leg next to the feet (in the grouse family this is feathered) by holding it against a solid table edge, and giving it a sharp tap with the back of a knife. Pull the foot away. It will come readily enough from a young bird; old birds and large ones, and waterfowl, may be more reluctant to part with their feet, and a pair of pliers and a helper may be necessary. Trim the leg at the first joint.

Remove the pin feathers by pinching them against the blade of a knife; tweezers are useful on sticky pin feathers, and pliers will do the job for the more stubborn ones in waterfowl. Probe for and remove shot, and trim away shot spots. Remove any bone splinters. If the tail is still on the bird, cut it off, *or* cut out the oil sack, a hard small bump embedded in the flesh at the base of the tail.

To remove down, singe the bird over a clean alcohol flame or a piece of burning crumpled newspaper. To singe a number of small birds, simply stick them on a long skewer, four or six at a time, and pass them over the flame. With a small brush, wash the plucked and trimmed bird in warm, sudsy water, rinse thoroughly, and pat dry.

SKINNING

Under certain circumstances, the bird should be skinned rather than plucked. If, for instance, the skin has been badly torn or damaged, a good plucking job will be next to impossible. Skinning is also preferred if there is a suspicion or certainty of strong diet-flavor about the bird, as may be true of late-season grouse, fishy ducks, or muddy coots. In this case, by skinning, the layer of fat under the skin may be removed, and most of the undesirable diet-flavor along with it, making the bird palatable when cooked with seasonings. Merganser, a notoriously fishy duck, has been treated this way with reasonable success.

The veteran bird with tougher skin and reluctant feathers is more easily skinned than plucked. But with the skin goes much of the fat, and for the sake of the bird's natural flavor, plucking may be well worth the trouble. If tough, the skin may be removed in the course of moist-heat cooking, once it has lent its fine flavor to the dish.

Finally some small birds such as starlings, blackbirds, and pigeons, which are cooked in moist heat (e.g., pies) are skinned as a matter of course to avoid a very tedious plucking job. Here, too, some loss of natural flavor is inevitable.

To skin fowl, remove the wings at the first joint and cut off the head. Slit the skin, through the feathers, down the back and along the legs and wings, and peel it off. Draw or trim the legs.

SPLITTING AND CUTTING

Splitting is the basic cut used when eviscerating very small plucked or skinned birds, cutting up fowl for cooking, or boning whole birds.

To split a dressed bird, use a very sharp knife and cut through the skin from neck to tail in a line with the backbone. Cut up through the ribs at the backbone, using a knife, poultry shears, or, for a small young bird, small sharp scissors. Take care not to puncture the entrails. Spread the bird open.

To clean small birds, such as quail and woodcock, first pluck or skin the birds, and then split them. Cut around the tail and vent, spread the bird open, and remove the entrails. Wash the bird well and wipe it dry with a clean cloth.

To cut up a split bird, cut the wings and legs away at the body. Separate the breast by cutting down each side below the ribs. The breast may be boned as described in the next section. When cutting, check all birds for broken bones and remove any splinters; remove any shot.

BONING

When boning fowl, the idea is to remove the entire skelton, leaving the flesh inside the skin, so that when stuffed the bird will appear to be intact. Any bird can be boned, but the bigger the bird, the easier the job.

Although boning is not difficult, the beginner will probably find it a painstaking process. The results, however, are rewarding, and boning is a good way to make one lone bird go a long way (see Pheasant Galantine). As an added dividend, the bones can be used to make stock.

Attempt to bone only the cleanly shot bird, as there should be no breaks in the skin other than the split up the back, and care must be taken to avoid puncturing the skin, especially around the wings where it is very thin.

Using a very sharp boning knife, cut the wings from the body at the first joint. Open the split bird and spread it out on the table, skin-side down. Slip the knife between the bone and muscle, and separate the flesh from the back (which is skinny) and from the ribs, working toward the center of the breast. Cut only where necessary, easing the flesh away from the bones with the back of the knife wherever possible.

Separate the wing and leg bones from the body by sticking the knife point into the joint and then twist-cutting to separate. Work the breast bones, cartilage, and keel bones free and remove the whole body skeleton.

In small birds, the leg and wing bones are usually left in for neater trussing. However, if you wish to remove these bones, grasp a thigh in one hand and, working from the inside, insert the knife into the thigh and against the bone, working it around the bone to free the flesh. Push the thigh bone upward and work the flesh down. Bend and snap or cut the knee joint, and remove the bone. Loosen the skin around the hock with the point of the knife, and proceed in the same way with the drumstick.

Repeat on the other thigh and leg. Bone the wings in the same manner, being extra careful with the thin skin.

The boned bird, when stuffed, is closed up the back with poultry lacers or with lacing thread run over rustproof pins.

FREEZING

Chill oven-dressed birds in ice water for 24 hours before packaging. Small birds, such as quail and woodcock, are best blocked in ice (see "Freezing Fish" in Chapter 8), as very small packages tend to dry out in the freezer. For birds the size of ducks and larger, use a heavy leakproof plastic bag of the cry-o-vac type, which shrinks to the contour of the bird when plunged into hot water, thus pressing out all air pockets.

Oven-dressed birds are best packaged whole, or they may be cut and frozen in recipe-size quantities. The packaged fowl should be promptly and thoroughly chilled before being put into the freezer.

Lean upland birds, properly shot and bled, dressed and prepared, may be freezer-stored for 8 to 10 months. Waterfowl and fat birds should not be stored longer than 3 to 6 months, as their fat has a tendency to become rancid.

Young birds from the freezer may have darkened bones. This is due to seepage of hemoglobin from the marrow during freezing and thawing; it has no effect on the quality of the meat or its flavor.

Check possession period regulations for all birds.

Do not freeze wildfowl uneviscerated or in the feathers.

Do not stuff birds before freezing.

TRUSSING

Birds to be cooked whole are usually trussed; those that are to be served whole on the table should *always* be trussed. Trussing is a matter of restraining the bird, and forcing its limbs into compact form for even cooking and attractive appearance. If the bird is to be stuffed, it should be trussed after stuffing.

Trussing may be done by any means that achieves the desired end. Two methods are given here: trussing with skewers and string (recommended for ducks and for quail, doves, and other small upland birds), and trussing with needle and string (*not* suitable for ducks with their short, low-set legs).

Trussing with Skewers and String: Use skewers that are a little longer than the bird is broad through the thighs. Place the bird on its back. (If desired, strips of fat may be inserted into the thighs against the bone for larding.) Hold the thighs close to the body, at the same time pressing down with the heel of the hand. Run a skewer through the middle of one thigh, through the body, and out through the middle of the other thigh.

Fold the wings across the back. Bring the neck skin down the back of the bird, tucking it under a wing. Run a skewer through the wings, passing it under the breast and pressing the wings close to the body.

Hold skewers securely by lacing a white cotton string or tape around the ends of one skewer, crossing it over the bird's back and around the other skewer. Draw the string taut and tie the ends together. Cross the legs at the ends and tie.

Trussing with Needle and String: Thread a trussing needle with a piece of white cotton string whose length is four times the girth of the bird. On very small birds, use tough white cotton or linen thread.

Bend the wings across the back, rounding the breast and tucking the neck skin under the wings. Hold the legs evenly upright with one hand, pressing down with the heel of the hand. Refer to the accompanying diagrams and proceed as follows:

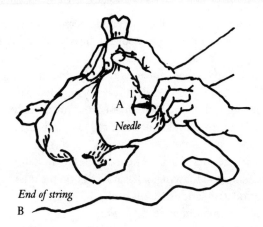

With the other hand, put the needle (A) through the flesh of the thighs at (1) just inside the bend of the drumstick elbow, through the body, and out the other thigh in the same place. Turn the bird on its side.

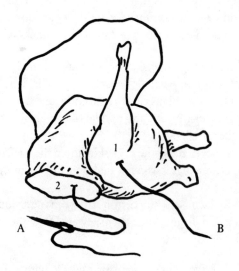

Push the needle (same string) through the wings at the elbow joint (2), catching the neck skin and passing between the skin and backbone en route. Turn the bird over. Draw the string tightly and tie in a knot with the other end of the string (B) at (1). Don't cut the string.

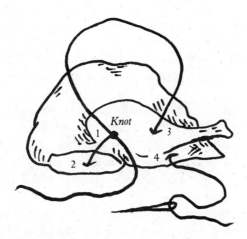

Lay the bird on its back again, and bring down the legs, pressing down on the thighs with one hand. Run the needle through the flesh (3) at mid-length of the drumstick *over* the bone; pass the needle between the breast and skin and keel bone, and out through the other drumstick in the same place. Return the needle and string, passing through the body only, just below spot (3) in the drumstick.

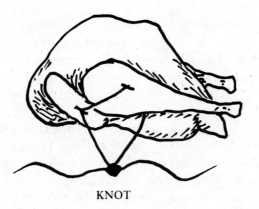

KNOT

Draw the string tightly and tie in a knot with the other end (B) at (1). Both knots being on the same side, they are easily snipped and the entire string neatly pulled out when the bird is cooked.

UPLAND GAME FOWL

You are now presented, kind reader, with a species of Grouse, which, in my humble opinion, far surpasses as an article of food every other land-bird which we have.
—John James Audubon
Ornithological Biography, 1834

The upland birds most commonly hunted in North America are of the gallinaceous order: the wild turkey, the various species of the native grouse family, including the prairie chicken and ptarmigan; and their kin, members of the pheasant family (who differ in having unfeathered legs and exposed nostrils), including the native quail or American bobwhite, the imported pheasant, and the partridge.

While there's no mistaking a wild turkey by name, or even a pheasant or quail, it's not so simple with grouse and partridge. An extravagant profusion of folk names for members of the grouse family adds to the charms of the hunt but can cause confusion. In W. L. McAtee's *Folk Names of Canadian Birds*, for example, one can note twenty-seven commonly used folk names under "Ruffed Grouse," and fifteen of these call the bird "partridge"—birch partridge, copper ruffed partridge, spruce partridge, gray partridge, and so on.

The overlapping of folk names can sometimes lead to misunderstandings with the game warden. For instance, the sharp-tailed grouse, once known as *faisan* (the French word for pheasant), is often called "prairie chicken." But the common prairie chicken is a species in its own right. Then again, the common prairie chicken is known in some locales as a pinnated grouse, and may be protected under that name. So the hunter should study the birds as well as the game laws.

Quality and Cooking Guidelines

The cooking of upland gamebirds is influenced by their natural flavor, texture, age, and general condition. The generally excellent natural flavor of prime upland birds is best preserved by simple cooking. This flavor is affected to some extent by the birds' dietary habits, but not as much as by the hunter's habits of caring for the birds.

The sage grouse of the West shows evidence of its sagebrush diet, sometimes to the point of overseasoning. Evergreen buds or resinous vegetable matter can flavor the grouse that feeds on such fare, but if the bird has been cleanly shot and promptly dressed out, this flavor should be no more than slightly noticeable, and it can be toned down by seasoning. If the dietary flavor is very strong, most of it can be removed by skinning the bird, and trimming away the flavor-laden fat, then larding the bird, to replace its natural fat.

Wild upland birds are inherently lean. However, all healthy animals have a certain amount of fat, and the plumper the bird, the better its texture and flavor. Lean meats tend to dry out during cooking and should be generously supplemented with fat. Avoid the direct application of moisture-drawing salt, especially when using dry heat; salt can always be added to taste at the table.

The flesh of upland birds is relatively fine grained; that of the smaller ones even more so. Within a species, the young bird is fine and tender; as the bird grows older and bigger, the flesh coarsens and becomes tough, requiring tenderizing.

The prime upland birds respond best to simple cooking methods that fully retain their natural juices and flavors. Seasonings, except in the special "diet cases," should be understated. Marinades may enhance the flavor of a dish, but they will *not* correct the effects of inadequate field care of the birds—no recipe will do that.

Young tender birds can be cooked whole by roasting covered in a moderate-to-hot oven. They also may be split (or use just the breast) and then broiled, fried, sautéed, or used in casseroles, with the remains used to make stock. Older, tougher birds can be cooked whole or cut, but they should be tenderized and/or cooked in moist heat. The following cooking guidelines apply to all upland game-birds:

- Frozen or chilled birds should be brought to room temperature for even cooking.
- Tenderizing marinades or commercial tenderizers may be used during refrigerator aging of older birds. Marinades given with individual recipes are interchangeable. Buttermilk is an excellent tenderizer.*

Upland gamebirds such as pheasant (top) *and chukar may be broiled and barbecued, but avoid overcooking them. Lard if necessary to prevent drying out.*

*The not-so-young upland bird responds nicely to a tenderizing treatment in buttermilk, without altering its flavor. Put the birds in a deep bowl, with little room to spare, and pour in a quart of buttermilk. Turn the birds over several times to coat them well. Let stand for 2 to 3 hours, turning the birds from time to time. Drain, rinse in cold water, and wipe dry before proceeding with the recipes that follow.

- Larding is done with butter (or margarine), oil, strips of bacon, or bards of fat salt pork, cut to size as required. The smoky flavor of bacon may be subdued by blanching (see Glossary). The crackling rind from a baked ham makes a fine larding cover under which to roast a bird.
- Avoid direct dry heat for all but the young, plump, tender bird.
- Cook well, but don't overcook.

Grouse and Partridge

The French make a nice distinction between *perdrix*, the feminine form, which refers to any partridge, and *perdreau*, the masculine, which refers to a young one; and as mentioned before, the "partridge" is usually a grouse. *Perdrix*, or *perdreau*, was certainly a grouse in the early French-Canadian recipes, since the recipes preceded the arrival of the partridge in North America by some two hundred years.

Age and tenderness, rather than species, are the deciding factors in choosing a recipe. Grouse and partridge recipes are interchangeable, and may be scaled to pheasant as well.

Perdrix au Choux (Partridge and Cabbage)

A traditional dish of French Canada, *perdrix au choux* dates back to the *coureurs de bois* of the eighteenth century. The following recipe was a favorite of the late Alphonse Didier, who for years was Executive Chef of the Royal York Hotel in Toronto. The recipe may be tailored to fewer birds. Pheasant or unusually large grouse may be split for cooking.

6 partridge or grouse,
   dressed and plucked or skinned
3 small cabbages, quartered
½ cup seasoned flour
6 strips bacon, cut in half
½ cup butter
2 cups beef bouillon
1 onion, stuck with 2 cloves
½ pound salt pork
1 tablespoon chopped parsley

Preheat the oven to 375° F (190° C). Wash the birds well in cold water and pat dry with towels. Wipe the cavities clean and lightly truss the birds. Blanch the cabbage quarters in boiling salted water for 3 minutes, and then drain.

Dredge the birds in the seasoned flour, shaking off the excess. Place 2 pieces of the bacon over each breast and tie them down with string. Melt the butter in a heavy frying pan and quickly brown the birds on all sides. After each bird browns, remove it to a large, well-greased Dutch oven. Trim the cores from the cabbage and arrange the cabbage around the birds in the Dutch oven. Swish the beef bouillon around in the hot frying pan and pour it over the partridge and cabbage. Add the cloved onion and lay the salt pork on top of everything. Cover tightly, bring to a boil, then bake for 1¼ hours.

Remove the cabbage from the pot and place it in the middle of a large, warm platter. Remove the string from the birds and arrange them around the cabbage. Slice the salt pork very thinly and place on top of the cabbage. Reduce the remaining pan juices by about a third, add parsley, and serve separately. *6 or more servings.*

Larded Grouse

Bring 2 young grouse (or pheasant), dressed and plucked, to room temperature. Preheat the oven to 425° F (220° C).

Wash the birds well in cold water and wipe dry. Wipe the cavities with a vinegar-dampened cloth, then rub the birds all over with fat. Push strips of bacon fat into the legs against the bone. Roll up bacon strips and place one in the neck and two or three in the cavity of each bird. Cover the birds entirely with thin strips of bacon, crackling pork rind, or chicken fat. Tuck pieces of fat between the thighs and body, and the wings and body. Truss loosely with skewers and string. Arrange the birds, breast up, in a shallow baking pan, and add enough water (about ½ cup) for basting. Tuck aluminum foil lightly over the pan and birds.

Bake until barely tender (25 to 35 minutes, depending on the size of the birds), basting frequently with the juices from the pan. Add a little water or wine if necessary for basting—or use Rosewater Glaze for Wildfowl.

Take the pan from the oven, remove the foil, untruss the birds, and remove all the bacon and other larding. Brush the birds with melted butter, dust lightly with seasoned flour, and return to the oven for a few minutes until they are very tender and turn a rich golden brown. Make a brown pan gravy, season lightly with salt and pepper, and stir in ½ cup of port wine or sherry for a winy sauce.

Variation: Prepare and lard the birds as above, but instead of tucking bacon into the cavity, fill it loosely with your favorite moist and savory stuffing or one from Chapter 11. Bake as directed above.

Staheli Partridge

Use young partridge, cleanly shot, dressed, and plucked, with undamaged breast skins. (Allow 1 bird per person.) Split and bone the birds, leaving the drumstick and wing bones in to allow for neater shaping when the bird is stuffed and trussed (see directions for boning earlier in this chapter). Wipe with a damp cloth.

Make the stuffing, using ½ cup of cooked wild rice and 1 tablespoon of liver paste for each bird. (The paste can be a commercial preparation of good-quality soft liver sausage.) To the paste add just enough cognac to give a rather loose consistency. Add the paste to the wild rice and mix lightly until evenly blended and somewhat cohesive. Season to taste with salt and pepper.

Preheat the oven to 400° F (205° C).

Spread the boned bird out flat, skin-side down, and heap the stuffing in the middle. Shape the bird neatly round the stuffing, rounding the breast smoothly, and fold the wings and legs over the back, tucking in the skin. Truss the bird. Arrange the birds, well spaced, in a baking pan.

The small, boned birds, with precooked stuffing, bake quickly. They are not larded in the manner usual for slow-cooking birds. Instead, soak strips of white paper in melted butter and encircle each bird, fastening the paper with a small poultry pin or toothpick. Brush the surface of each bird with melted butter and put the pan into the oven. After about 10 minutes, baste with melted butter, lower the heat to about 350° F (175° C) and bake for another 15 to 20 minutes, or until the birds are tender and golden brown. Serve with parsleyed potatoes and buttered fiddleheads.

—Fred Staheli
Toronto, Ontario

Roast Ptarmigan

6 to 8 ptarmigan
1 pound salt pork, sliced

Dressing:
1 loaf stale bread
4 medium onions, chopped
1 teaspoon poultry seasoning
Salt and pepper to taste

Skin and clean birds that you intend to roast. Soak them in salted water overnight.

Make the dressing: In a large bowl, break up the bread, add the chopped onion, poultry seasoning, and salt and pepper to taste. Add enough water to make a really moist dressing.

Towel-dry the ptarmigan. Tack 2 slices of salt pork on each side of the birds, using toothpicks. Place the birds close together in a roasting pan. Cover them with an ample amount of dressing. The dressing flavors the birds and keeps them moist.

Pour water in the bottom of the roaster to a 1-inch depth, and maintain this during cooking. Cover the roaster. Bake in a slow oven at 275° F (135° C) for about 4 hours. The water in the bottom of the roaster makes a rich gravy.

—Homer Homemakers
Cooking Up a Storm in Homer, Alaska

Spruce Grouse Marinated

This recipe is good for late-season old birds, which may taste of evergreen, and for sage grouse, as it tones down the excessive natural seasoning of such birds.

> 2 dressed grouse
> Marinade
> Flour, seasoned with pepper and garlic powder
> ¼ cup olive oil or bacon fat
> 1 large onion, sliced
> 20-ounce can tomatoes
> ½ cup wine
> 1 tablespoon sugar
> 1 green pepper, cut in rings
>
> *Marinade:*
> 2 tablespoons lemon juice
> 1 cup tomato juice
> ½ cup dry white or red wine

Skin the dressed grouse and discard the skin. Split the birds, cut into serving pieces, and carefully scrape and trim away as much fat as possible. Place the meat in a ceramic bowl. Combine the marinade ingredients and dribble over the meat. Cover and let stand for several hours, turning the pieces over from time to time. Drain the meat and pat dry between towels. Dredge the pieces in the seasoned flour and let them rest on a rack.

Heat the olive oil or bacon fat in a Dutch oven. Separate the onion rings and lightly brown until translucent. Remove the onion and reserve. Brown the floured meat on all sides in the hot fat. Scrape up from bottom of pot as you turn the meat to loosen the browned bits and prevent sticking. Add the tomatoes and scatter the pepper rings and reserved onion over the top. Cover tightly and simmer over a low heat for 1 hour or until the meat is very tender, or finish in a moderate oven. Serve the grouse in its own sauce. *4 servings.*

Pheasant

Pheasant, a relatively recent import to North America, may be found in the wild or on publicly or privately managed preserves. The farm pheasant is usually fatter than the wild one that must fend for itself, although they're all relatively lean birds and require additional fat in the cooking. Pheasant is cooked like other upland birds of comparable size and age (see recipes for grouse and turkey).

Roast Wild Pheasant

> 1 young pheasant, dressed
> Lemon juice
> 1 cup chopped celery
> 1 onion, chopped
> Pinch salt and pepper
> Butter
> ½ cup sherry or melted tart jelly

Wipe the cavity of the pheasant with lemon juice. Mix the celery, onion, and seasoning with 1 cup of crumbled hard butter, and stuff the cavity with as much of the mixture as it will hold. Do not close the cavity. Placing chunks of butter in the creases, fold the wings over the back, tucking in the neck skin, and hold with a skewer; tie the legs together.

Preheat oven to 375° F (190° C).

Soak doubled cheesecloth in melted butter or fine cooking oil and tuck loosely over the bird. Place, breast up on a rack or trivet in a roasting pan. Cover the bird with foil and roast in the oven, basting frequently with melted butter or oil, until tender (about 15 to 20 minutes per pound). Remove the foil and the cheesecloth, and add the sherry or jelly to the pan. Baste from the pan and brown for 10 to 15 minutes, until golden. Transfer the bird to a warmed platter. Remove the skewer and string. Discard the stuffing. Make a brown gravy from the pan drippings, or Wildfowl Giblet Gravy.

Variation: Stuff with moist wild rice stuffing that has medium or mild seasonings (see "Stuffings" in Chapter 11) and truss. Roast as above. Brush the breasts of roasted birds with crabapple jelly, and let glaze in the oven; or garnish with brandied apricot halves, using some of the brandy syrup for the final basting.

Pheasant in Sour Cream

1 pheasant, dressed
Flour, seasoned with salt and pepper
Clarified butter or cooking oil
1 tablespoon onion juice
1 cup commercial sour cream

Cut the pheasant into serving-size pieces, and dredge in the seasoned flour. Heat clear butter or mild cooking oil in a frying pan over high heat, and brown the pheasant well on all sides. Cover, and cook over moderate heat for 10 minutes. Reduce heat to a simmer.

Mix the onion juice with the sour cream and pour over the bird. Continue cooking, covered tightly, until very tender. Serve the meat in its own sauce, salting lightly to taste. *2 to 4 servings.*

—Mrs. Stuart Gordon
Montreal West, Quebec

Braised Breast of Pheasant

Braising is a method ideally suited to pheasant and grouse, especially the older birds, because it retains and enhances the meat's natural succulence. This recipe uses the entire bird in its preparation and requires cleanly shot birds with undamaged breasts.

2 pheasant, or 4 grouse, dressed and plucked
Marinade
½ cup flour, seasoned with black pepper
  and a trace of cayenne
Cooking oil or clarified butter
Stock
Salt to taste
½ cup sliced mushrooms
Pineapple chunks (optional)
6 cups steamed wild rice

Marinade:
1 cup red or white wine
1 teaspoon honey
Juice of 1 orange
Sliver of garlic, crushed

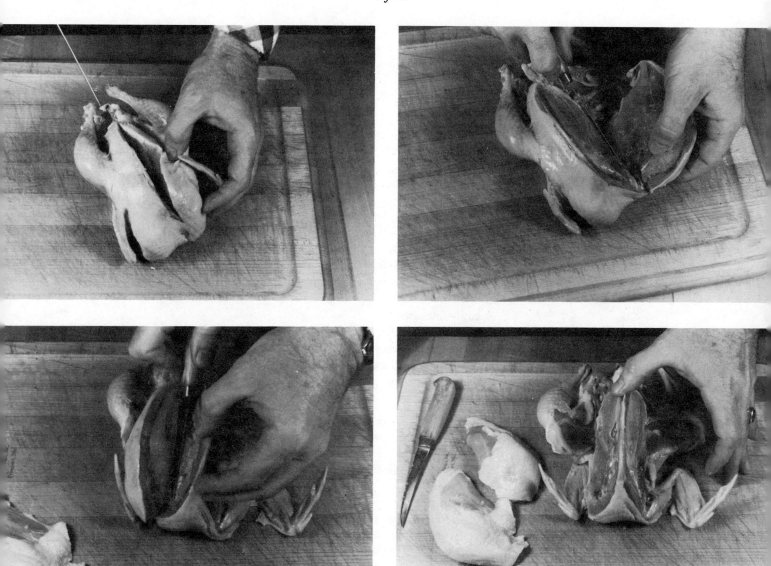

Removing breasts from a pheasant. Top left, make the first cut on one side of the breast with a flexible fillet knife. *Top right,* allow the knife to ride along the bone to free as much meat as possible, then cut through the skin at the bottom to free the breast. *Bottom left,* remove the breast from the other side in the same way. *Bottom right, boneless pheasant breasts are useful in many recipes.*

Split the birds, and with a fine, sharp boning knife cut away the breasts, taking care to leave no bone fragments or shot in the meat. Make a strong stock (see Glossary) from the remaining carcasses and season it lightly with *fines herbes,* tarragon, or fennel.

While the stock is cooking, combine and heat the marinade ingredients. Place the breasts in an earthenware or glass bowl and pour the hot marinade over the meat. Cover and let stand for 3 to

[151]

4 hours, turning the meat over once or twice. Lift the meat from the marinade and let it drain well. Reserve the marinade, discarding the garlic. Dredge the breasts in the seasoned flour.

In a large iron skillet heat oil to about a ⅛-inch depth and brown the meat skin-side down to a golden crustiness. Turn and brown the other side. Add the reserved marinade; add hot stock until the meat is just about half under. Salt lightly, cover tightly, and let simmer gently until the meat is tender, about 30 minutes. Gently run the edge of a spatula under the meat, scraping the bottom of the skillet once or twice during cooking to prevent sticking or scorching. About 10 minutes before the meat is done, add the mushrooms. Add a few small chunks of fresh or canned pineapple (optional but a noteworthy touch).

On a deep platter arrange the hot wild rice, making a broad nest in the middle. Arrange the breasts in the nest, and spoon the pan sauce over everything. Garnish with sprigs of parsley, or whatever takes your fancy.

Pheasant Galantine

5- to 6-pound pheasant or wild turkey,
   cleanly shot with skin unbroken
Stuffing
½ cup white wine
Bouquet garni, including a pinch of tarragon
2 carrots, very thinly sliced
1 onion, stuck with 2 cloves
2 tablespoons gelatin

Stuffing:
1 cup finely ground veal
1 cup finely ground pork
Pheasant giblets, finely ground, or ¼ pound
   uncooked calf's liver
½ cup suet
Salt and pepper
½ teaspoon ground poultry seasoning
¼ teaspoon powdered garlic
1 tablespoon finely minced onion

Bone the pheasant as described in the previous recipe, and make a lightly seasoned stock from the bones (see Glossary).

To prepare the stuffing, grind the veal and pork together, adding the giblets and suet. Mix with the seasonings and onion and blend well.

Spread the boned bird out, skin down, on a large square of cheesecloth. Pile half of the stuffing on the bird and fill the legs closely, but not the wings. Add the remainder of the stuffing. Sew up the bird with needle and thread, easing it into its original shape. Round out the breast and draw the neck skin down on the back; fold the skin of the wings over the back, pin to secure, and snip off excess skin. Pressing the legs close to the body as though trussed, bring up the cheesecloth, wrap closely, and tie securely with cotton tape or gauze bandage.

In a deep pot, just big enough for the bird, bring the stock (made from the bones) to a boil. Add the wine, and carefully place the bird in the pot. It should be completely immersed—if necessary, pour in other boiling stock or water to cover. Add the *bouquet garni*, carrots, and cloved onion. Cover the pot tightly, and cook gently over low-to-moderate heat for 5 to 6 hours, or to an internal temperature of 185° F (85° C). Do not replace lost moisture. Let cool to tepid in the stock.

Carefully remove the bird and lay it on its back on a platter. Press lightly so it doesn't settle to one side, then let it rest at room temperature until cool. Unwrap the bird carefully and snip and remove the thread. Place in the refrigerator to chill.

Strain the stock and let it cool. Skim off the fat and clarify (as directed for Beaver Tail Soup). Reduce to about 2 cups. Dissolve the gelatin in ½ cup of cold water and stir into the boiling stock. Set aside to cool. Keep an eye on it. When the cooled broth has thickened to the point where it will just pour in a thin stream, pour it over the chilled bird, just enough to glaze it thinly all over. The gelatin-broth should set on the chilled bird. Repeat the glazing and return the bird to the refrigerator to set. Serve cold, garnished with a variety of colorful fruit condiments and pickles. Cross-slice at an angle.

Turkey

The Turkey is a much more respectable Bird, and withal a true original Native of America.
—Benjamin Franklin

Thus Ben Franklin compared the wild turkey, his candidate for national emblem, with the bald eagle. The turkey lost the title to the bald eagle as national emblem and some nature philosophers claim it was probably for the best, or the turkey would doubtless be an endangered species today. The turkey (maintained through successful domestication) did win a permanent place on the Thanksgiving table as a symbol of the bounty of the land. Successful conservation programs during the twentieth century have been restoring the once-threatened wild turkey, so hunters may once more celebrate Thanksgiving in the original traditional manner.

Wild turkeys, which 200 years ago tipped the scales at 30 to 40 pounds, now average around 16 pounds for toms and 9 to 10 for hens. Young birds (6 months old) run 6 to 13 pounds, but they are not necessarily more tender than older and bigger birds. The fall-into-winter turkey, fattening on mast, fruits, and seeds before breeding season, is considered the most succulent table bird.

For cooking purposes, a wild turkey is comparable to a free-range domestic farm turkey, though it may not be as fat, and general turkey recipes may be used.

Roast Wild Turkey

Bring an oven-dressed turkey (8 pounds or more) to room temperature. If it's frozen, thaw slowly in the refrigerator or other cold place. Wash the bird well, inside and out, and towel-dry. Probe for and remove shot and bone splinters; trim damaged flesh.

Brush the cavity with melted butter and stuff two-thirds full with Tom Schirm's Chestnut Stuffing, Corn Bread Giblet Stuffing, or Fruity Stuffing (see Chapter 11). Preheat the oven to 450° F (230° C).

Sew up and truss the bird, tucking chunks of butter into the creases under the legs and wings. Rub all over with butter. Place on a rack or a bed of carrots in a roasting pan.

In a saucepan melt 1 cup of butter, and add 1 cup of dry white wine to it. Cut a piece of cheesecloth or cotton gauze, large enough to cover the bird, and soak it in the butter-wine mixture. Spread the dripping gauze over the bird, tucking it under. Baste again with melted butter and wine, letting some run into the pan. To prevent the drumsticks from browning too quickly, cover them lightly with foil, securing it with pins or toothpicks.

Put the turkey into the hot oven. After 10 minutes turn the heat down to 350° F (175° C). Baste every 30 minutes or so, first with the melted butter and wine, and when that is used up, with pan drippings. If the bird browns too quickly, lay a piece of foil loosely over the top, shiny side up (remove foil from drumsticks). Remove all foil about 1 hour before the roast is done.

Allow 20 to 25 minutes per pound, or cook to an internal temperature of 190° F (88° C). The meat thermometer should be inserted between the thigh and body, taking care that the tip does not touch bone. Don't let the bird overcook—it is done when no pink shows in the juice when the meat is pierced with a fork, the drumstick is freely movable, the bird is brown all over, and the aroma is irresistible. Remove the gauze. Baste from the pan, and place the turkey on a large warm platter. Serve with Brown Pan Gravy.

Barbecue-Smoked Turkey

Throughout the South and Southwest, a smoky barbecue-roasting over the coals is a favored way to cook wild turkey. Native woods lend regional distinction to the product.

L. J. "Touch" Touchton, owner-operator of the Mullet Inn and its famous smokehouses on the Clearwater-Tampa causeway in Florida, simply oils and seasons the turkey with pepper and sage, wraps it in foil, and puts it into the smoke ovens. In a deep rack over Florida oak (blackjack) at about 350° F, a 10-pound bird cooks in about 4 hours (allowing 20 to 25 minutes per pound). Moderate heat is maintained by opening and closing the door. The turkey cooks in the hot smoke for about 2 hours; then the foil is opened and the turkey is basted with oil and lots of white pepper, and left to brown, with frequent basting until done. The blackjack gives the meat a distinctive reddish gold color and a wonderful flavor.

Jim Mosley of G & M Catering in Austin, Texas, and a specialist in outdoor and game cookery, barbecue-smokes the turkey over mesquite. The dressed bird is lightly stuffed with orange sections, apples, and onions and is put into the covered barbecue to bake entirely over the hot mesquite smoke. It is basted frequently with an oily barbecue sauce. This turkey shouldn't be left too long. Mosley advises using a meat thermometer if in doubt about doneness.

Various home smoking appliances are on the market and should be used according to instructions. A conventional home barbecue can be adapted to smoke a turkey, other wildfowl, and some fish (see Barbecue-Smoked Lake Trout).

Note that barbecue-smoking is not a preservative method. It simply bakes the game over the coals in smoky heat.

Fried Turkey Breasts with Running Gear Gravy

This recipe, which feeds 8 to 10, is for a 12- to 15-pound turkey, but it can also be adapted to grouse or pheasant.

The bird should be skinned rather than plucked. Cut away the breasts and set aside. Disjoint and cut up the rest of the carcass—legs, thighs, neck, back, and wings. Cover with water and slow-boil, or wrap in foil and bake, until the meat falls from the bones (the meat and stock are used in the gravy).

Angle-cut the breasts across the grain in ¼-inch slices. In a bowl, combine 1 cup of fine dry bread crumbs with seasoning—salt, pepper, and a pinch of cayenne. Double bread the slices of breast meat (that is, dip in milk, dredge in crumbs, and repeat). Let the breaded slices rest on a rack.

In a large heavy skillet heat oil, a good ½ inch deep, until it browns a bread cube in 1 minute. Add the breaded meat slices. Cook in two or more lots if necessary—don't crowd the slices in the pan. Be sure the oil is hot and deep enough before adding more meat. Cook each side to a crusty brown, flipping once, about 10 minutes in all. Place on a paper-lined platter and keep warm while making the gravy.

Running Gear Gravy: "Running gear" is the term for drumsticks and thighs, hence the name of this gravy. Strip the cooked meat from the bones and chop finely. Reserve the stock.

Pour off the excess oil from the frying pan in which the breasts were cooked, leaving the brown drippings with a coating of fat. Add about 2 tablespoons of flour to an estimated 1 cup of drippings. Stir until brown and bubbly. Add the hot stock and stir until thickened. If too thick, mix in some hot water. Blend in the chopped meat. Cook, stirring occasionally, for about 5 minutes. Season to taste. Pour over the fried meat, or over potatoes or rice, and serve.

> —Rob Keck
> Executive Vice President and World Champion Caller
> National Wild Turkey Federation

Quail, Woodcock, and Other Small Gamebirds

Along with quail and woodcock, the following small gamebirds are included here for convenience: snipe, rails, doves, pigeons, and blackbirds. Snipe and rail are not upland birds, but they fit in well with this group for cooking purposes. Usually weighing less than a pound, all these birds are relatively lean. They generally are split for cleaning rather than drawn (see Splitting and Cutting under "Home Care" earlier in this chapter).

QUAIL

Quail, also known as bobwhite, though kin to the pheasant and peacock, is a small bird; one or even two are required to a serving. Its delicate flavor and moisture are best preserved by quick cooking.

Golden Quail

Use 4 young plump quail, plucked, split, and flattened. Wipe the meat with a damp cloth, and rub well with butter. Put 2 cups of water in the bottom of a steamer. Arrange the split birds, skin up, on a rack in the steamer and pour ½ cup of dry white wine over them. Cover and steam gently until just tender.

Transfer the birds to a buttered baking pan. (Save the steamer liquid for sauce or braising stock.) Brush with ½ cup of melted butter, sprinkle lightly with flour, and brown under the broiler until golden. (If the oven happens to be hot, the quail may be browned in the oven.) Season lightly with salt and pepper. Serve with lemon wedges and a tart jelly.

Roast Quail

Bring 4 or 5 dressed and plucked quail to room temperature. Wash the birds well in cold water and towel-dry. Wipe the cavities with a vinegar-dampened cloth. Make Fruity Stuffing (use wild rice), and stuff the birds.

Preheat oven to 425° F (220° C). Rub the birds well with melted butter. Arrange them breast up on a rack in a baking pan. Soak a double thickness of cheesecloth in melted butter and lay it over the birds. Cover with foil.

Put the birds into the oven. Baste often with hot melted butter and white wine, and bake for

15 to 20 minutes, or until tender. Remove the foil and cheesecloth. Baste well from the pan, dust lightly with flour, and bake to a delicate gold. Serve with Bread Sauce (see Roast Woodcock with Bread Sauce) or Brown Pan Gravy, or place each bird on a round of toast on a platter, and pour the pan drippings into the platter to be soaked up by the toast. Serve with spiced crabapples or citron preserves, with a slice of orange for color.

Broiled Quail "Pineburst"
4 quail, split-dressed
Salt and freshly ground black pepper
2 tablespoons soft butter
1 cup hot chicken stock
4 teaspoons flour
4 teaspoons butter
¼ cup heavy cream
1 tablespoon red currant jelly

Season the quail with salt and pepper, then spread with soft butter. Put the birds, skin-side down, under the hot broiler for 5 to 6 minutes. Turn and broil for another 5 to 6 minutes, until nicely browned. Remove the birds to a heated platter and keep warm.

Pour off the excess fat from the broiler pan, leaving the brown drippings. Add the chicken stock to the pan to loosen the drippings (don't cook). Mix the flour and butter in a saucepan; heat and stir until bubbly. Add the chicken stock and drippings, and stir until thick and smooth. Cook for 5 minutes, stirring frequently. Stir in the cream and red currant jelly and cook to desired thickness. Season with plenty of freshly ground pepper, and salt if necessary. Serve separately or over the birds. This dish is excellent with wild rice sautéed with minced scallions and chanterelles. Or serve with croutons made from hominy grits.

— Pinehurst Hotel and Country Club
Pinehurst, North Carolina

Castle Quail
4 quail, dressed and plucked
1 teaspoon dried tarragon
½ cup dry white wine
Clarified butter (see Glossary)
Salt and pepper

Wash the quail, pat dry, and bring to room temperature. Clip off the wings, leaving enough skin to tuck under the back. Cut the legs off at the first joint and truss to the body.

Soak the tarragon in the wine for about 1 hour.

Melt clarified butter to about a ¼-inch depth in a large, heavy skillet. Fry the quail until browned on all sides, turning as one side browns. Pour the tarragon-wine over the birds. Place a close-fitting lid on the skillet, and lower the heat. Simmer for 1 hour, or until the birds are tender. Season to taste with salt and pepper.

— Estelle Warmbrod
Whispering Pine Shooting Preserve and Kennels
Carthage, North Carolina

Wildfowl

WOODCOCK

The fine flavor and general distribution of the woodcock make this bite-size bird a worldwide favorite. It goes by many names in America—timberdoodle, big-eye, and mudsnipe are just a few. By whatever name, the delicate flavor of the strange little bird dictates that the succulent morsel be cooked simply and quickly, with lots of butter but little or no seasoning.

Woodcock Roasted Before the Hunter's Eyes

Pluck and draw or split the birds to clean. Get a good hardwood fire going in an outdoor fireplace—or a wood cookstove or indoor fireplace—and build up a bed of coals. Wash the dressed birds in clear cold water, drain, and pat dry with a towel. Probe for and remove any shot, and trim damaged parts.

For drawn birds, insert a marble-size chunk of hard butter or margarine or a small curl of fat bacon into the cavity of each bird. Truss, wrapping a thin slice of bacon, spiral fashion, around the bird and securing it with pins or pegs. Fasten the bird onto a spit or forked pole. Rub with butter, and broil over the coals, turning and basting with melted butter almost constantly for 15 to 18 minutes, or until the bird is tender and golden.

For split birds, flatten and rub all over with butter. Place in a hinged wire toaster or grill and hold over the hot coals, skin-side up, for a couple of minutes to sear the underside. Baste the top with butter, and turn to sear the skin side. Baste almost constantly and turn frequently until the birds are tender and golden. The split birds broil very quickly—in 10 to 12 minutes. Don't overcook.

Roast Woodcock with Bread Sauce

Preheat the oven to 425° F (220° C). Remove the heads from 4 plucked and split-dressed woodcocks, leaving a good piece of neck skin (or skin the head, to be tucked under a wing). Wipe the birds with a lemon-juice-dampened cloth. Place 2 or 3 small chunks of hard butter in each cavity, and push a small chunk of butter under the neck skin to the breast. Truss with string and skewers, legs close to the body and wings snapped and folded over the back, tucking in the neck skin (or head). Trim off the excess skin. Tie a thin bard of salt pork around each bird and score the pork.

Put the birds on a rack in a baking pan, placing a piece of stale, dry bread under each bird to catch the drippings. Baste with melted butter and bake until tender, 20 to 25 minutes. Remove the bards of pork. Baste the birds with more melted butter, dust lightly with flour, and return to the oven until evenly browned. Remove the birds.

Trim the bread to a diamond shape, each piece just large enough to support a bird, and arrange on a heated platter. Add remaining pan drippings, no more than the bread will absorb. Place a bird on each, garnish with sprigs of fresh parsley and slices of lemon. Serve Bread Sauce on the side.

Bread Sauce:
1 cup fine dry white bread crumbs
2 cups milk
1 medium onion
3 tablespoons butter
Salt and pepper

Sift the crumbs through a coarse sieve, then sprinkle them over the milk in a saucepan. Set remaining coarser crumbs aside. Add the whole onion to the milk and scald over a low flame for 12 minutes after

[157]

skin forms on milk. (This must not scorch—use a double boiler if necessary.) Remove onion. Add 1 tablespoon of the butter, and salt and pepper to taste.

Meanwhile heat the remaining butter in a saucepan; when brown, add reserved coarse bread crumbs and fry to a rich brown, stirring quickly to avoid scorching. Remove from the heat.

Put the sauce in a gravy boat and sprinkle the browned crumbs on top. Serve at once. Bread Sauce is excellent with all very small birds (roasted or broiled)—snipe, rail, squab, dove, quail—any of which may be cooked by this recipe for woodcock.

Variation: Skewer the trussed, barded birds on a long spit, and broil them over hot coals in the fireplace. Serve with Bread Sauce.

SNIPE AND RAIL

Simple cooking is also recommended for snipe and rail. Use butter generously but little or no seasoning, and add no salt during cooking. Recipes for quail, woodcock, snipe, and rail are interchangeable.

Snipe or Rail in Casserole

Preheat oven to 375° F (190° C). Split and clean 4 to 6 plucked birds (all of one kind or mixed), and press with the palm of the hand to flatten. Dip each piece in milk and dredge in plain flour. Brown well in deep, hot clarified butter or mild cooking oil, or in a mixture of oil and butter.

Arrange the birds in a heated ovenproof casserole. Pour the remaining butter from the pan over the birds, lightly dust with pepper, and add a little white wine or water to moisten. Cover and place in oven. After about 20 minutes pour commercial sour cream over the birds and continue baking, covered, until tender. Serve very hot on rounds of dry toast, with the birds' own sauce from the baking dish.

PIGEONS AND DOVES

Pigeons and doves belong to the same family. The common pigeon is called dove in some locales, and the young or fledgling pigeon is known as squab. Pigeons are widely distributed throughout North America. Generally there is no closed season on pigeons, but those taken in late summer through early winter provide the best table fare. The migratory doves are protected and their hunting confined to open season.

The meat of pigeons and doves is dark and fine of flavor; the adult pigeon tends to be not quite as tender as the dove and is best braised. Otherwise the two are cooked alike. The lifestyle of wild city pigeons is not conducive to producing good meat; use only country pigeons in the following recipes.

Braised Doves

Flatten 6 split-dressed doves (or pigeons), preferably plucked.* Wipe with a cloth dampened in lemon juice or vinegar. Dredge the birds in a mixture of fine corn meal and flour seasoned with garlic salt and pepper.

In a large, heavy skillet or Dutch oven, heat a mixture of cooking oil and butter, about ¼ inch

---

*The breast only may be used in this recipe. Many dove hunters in the United States, especially in the East, use just the breast, which contains most of the meat, when cooking dove.

deep. Brown the birds on both sides. Draw off excess fat. Sprinkle each bird with a pinch of fennel or tarragon. Add a few wisps of pimento for color. Add ½ cup of white wine. Cover and simmer over low heat for 1 hour, or until the birds are tender. Serve the birds hot on squares of dry toast and pour the sauce over them. Surround with sautéed mushrooms and garnish with sprigs of fresh parsley.

Pigeons in Sour Cream

6 young pigeons (doves)
Clarified butter (see Glossary)
1 teaspoon finely chopped onion or shallot
1 teaspoon chives
4 large mushroom heads, thinly sliced
1 cup canned tomatoes
Pinch thyme
1 bay leaf
2 sprigs summer savory
Salt and pepper to taste
1 teaspoon paprika
1 cup sour cream or yogurt

Split the birds down the back, but don't separate the halves. Wipe them with a brandy- or wine-moistened cloth and rub with salt and pepper to taste. Sauté the birds in about ¼ inch of clarified butter over low heat until golden brown on both sides and tender—about 30 to 40 minutes. Lift the birds out of the pan, cover with foil, and keep hot.

To the pan add the onions, chives, mushrooms, and tomatoes. Simmer for 4 to 5 minutes, stirring constantly. Add the thyme and other seasonings. Simmer for another 4 to 5 minutes, then gradually add—stirring constantly—the sour cream or yogurt. Bring to a boil and pour the sauce over the birds just before serving. Serve with broiled mushroom caps and garlic-flavored croutons.

—Angelo P. Casagrande
Chef, Chateau Laurier
Ottawa, Ontario

Pigeons with Sauerkraut

4 pigeons, cleaned, plucked, and split
2 cups white or red table wine
2 tablespoons bacon fat
Flour
Pepper
4 cups sauerkraut
5 or 6 strips bacon
Salt

Wipe the pigeons well with a vinegar-moistened cloth. Put the birds into a deep earthen bowl, pour the wine over them, and turn them a few times. Marinate the birds for 1 or 2 hours, turning them occasionally. Remove the birds and reserve the wine.

Heat the bacon fat in a Dutch oven or heavy, covered skillet. Dust the birds with flour and pepper, and brown them well on all sides in the hot fat. Arrange the birds skin-side up, spread the sauerkraut over them, add the reserved wine, and place the bacon strips on top. Cover tightly. Simmer slowly on the stove, or bake in a 375° F (190° C) oven, until the meat is tender, about 1 hour. Test for salt and add to taste.

BLACKBIRDS

Blackbirds are seasonally abundant in agricultural areas to the point of nuisance. Fattened in cornfields, vineyards, and orchards, the young birds brought down from their early autumn feast or flight are at their choicest. On the other hand, where nuisance birds are concerned, a pair in the spring is worth ten in the fall, and if enough pies were filled with blackbirds in the spring, presumably it would help control the population of the tasty little bird.

Blackbirds are easily dressed by splitting, and may be plucked or skinned (though with the skin goes flavor-laden fat). However dressed, they are delicious when braised like pigeons and doves, broiled in a toaster over the coals like woodcock, or baked four-and-twenty in a pie.

Blackbird Pie

24 blackbirds, plucked or skinned,
  split, and cleaned
¼ cup vinegar
¼ teaspoon mace
1 lemon, juice and grated rind
¼ teaspoon sugar
1 onion, stuck with 2 cloves
Dry red wine or claret
Pastry for 2-crust 12-inch pie
3 tablespoons butter
Flour
Salt and pepper
Pinch freshly grated nutmeg
Milk

Soak the dressed blackbirds in water and the vinegar for a couple of hours. Drain, rinse, and put the birds into a deep kettle. Barely cover with water, adding the mace, lemon juice, a little grated rind, and the sugar. Bury the onion in the meat. Bring to a boil, skim, and reduce the heat. Simmer until the meat is ready to fall from the bones, adding wine to keep the birds covered with liquid. Take out and remove the breasts intact and the smaller bits of meat. Reserve the liquid.

Line a 12-inch round baking dish or deep pie plate with pastry and add the meat. Preheat the oven to 425° F (220° C).

Boil the reserved liquid in the Dutch oven until about 2 cups are left. Discard the onion. Rub the butter in flour, using as much flour as necessary to make a mealy mixture. Sprinkle the butter-flour mixture over the top of the boiling liquid. Stir until blended and thickened. Season with salt and pepper to taste, and add a pinch of grated nutmeg.

Pour the sauce over the meat. Cover with pastry, pinching the edges of both crusts to the sides of the dish. Brush with milk. Score and bake in the hot oven for 10 minutes. Reduce the heat to 375° F (190° C) and bake for 45 minutes, or until the pie is evenly browned all over. (A glass dish allows one to see how the bottom crust is browning.) Instead of one large pie, two smaller ones may be made. Either way, this recipe yields *10 to 12 servings*.

Variation: "Eating crow" need not be a figurative penance—it can be a quite satisfying meal when prepared in the same way as Blackbird Pie. However, unlike blackbirds, hungry crows are carrion eaters; therefore, they should be used for the table only at the peak of agricultural plenty, and they should be well cooked. Crows are big birds, and half a dozen or so will fill the pie.

Mixed Bag

Many great recipes have evolved from combinations of wildfowl and other small game. The following traditional classics are fine for using damaged game or a mixed bag (also see Poacher's Potage).

Salmi of Upland Birds

Use 2 young grouse, 1 pheasant, 4 or 5 quail, or a combination. Partially roast the dressed birds, covered, in a 375° (190° C) oven. Carve the meat from the breasts, removing the skin, and set the breast meat aside.

Put the remainder of the carcasses with the skins and giblets in a saucepan. (If the giblets have not been saved, use a chicken liver or a small piece of beef liver.) Barely cover with water and cook until any remaining meat can be stripped from the bones and the liquid is reduced by half. Discard the bones and skin. Put the stripped meat and the cooked giblets, about ½ cup at a time, into a heavy-duty blender along with a little of the bouillon, and blend to a smooth paste. Dilute the paste with 1½ cups of red wine and ⅓ cup of the bouillon. Rub through a sieve into a saucepan. Add a heaping teaspoon of butter. Season lightly with salt, a few grains of cayenne, and a bit of grated lemon rind. Cook gently for 1 hour.

To the cooked sauce add the breast meat, and heat just to the boil. Simmer a few minutes until the meat is tender. The sauce should be thin but not watery. If it's too thin, rub a little butter in flour and stir into the sauce, a sprinkling at a time, until the desired consistency is reached. Place strips of dry toast in a hot, deep platter. Arrange the breast meat on the toast and pour the sauce over it.

Potted Wildfowl

Potting, or making a pâté, is an excellent way to use 1 or 2 lone small fowl, or the bird with missing parts. Leftover fowl may be used this way, also. The preparation of a pâté is a matter of taste and judgment rather than precisely measured ingredients. With the aid of a blender, the mixing can be done in minutes.

Rub the oven-dressed birds all over lightly with butter or margarine. Sprinkle with salt inside and out. If the birds have been skinned, salt them first, then wrap in thinly sliced bacon or in cheesecloth dipped in melted butter. Place in a well-buttered cake pan. Lay a piece of aluminum foil over the top, shiny-side up, to prevent browning. Do not pinch the foil to the pan. Bake in a 320° F (160° C) oven until the meat falls from the bones. The birds will appear overcooked and dry, as they should be for potting.

Take the birds from the oven, and remove the bacon or cheesecloth. Strip the meat from the bones. Put the meat, about ½ cup at a time, into a blender, and process at medium speed, adding enough butter to make a smooth paste. Blend in a pinch each of cayenne, freshly ground black pepper, and mace, and a trace of allspice (or spices and seasonings to taste). Add ¼ teaspoon of sugar. Blend and test for seasonings.

Spices may be adjusted one way or the other when you blend the next lot, and salt added to taste. Remember that spices develop during storage, so don't overdo it. Adjust the amount of butter in the same way. The mixture should be soft but not oily—it will firm up when chilled.

Repeat the process until all the meat has been used. Mix the batches together. Add a few slivered hazlenuts or almonds, or try pine nuts for a tangy flavor. Pack the paste into small bowls, pressing the meat down firmly to eliminate air pockets. Cover completely with melted butter. Allow to ripen in the refrigerator for 5 to 7 days.

Check the bowls during storage. If the butter cracks or draws away from the sides of the bowls, add more melted butter. Properly covered and stored, the potted fowl should keep for as long as

1 month. However, once opened, it should all be used immediately. To serve, turn out on a plate, garnish, and surround with thin crackers or melba toast.

Small-Game Fricassee

2 partridge or small grouse, or 1 large grouse
  or pheasant (plucked or skinned)
1 rabbit, or 2 squirrels
Marinade
Butter and cooking oil
1 large onion, sliced
Flour seasoned with pepper and a few grains of cayenne
1 tablespoon tomato paste

Marinade:
1 cup red or white wine
1 teaspoon sugar
1 tablespoon mixed pickling spices, tied in cheesecloth,
  or ½ cup pickle juice
1 clove garlic, crushed

This recipe is suitable for small game with damaged parts. Trim the usable parts of the game and cut into serving pieces, taking care to remove any bone splinters and shot. Wipe the pieces with a damp cloth.

Combine the marinade ingredients in a saucepan and heat (don't boil). Lay the pieces of fowl and rabbit or squirrel in an earthen bowl, and pour the hot marinade over the meat. Add hot water if necessary to keep the meat wet. Cover and let stand 3 to 4 hours, turning once. Drain the meat and reserve the marinade, discarding the spice bag and garlic.

Heat a mixture of butter and cooking oil, ¼ inch deep, in a heavy frying pan. Separate the onion slices into rings and brown lightly. Remove and reserve the onion. Dredge the pieces of fowl in the seasoned flour and brown well on all sides in the hot fat. Scatter the onion rings over the top.

Stir the tomato paste into the reserved marinade. Add it to the pan, along with enough water or stock to just show through the meat. Cover tightly and simmer for 1 hour, or until the meat is very tender. Scrape up from the bottom of the pan from time to time. After the first ½ hour, a few sliced mushrooms may be added. Serve the meat in its own sauce.

Poacher's Potage

A combination of any of the following will make a tasty dish: hare, grouse, partridge, pheasant, squirrel, and/or any other delectable small gamebird or game animal, dressed for cooking. The measurements below are for the equivalent of a hare and a couple of small grouse. Adjust as necessary for more or less meat.

¼ cup vinegar
¼ cup butter
¼ pound salt pork, diced
Flour
Red wine
1 faggot (see Glossary)
1 onion, stuck with 2 or 3 cloves
6 large tomatoes, quartered (or 1 20-ounce can)
1 teaspoon salt
Pepper
1 tablespoon sugar
6 to 8 small onions
1 cup sliced whole mushrooms (caps and stems)

Cut the game into pieces for cooking. Soak the meats overnight in the vinegar and enough water to cover. Rinse well and pat dry.

Melt the butter in a large, heavy pot with a tight-fitting cover, then lightly brown the salt pork in it. Remove the pork. Dust the pieces of meat with flour and brown well on all sides in the hot fat, scraping the browned bits up from the bottom. Just when it's beginning to smoke, stir in equal parts of water and wine to just barely cover the meat. Return the browned pork to the pot, and add the faggot, onion, tomatoes, salt, pepper, and sugar. Bring to a low boil, cover, and cook gently until the meat is almost tender. Remove the faggot and clove-onion when sufficiently seasoned.

Add the small onions and mushrooms; cook until they're tender and the meat is ready to fall from the bones. Lift out the meat, strip it from the bones, and return it to the brew. The stew may be thickened by kneading 2 tablespoons of butter in 2 tablespoons of flour and sprinkling the mixture over the simmering stew. Stir and cook uncovered until slightly thickened—a minute or two. Serve the stew in a deep tureen. Sprinkle the surface with croutons fried in garlic butter. *6 servings.*

Variations: For Poacher's Pie, thicken the stew, cover with pastry, and brown in a hot oven. Or, make dumplings from biscuit mix; add them to the unthickened stew, cover, and cook as directed on the package.

WATERFOWL

But the fact is, duck hunting is the one sport above all others for me.
—Jack Miner
Jack Miner and the Birds

From the vast breeding ground "beyond the North Wind" to the hospitable wintering grounds in the South, the whole North American continent is the natural home of migratory waterfowl. On a continental scale, waterfowl commonly hunted are ducks and geese, although in parts of the West, some hunting of sandhill crane may be permitted.

Wild Ducks

The influence of the haunts and dietary habits of waterfowl on its flavor is particularly noticeable in wild ducks, which range from vegetarians to outright fish eaters. The game ducks* of table renown

are the vegetarians, and for culinary purposes, these are separated here into two groups: *select* and *choice*, determined simply by whether the duck shuns fish in its diet, or eats it occasionally.

The select group includes the gadwall (grey duck), green-winged teal, pintail, redhead, widgeon, and wood duck. Choice ducks are the black duck, blue-winged teal, canvasback, mallard, and ringneck. All of these select and choice ducks may usually be depended upon for fine flavor in regions where they feed on inland lakes, swamps, and marshes, especially in the richly vegetated western plains and prairies and here choice ducks may become select.

Young, tender ducks may be roasted, broiled, sautéed and/or cooked in moist heat. Older, less tender birds may be marinated and baked covered; they also benefit from a commercial tenderizer and moist-heat cooking. Tough old veterans are best made into duck soup.

Some other game ducks, whose diet consists of a high percentage of animal matter, need not be overlooked as table fare. Depending on how much fish they have consumed, and how recently, the goldeneye (whistler), the scaups, and the hooded merganser may be made palatable, if not gastronomically outstanding, when treated for their dietary indiscriminations.

The coot, or mudhen, although not a duck or even closely related, should be mentioned here. A very palatable bird when properly prepared, the young coot should be skinned rather than plucked and treated as a fishy duck, thus removing lingering traces of the bird's muddy haunts. The coot may then be cooked by any of the moist-heat recipes recommended for the choice group of ducks.

General kitchen preparation procedures for wildfowl are given at the beginning of this chapter. Fishiness is a problem peculiar to wild ducks and is dealt with here.

FISHY DUCK TREATMENT

If fishiness is detected during the cleaning of the birds, this information should be passed on to the cook. Since dietary flavors are concentrated in the duck's fat, they can be largely eliminated by removing the fat, using a flavor-aid treatment, and cooking the bird in moist heat with seasoning.

---

*These ducks are not always all on the open-season list; restrictions vary across the continent as conditions or population levels dictate. Consult the migratory gamebird regulations.

Skin the freshly killed bird. Carefully scrape away as much surface fat as possible. Wipe the bird with a lemon- or vinegar-moistened cloth before trying either of the following two flavor aids:

1. Place a whole peeled onion and a quartered lemon in the bird's cavity; cover and refrigerate for 12 hours. Discard the onion and lemon and replace with fresh ones. Turn the bird over, and refrigerate another 12 hours. Wipe the bird again with a lemon- or vinegar-moistened cloth.

2. Immerse the skinned bird in a deep bowl of tomato juice; cover and refrigerate overnight. This is both a flavor aid and a tenderizer. The bird may be split and cut first.

After either of these treatments the duck should be cooked in moist heat with plenty of seasoning. If the meat is extremely fishy, use the breasts only.

Following are two recipes for Roast Duck, Select and Choice, and a selection of North American hunters' favorite duck dishes.

Roast Duck — Select

The natural flavoring of the young select vegetarian duck is best captured by quick roasting. Roast only very young birds by this quick method, and cook them until just tender and nicely browned, never overdone. To roast older birds, follow instructions for Roast Duck — Choice.

A mild moist stuffing may be used if desired — it will make the bird go further. However, plump young select ducks* are at their very best without embellishment. They require nothing but a mixture of melted butter or mild cooking oil and dry white wine to help their own basting juices along.

Preheat oven to 425° F (220° C).

Stuff if desired and truss the birds. Place them breast up, uncovered, on a rack in a small roasting pan. Determine roasting time from the chart for young select ducks. Baste the birds frequently, first with a mixture of melted butter and wine, then with pan juices as they collect. Good accessories for roast duck are light, tart sauces or fruit condiments (see Game Sauce, Orange Sauce, Spiced Cranberries, and other recipes in Chapter 11).

ROASTING TIMES FOR YOUNG SELECT DUCKS

Species	Average live weight*	Total time at 425° (220° C) for 2 to 4 birds†
Canvasback (inland)	3 pounds	30 minutes
Gadwall (grey duck)	2 pounds	30 minutes
Green-winged teal	under 1 pound	20 minutes
Pintail	2 to 2½ pounds	30 minutes
Redhead	2 pounds	30 minutes
Widgeon	1½ pounds	25 minutes
Wood duck	2 pounds	30 minutes

*Dressed weight is approximately two-thirds of live weight.
†Timing is approximate and varies slightly with the number of birds in the pan. Roast until tender and nicely browned.

*If the duck is quite lean, place 2 strips of (blanched) fat bacon on the breast and cover the bird for the first half of the cooking time. If the duck is unstuffed, a couple more strips of bacon may be rolled up and placed in the cavity as well. Remove the bacon when the bird is done. Baste well, dust lightly with flour, and return the bird to the oven for a minute or two to brown.

Roast Duck – Choice

Unless they are very young, choice ducks should be marinated overnight. Use the buttermilk treatment described under "Quality and Cooking Guidelines" in the upland game fowl section earlier in this chapter; or cover the birds with milk to which ½ teaspoon of baking soda per quart has been added. (If the birds are suspected of having eaten fish recently, they are no longer choice – don't roast them. See "Fishy Duck Treatment" above.)

The proper stuffing will enhance the bird's flavor. Use Peanut Stuffing for Ducks, Apple Stuffing, or one of the other savory stuffings in Chapter 11, all of which are good to eat.

If an edible stuffing is not used, place 1 or 2 curled strips of bacon, 1 whole peeled onion, and 1 teaspoon of crushed black pepper in the cavity of the dressed bird, and pour in ½ cup of claret or red wine. Another such method is to rub the bird inside and out with lemon juice, pepper, and garlic, and then place a cored apple, a few cranberries or raisins, and a few chunks of hard butter in the cavity (any combination of apple, orange, lemon, and grapefruit wedges, chunks of celery and carrot, and sliced onion may be used instead). These stuffings are removed from the bird before serving.

Preheat the oven to 375° F (190° C).

Stuff and truss the bird, and oil it all over. Place breast up on a rack in a roasting pan, cover and cook until tender (see chart for roasting times for choice ducks). Baste frequently with a mixture of wine and melted butter or cooking oil, then with pan drippings as they collect. If the bird is plump, wine or plain orange juice is fine for basting. During the last 20 minutes of roasting, remove the cover. Baste well, dust lightly with flour, and let brown. Tart and spicy sauces and fruit condiments go well with roast choice ducks: try Curry Sauce, Sweet and Sour Sauce, Spiced Grapes, and other recipes in Chapter 11.

ROASTING TIMES FOR YOUNG CHOICE DUCKS

Species	Average live weight*	Total time at 350° F (175° C) for 2 to 4 birds†
Black duck	2½ to 3 pounds	1½ hours
Blue-winged teal	under 1 pound	¾ hours
Canvasback	3 pounds	1½ hours
Mallard	2½ to 3 pounds	1½ hours
Ringneck	2½ pounds	1¼ hours

*Dressed weight is approximately two-thirds of live weight.
†Timing is approximate and varies slightly with the number of birds in the pan. Roast until tender and nicely browned.

Breast of Duck

The following dish was served to Prince Philip at the Royal Military College in Kingston, Ontario. The combination of western prairie ducks and Mrs. Ironside's creative treatment so impressed the prince that he requested the recipe.

Wipe the duck breasts with a damp cloth. Make a well-seasoned mixture of flour and poultry seasoning, salt, and pepper. Dip the breasts in milk, then roll them in the flour. Heat butter in a skillet, and brown the duck breasts on both sides. Place in a casserole.

Preheat the oven to 275° F (135° C).

To the skillet drippings, add 1 package of dry onion soup mix and a bit more flour, and stir to make a bubbly roux. Add hot water to make a nice gravy, stirring until smoothly thickened, and pour over the duck breasts. Bake covered until tender, about 2 hours.

—Mrs. J. D. Ironside
Swift Current, Saskatchewan

Coral Cay Ducks with Oyster Stuffing

4 ducks (1 per person), cleaned and plucked
2 teaspoons baking soda
Oyster stuffing
Garlic
Butter
Pepper
Salt
¾ cup orange juice, freshly squeezed, and pulp

Oyster stuffing:
3 cups stale bread crumbs
2 teaspoons thyme
½ teaspoon salt
¼ teaspoon white pepper
¼ cup melted butter
2 tablespoons minced onion
1 pint oysters (fresh or canned) and juice

Wash the ducks well and trim oven-ready. Cover with water, add the baking soda, and refrigerate overnight.

Make stuffing the next day. Toss the seasonings and bread crumbs together. Sauté the onion in the melted butter until just translucent. Add the onion and butter to the crumbs. Toss lightly. Drain the oysters, add about ½ cup of the juice to the stuffing, and toss again. Chop the oysters coarsely and add to the stuffing. Toss until evenly distributed. Let the stuffing rest in the refrigerator for about ½ hour.

Rinse the ducks in cold water and pat dry. Rub the skin of the birds all over with slices of fresh garlic. Insert a sliver of the garlic into the cavity of each. Stuff lightly, allowing room for the stuffing to swell, and close the cavity with toothpicks. Put the birds into a roomy baking pan, breast up. Place a good dab of butter on each bird and dust with pepper. Pour in about ¾ cup of freshly squeezed, strained orange juice (reserve the pulp). Cover the birds closely with foil and put into a preheated moderate oven (350° F, 175° C) for about 30 minutes. Remove the foil and baste well from the pan. Lay the foil over the birds. Return them to the oven and baste every few minutes for another ½ hour. Jab the skin with a skewer; when no blood shows, remove the foil.

Salt the birds lightly. Spread the pulp from the strained orange juice over the breasts and return the ducks to the oven until just browned. Don't overcook. Serve with mint jelly. A gravy may be made from the pan drippings and served on the side.

—Bill Cobb
Coral Cay
Port Aransas, Texas

Tombigbee Swamp Ducks

Pluck and clean the ducks and soak them overnight in a weak solution of salt and baking soda. Rinse under cold water and towel-dry. (If the ducks seem to be old, it may be wise to parboil them about 20 minutes.) Season with salt and pepper inside and out. Rub all over with butter.

Put 2 small apples, 1 sliced orange, and a handful of celery leaves in the cavity of each duck. If the duck is on the lean side, lay a strip or two of fat bacon over the breast. Place the ducks, breast up, in a shallow baking pan.

Add 1 inch of hot water to the bottom of the pan, cover, and bake in a preheated 350° F (175° C) oven for 1 hour, or until tender. Baste from the pan occasionally. Remove the cover during the latter part of the cooking time (about 20 minutes) so the ducks can brown well.

Variation: The birds may also be baked in foil. Prepare them as above. Salt the cavity heavily and season with pepper. Put into the cavity 1 peeled onion, 1 carrot, and a few celery leaves. Prick a small juicy orange with a fork, and place the orange in the cavity opening to seal it. Rub the outside of the ducks well with butter.

Wrap in foil, tucking the ends up so the package may be opened for checking and basting. Put into a preheated 375° F (190° C) oven and bake until done (meat is tender and beginning to leave the breastbone). When checking to see if the ducks are done, baste with juices accumulated in the bottom of the foil wrapping.

–Kathryn Tucker Windham
Treasured Alabama Recipes

Mallards in Sauerkraut

Plump mallards from the western prairies, famous for their grain-fed flavor, can be just as tough as any other old ducks when past their prime. This recipe calls for "two old birds" and turns them into a succulent dish. It may be used for any old table ducks (or geese), as long as they're plump.

Split 2 dressed, plucked birds through the back. If they're badly shot up or otherwise unpresentable, use the breasts only, but do try to save the skin for flavor. Remove all bone splinters; probe for and remove shot. Wipe each piece with a damp cloth and dust with flour. Sear lightly on all sides in hot cooking oil.

Preheat the oven to 400° F (205° C).

Spread sauerkraut (20-ounce can) over the bottom of a large casserole or Dutch oven. Add 4 thin slices of ham and arrange the ducks skin-side up on the ham. Add 1 cup of dry white wine and 1½ cups of water. Cover tightly, and bake for 45 to 60 minutes, until the meat is tender. Serve the duck on the ham slices and top with sauerkraut. *4 servings.*

Braised Breast of Goldeneye, Scaup, or Hooded Merganser

Given a flavor-aid treatment, these divers may be acceptable table fare. Their diets are high in animal matter—crayfish, tadpoles, insects, and other small aquatic life, including fish. Whether fishy or not, the flavor of these ducks is likely to be stronger than that of a vegetarian duck and is improved by the Fishy Duck Treatment described earlier.

This recipe is scaled to 2 goldeneyes or scaup, or 4 of the smaller hooded mergansers. Breasts of any table duck may be prepared by this recipe (the tomato juice treatment may be omitted for tender vegetarian ducks).

Skin and cut the breasts from the ducks, removing as much fat as possible. Wash, pat dry, and put into a deep bowl. Heat to boiling enough tomato juice to cover the meat. Pour it over the breasts. Cover and refrigerate overnight. Drain and wipe each piece with a damp cloth.

Season ½ cup of flour generously with pepper and garlic powder and a good pinch of cayenne. Dredge each piece of duck in the flour, coating it well on all sides. In a large skillet, heat 3 tablespoons of olive oil or cooking oil. Add a large clove of garlic, finely minced. Brown the meat quickly on all sides. Sprinkle 1 teaspoon of dried thyme or savory over the meat. Slice a medium-size carrot, a large onion, and a green pepper, and scatter the vegetables over the meat. Add a few slices of celery.

In 1 cup of boiling water, mix 2 tablespoons of tomato paste and pour it over the meat and vegetables. Add red wine until the liquid barely shows through the meat. Bring to a boil, cover, and reduce the heat. Simmer until almost tender, occasionally running a spatula under the meat to keep it from sticking. Moisten with a little hot water only if necessary. Add salt to taste.

Sauté a cupful of sliced mushrooms in a little butter, or open and drain a can of mushrooms, and add to the meat. Cover and continue cooking until the meat is tender. Serve the duck in its own sauce with fluffy hot rice.

Duck and Squirrel Cacciatore

Ducks that are small by nature or tender age, such as the teals and young pintails, carry practically all of their meat on the breasts. They are thus best cooked by a method that makes the most of this delicious mouthful without entirely wasting the rest of the bird. Such a preparation is Emmitt Briand's cacciatore-style dish. Briand, of Toronto, Ontario, says it's great when made of duck, even better when a couple of squirrels are added.

Pluck or skin the ducks. Split up the back and clean. Cut the breasts away from the bones. Probe for and remove any shot with tweezers. Skin and clean the squirrels, and cut away as much meat as possible. Wash all the meat in cold water, pat dry between towels, and put aside.

Trim and wash the remaining carcasses and put them into a deep saucepan or small stockpot. Cover with cold water and bring to a boil. Skim. Add a little salt, plain or seasoned, and about 1 tablespoon of vinegar. Boil down gently for about 1 hour. Strain the stock. (Note: If the ducks or squirrels have been damaged by shot, simply skin at once, cut away the unaffected meat, and discard the remaining carcasses. Chicken stock, home-made or canned, may be used.)

While the stock is boiling down, get the meat under way. The following proportions are for 3 or 4 ducks and 3 or 4 squirrels, or whatever combination is on hand. Adjust proportions for more or less total meat.

½ cup flour, seasoned with salt and pepper
Olive oil
1 garlic clove, crushed
1 onion, sliced
1 green pepper, sliced
20-ounce can plum tomatoes
½ cup dry white wine
½ cup stock
2 tablespoons tomato paste
Salt and pepper to taste
1 bay leaf
¼ teaspoon each thyme, marjoram, and/or
  other herbs to taste
1 cup mushrooms, fresh or canned (optional)

Dust the meat in the seasoned flour. Place a large, heavy skillet or Dutch oven over medium heat and add olive oil to about a ¼-inch depth. Add the crushed garlic and stir it around while the oil heats. Discard the garlic. Lightly brown the meat in the hot oil, turning it to brown evenly on all sides. Add the onion and pepper slices. Stir and cook, mixing the vegetables in with the meat, for 3 or 4 minutes, until the vegetables are soft and the meat is partially cooked. Add the plum tomatoes. Cover lightly and let simmer on low heat for about ½ hour.

In another saucepan, heat just enough oil to coat the pan well. Add the wine, stock, and tomato paste, and mix well. Add salt and pepper and any other seasonings to taste. Stir while the mixture comes to a bubble, and then pour it all over the meat. Mix gently. Cover the brew and let it simmer for at least a couple of hours. If necessary, moisten with hot stock or water. About 15 minutes before serving, add the mushrooms. (This dish may be cooked a day ahead and refrigerated. The next day, simply heat it to a simmer and serve.)

Wild Geese

Wild geese are vegetarians, and in their prime they are the aristocrats of the festive board. From the Gulf of Mexico and the coast of California to the Arctic deltas and tundra, wild geese thrive on diets ranging from wild millet, bulrushes, and eel grass to tundra grasses, wild grains, nuts, and berries—and on the flyways they feast on tender new shoots of grasses and weeds, and the waste grains of cultivated lands.

Field and home care techniques described earlier in this chapter are applicable to wild geese. Because of their size,* the larger geese are more conveniently aged before plucking; they should be hung, heads up, in a cold, well-ventilated place, protected from insects.

Wild geese often live to a rather old age, and thus are not always tender. If the breastbone and rib cage are rigid and the plumage coarse, the goose is not young. A bird somewhat past its first tenderness will respond to a mild marinade, and even a tough old goose can become remarkably fine table fare when treated with a pickle-smoke cure (see Pickle-Cured Smoked Wild Goose).

How you cook your goose may depend on where it was bagged. For example, Jim McLaughlin, of the Old Roadhouse Inn in Nome, Alaska, says he pricks the skin in several places and puts the goose into a very slow oven for the first hour or so to render out excessive fat. Of course, hunters in the upper reaches of Alaska have the advantage of being where the wild geese grow fat and succulent after summering on the profusion of berries and other lush tundra vegetation.

Once the geese take to the flyways in migration, however, they begin to burn up the fat rapidly; they become progressively leaner until they reach their destination pretty well depleted of succulence, and settle in to recover it.

The rich, dark meat of the wild goose requires simple cooking, with seasoning to enhance rather than overpower its natural flavor. The recipes in this section are applicable to all species of game table geese. They may also be used for the sandhill crane, a tasty 10-pound bird that can be dressed, prepared, and cooked like wild goose of comparable age and size.

*Average live weights of geese are: common Canada, 10 pounds; lesser Canada, 6 pounds; Richardson's Canada, 4 to 5 pounds; white-fronted, 6 to 7 pounds; American and black brants, 3 pounds; greater snow, 7 pounds; and lesser snow (blue phase), 5 pounds.

Roast Wild Goose

If your goose comes from near its northern summering grounds and is fat enough to provide its own basting, follow Chef McLaughlin's procedure, described above, for rendering out excessive fat. But from points farther along the migration route, it's a rare bird that doesn't need some help to keep it moist and succulent in the roasting pan. This may be provided by means of an oily basting, supplementary larding, or both; of further aid is a moist, rich stuffing such as Apple Stuffing or Fruity Stuffing (see Chapter 11).

Unless it's young and tender, soak the dressed goose overnight in the refrigerator in a solution of ½ cup of wine or vinegar to 1 gallon of water (or 1 cup of powdered milk and 1 teaspoon of baking soda to 1 gallon of water). Rinse under cold water and pat dry. Preheat oven to 325° F (165° C).

Stuff the goose lightly, about three-quarters full. Truss the bird and place it on a rack in the roasting pan. Soak a large piece of cheesecloth in a basting mixture of equal parts of white wine and melted butter or cooking oil, and lay it over the bird. If the goose is moderately fat, a frequent basting with the wine-butter mixture should be sufficient—the leaner the bird, the more basting required. If the bird is decidedly lean, lay a few slices of fat bacon over the breast and thighs before applying the cheesecloth.

Cover the goose for at least half of its roasting time, depending on its fattiness. Baste frequently with the wine mixture for about half the time, then baste from the pan. Allow about 25 minutes per pound of stuffed bird, or bake until tender and evenly browned. Make Brown Pan Gravy, and serve with Spiced Cranberries or Cranberry-Rosehip Sauce.

Cranberry Wild Goose

A cranberry and butter stuffing helps keep the goose moist during cooking and complements its natural flavor.

> 1 goose, dressed
> 1 cup cranberries
> 1 cup hard butter, coarsely chopped
> 1 tablespoon sugar
> 2 thick slices slab bacon
> 2 to 3 ounces sweet or medium sherry
> Flour
> 1 tablespoon cornstarch
> Salt and pepper

If the goose is frozen, thaw it in the refrigerator or a cold room. Wash it well both inside and out, removing any adhering membranes in the cavity. Wipe dry. Preheat the oven to 325° F (165° C).

To prepare the stuffing, combine the cranberries, butter, and sugar, and pack the mixture into the cavity, filling it as closely as possible. Mix more stuffing if necessary. Truss the bird with string and poultry lacers, closing the cavity completely. Rub the bird generously with butter or cooking oil.

Press a double thickness of heavy-duty aluminum foil, big enough to wrap the bird, into a roasting pan. Place the bacon slices side by side on the foil, and place the goose, breast up, on top. Pour the sherry over the bird. (A little apple or cranberry jelly, or just a little sugar dissolved in water may be substituted for the wine.) Fold the edges of the foil together, enclosing the bird completely.

Bake until tender, allowing about 30 to 35 minutes per pound. About 30 minutes before the time is up, tear open the foil, letting the juices run into the pan. Remove the foil. Dust the goose lightly with flour. Baste from the pan every 10 minutes or so for the last 30 minutes of cooking, letting the bird brown until it's tender and an even deep gold color. Remove it to a warm platter. Untruss the bird. Discard the stuffing if you wish; it has done its job of larding and flavoring the bird and its sauce.

Quickly boil the sauce down to about half its volume. Mix the cornstarch in ½ cup of water. Stir into the sauce. Stir and cook for a minute or so until clear and slightly thickened. Season to taste with salt and pepper. Serve the sauce in a gravy boat, along with the goose.

Breast of Snow Goose
The snow goose's Latin name, *Chens hyperborea*, means "Goose from beyond the North Wind."

> 1 snow goose
> ½ cup dry red wine
> Dash dry mustard
> 1 ounce olive oil
> ½ bay leaf
> Salt and pepper
> ¼ cup cream

Skin the goose, cut out both breasts, and slice them at an angle into thin steaks. Mix the wine with the mustard, add the olive oil and bay leaf and a little salt and pepper. Place the slices of breast on a flat platter and pour the oily mixture over them. Let stand for 2 hours, turning the meat over occasionally.

Remove the steaks and pan-fry them. When tender, transfer the meat to a warm serving platter and keep warm. Sprinkle a little flour in the frying pan, stir in the remaining oil mixture, cook for 5 minutes, then mix in the cream. Strain the sauce, and pour over the steaks. Top with maple-sugar glazed apple rings. Serve egg noodles on the side.

—C. Hitz
Chef, Château Frontenac
Quebec

PART FOUR

Fish

But yet, though while I fish, I fast,
I make good fortune my repast;
And thereunto my friend invite,
In whom I more than that delight;
Who is more welcome to my dish,
Than to my angle was my fish.

Izaak Walton
The Compleat Angler

8

Basic Care and Cooking of Fish

... we brought home our limit—80 speckled trout—in perfect condition ... it had been a five-hour climb into the mountains; at that elevation there was still ice around the shores. As we caught the fish, we cleaned them, all 80 of them, put them in poly-bags and packed them in ice in our packsacks ... the fish were perfect, still in rigor, and ice still left when we checked out our week's catch at the park gates.

— Clorice Landry
Shediac, New Brunswick
On spring trout fishing in Laurentide Park, Quebec

The few methods and principles on which all fish cookery is based are simple. However, there are several factors upon which their success depends. The nature of the fish itself, its field care, and its treatment in the kitchen all bear on its eventual triumph on the table. First and foremost is the quality of the fish when it reaches the cook; no recipe can overcome the damaging effects of improper field care and handling of the fish between the time it's caught and prepared for eating.

FROM CATCH TO COOK

Fish flesh is extremely perishable, and the care of the fish from the moment it's caught all the way to the cook is critical to maintaining its quality. To be acceptable in the kitchen, a fish must be fresh-smelling (or odorless) and firm or rigid in texture. Fresh fish of good eating quality exhibit the following characteristics:

- The flesh springs back to finger pressure.
- The scales are firmly attached and glisten like sequins.
- The eyes are well rounded and protruding, not sunken.
- No bones stick through the flesh inside the cavity of a dressed fish.
- The gills are bright red.
- The odor, especially noticeable in the gills, is mild, light, and fresh. In saltwater fish, there is a faint trace of iodine.

Conditions across the continent vary so drastically that it's impossible here to cover field care for all fishing situations. (State and provincial wildlife and/or fisheries agencies are usually a good source of regional information.) However, a few tips of a general nature bear emphasis: Kill the fish as soon as it's caught; not only is this the humane thing to do, but the flesh deteriorates more rapidly in fish left to die slowly. Don't put live fish in pails of water, or on stringers to struggle and drag after the boat. Don't put dead fish there either. Water impedes natural drainage of the fish. The relatively warm water at the surface interferes with rigor mortis, aids bacterial action, and altogether speeds up spoilage of the fish.

If you can't clean it right away, do bleed the fish immediately, especially if it's a big one—cut through the throat or cut off the head and let it drain. Wash the fish, keep it cold, and clean it as soon as possible. If there's no way to keep the catch cold, it should be cleaned, cooked and eaten, or returned alive and well to the water.

Cleaning, Skinning, and Scaling Fish

Preparation of the various forms of dressed fish described in the next section may require that the fish be cleaned and skinned or scaled.

Cleaning: The usual cut for gutting fish is through the abdomen. Exceptions are the gib (for very small fish) and the kipper cuts. Fillets are usually cut directly from the uncleaned fish.

Use a sharp, pointed knife. Push the point of the knife through the skin at the base of the throat. With a light, easy stroke, slit the skin as far as the vent. Separate the edges, and with the point of the knife, cut across the throat and free the gut. Cut the skin around the vent, taking care not to sever the intestine, and everything will come away intact. Cut out the gills. Separate the roe if present (in many fishes this is a delicacy), the liver, and other giblets as desirable, and dispose of the remaining entrails. Wash the fish and flush out the cavity with plenty of clean water, wiping out any blood or other matter clinging to the backbone, until the inside of the fish is glistening clean.

Very small fish are cleaned through the gills, a procedure called *gibbing*. Spread open the gill cover, slip forefingers in around the inner gill, and with a gentle pinch draw it out, bringing the viscera along with it.

Immediately chill the fish after cleaning it. If this is not possible, cook it or salt it (see Smoking in Chapter 3).

Skinning: Skinning a fish is facilitated by first dunking it in scalding water. Cut through the skin around the neck below the gills of the cleaned (dressed) fish. Slip the knife between the skin and flesh of the neck, and draw the skin back, easing it away from the flesh on one side with the blunt side of the knife and working toward the tail. Skin the other side by the same procedure. If the tail is to remain, cut through the skin around the caudal peduncle.

Scaling: To scale a fish, lay it on a solid surface and grip it firmly by the tail with one hand. Using the blunt edge of a knife, held at about a 45-degree angle to the fish, scrape away the scales, working from tail to head. It's easier to scale a semi-thawed fish, but the scales do fly.

All fish have scales, although some are scarcely discernible, like those of the salmon, trout, and mackerel. Scrape these with the blunt side of a knife when preparing to cook, and serve in the skins.

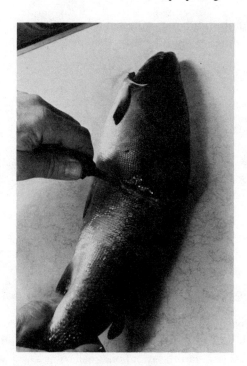

Scaling a salmon.

[179]

Dressing Fish

Fish as they come from the water ("in the round") may be dressed in several ways: whole dressed, head dressed, pan dressed, split, steaked, filleted, or boned. In some dressing procedures, the fish is first cleaned, and also skinned or scaled. In others (filleting, splitting, or boning), the fish is cleaned in the process.

Whole Dressing: A whole, dressed fish is simply one that has been cleaned in the conventional manner as described in the previous section. If the fish is to be skinned, it is done now before further dressing.

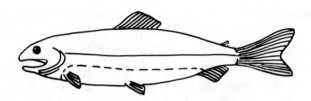

Head Dressing: To cut the head from a dressed fish, simply make a clean cut across the throat just under the gills. (Don't throw away the heads; they make great chowders.)

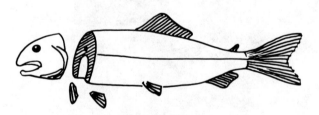

Pan Dressing: Remove the fins, scales, and tail from a head-dressed fish. With the point of a knife, cut through the flesh close to and around the fins. With a firm grip, using pliers if necessary, give the fin a sharp backward jerk. Fin and root bones will come away with it. Don't cut the fins off with scissors or a knife, or the roots will be left in the flesh.

Splitting: Head-dressed and pan-dressed fish too thick to fry or broil whole may be plank- or flat-split by cutting through the ribs to one side of the backbone. Flatten the fish or cut them in half.

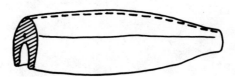

Steaking: Steaks are cut from large pan-dressed fish. Fish above, say, 8 pounds are cut into meal-size portions or steaks by cutting through the backbone into slices of any thickness desired.

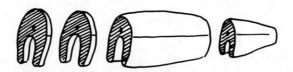

Filleting: Fish from 2 to 3 pounds and up are filleted. (Extra-large fillets are then cut into meal-size portions.) A cleaned, dressed fish may be filleted, or the cleaning step may be bypassed by simply cutting the fillets from a fish in the round. If the fish is skinned, there's no need to scale it. Otherwise, scale the fish before filleting.

In the general run of fine sportfishes with excellent skin, whether you skin or not depends on how you plan to cook the fish. It's best to leave at least some of the fillets unskinned until it's time to cook them. The skin provides added protection against drying in the refrigerator or freezer, and it's easily removed from a semi-thawed fish. Leave the skin on fillets that are to be smoked or broiled — it holds them together. (Also, fishing regulations may require a bit of skin for inspection purposes.)

Follow the accompanying photographs in which Norm Lee of The Pas, Manitoba, shows how to fillet a walleye. (All photos by John Power.)

Step 3: Slit along belly from pelvic fins to the vent.

Filleting, step 1: Insert fillet knife under pectoral fins below gills and cut to the bone.

Step 2: Cut across throat and under the pelvic fins.

Step 7: Cut through skin at tail and remove fillet.

Step 8: Remove fillet from other side in the same way.

Step 9: Skin each fillet.

Step 4: Grasp the head firmly and insert knife under flesh at bone.

Step 5: Run knife toward the back, shearing off along the backbone through the ribs.

Step 6: Continue all the way to the tail.

Step 10: Cut away the rib cage from each fillet.

Step 11: Trim the bony lower part. (Photo sequence by John Power.)

Boning Fish in the Round: Large fish (around 5 pounds or more) are more easily boned than small fish. In this procedure, the fish is not cleaned in a separate operation; instead, the entrails are removed as part of the boning procedure.

Scale the fish and cut out the fins. Cut along the back through the flesh to the bone, from just above the gill covers to the tail. Starting midway at the back, slip the point of the knife blade broadside between the flesh and bone, and cut, easing the flesh from the backbone and ribs and gently drawing it back as you work. Take care not to puncture the skin or abdomen. Continue working either way toward head and tail.

Turn the fish over and repeat on the other side.

With the point of the knife, cut through the skin around the vent. Cut through the backbone at the neck and sever the cords in the throat; cut through the backbone at the tail, being careful not to cut through the skin. With the knife blade, ease the backbone and ribs away from the fish and lift out, bring the entrails with them. Cut away any flesh adhering to the bones, and use it to pad any thin spots on the fish.

Boning Head-Dressed Fish: Scale the fish (dressed and with head removed) and cut out the fins. Before cutting off the tail, continue the slit from the vent to the tail. Cut across to the backbone. Put the fish on its side on a cutting board, and pressing the tail end down with one hand, bone the lower side first. Slip the tip of the boning knife broadside in between the flesh and ribs. Ease the knife toward the head, cutting the flesh away from the ribs. Now work back toward the tail end until the flesh is separated from the bones on one side. Turn the fish over and repeat. Cut off the tail, and lift out the bones and any flesh adhering to them. Use this flesh to pad thin spots in the fish.

Freezing Fish

Only fish in absolutely fresh condition, properly chilled and dressed, should be frozen for storage; and once frozen, they should remain so until thawed for cooking.* Depending on their size, game-fishes are frozen dressed whole or cut into steaks, fillets, or meal-size portions; panfishes may be frozen in the round in meal-size lots.

A constant temperature of $-5°$ F to $-10°$ F ($-21°$ C to $-23°$ C) assures the best results. At these temperatures, lean fish may be stored for 9 to 12 months; medium-fat fish for 5 to 9 months; and fatty fish for 3 to 4 months.

The freezer life of frozen fish can be extended considerably, and their quality maintained better, by encasing, or glazing, them in ice. The glaze may be a thin coating of ice (dip-glazed) used for whole lean fish or meal-size cuts, or a block of ice (block-frozen) built up around the fish, used for whole fish or meal-size lots of small fish or fillets. A more recent development is the gelatin-dip, great for any fish but particularly so for fatty fish.

Dip Glazing: Freeze the whole fish or meal-size portions hard. Dip the frozen fish in and out of ice water, repeating until a good coat of ice has formed over the entire fish (let it freeze hard in between dips). Wrap the fish well in butcher paper, food wrap, or aluminum foil, pressing out trapped

---

*If you are ice fishing in below-freezing weather, it may not be possible to clean the catch before it has frozen. (*Never* leave fish lying about a heated ice-fishing hut.) Should a fish freeze in the round, *don't* thaw it to clean, and then re-freeze, when you get home. Instead, leave it frozen and glaze it on the spot by dipping in and out of the fishing hole, or glaze it at home before freezer storage.

BRAISED BREAST OF PHEASANT, served with wild rice, makes an elegant, attractive main dish. Braising, which retains and enhances the meat's natural juices, is a particularly good method for cooking older pheasant and grouse.

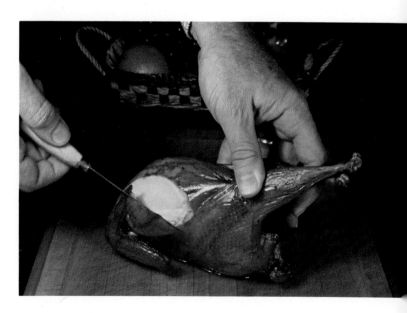

Old, tough wildfowl can be transformed into delectable viands by salt-curing and smoking. This SMOKED PHEASANT may be served hot or cold.

Older, less tender ducks are best marinated or given a tenderizing treatment, then baked covered or cooked by a moist-heat method. After the addition of some freshly squeezed orange juice to the pan, these CORAL CAY DUCKS WITH OYSTER STUFFING will be covered with foil and baked in a moderate oven.

Successful game-management programs have restored the once-threatened wild turkey to huntable populations throughout its native range and beyond. Though traditionally served at Thanksgiving, ROAST WILD TURKEY is such a fine dish that it deserves more than once-a-year treatment.

The rich, dark meat of wild goose calls for simple cooking and seasonings that enhance its natural flavor. In this recipe for CRANBERRY WILD GOOSE, a cranberry and butter stuffing provides larding and adds flavoring to the goose and sauce, which may be thickened and seasoned along with the meat.

The fine flavor of dove is accentuated by a simple but savory preparation of BRAISED DOVES, seasoned with garlic, salt, pepper, and a little fennel or tarragon. Many cooks use just the breasts, which contain most of the meat, when cooking doves.

A colorful preparation, Minuta a la Cazulla combines fish, shrimp, and clams in a wine sauce seasoned with garlic and hot red peppers. Any fine white-fleshed fish, such as Nassau grouper, flounder, halibut or walleye, gives excellent results with this recipe.

Small dressed fish, fillets, and steaks are suitable for pan frying. The fish are dusted with seasoned flour (à la meunière) or dipped in a sticking agent and rolled in crumbs (à l'Anglaise) before frying. The fat should be sizzling, and the fish should be fried uncovered on each side until golden brown.

Large, fatty fish like salmon may be poached in a deep court bouillon, then served immediately with a sauce or used in any of numerous recipes. The many variations of court bouillon all serve to enhance the fish's natural flavor and correct off-flavors. Oblong poachers with perforated trays for lifting the fish in and out are ideal for poaching or steaming fish.

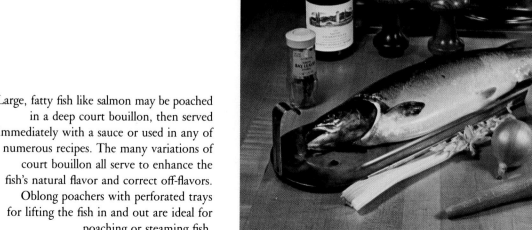

POACHED HALÍBUT DE PESCA is a simple, tasteful preparation of the firm-fleshed halibut, one of the most highly prized members of the flounder family. This recipe also is suitable for cooking red snapper, whitefish, trout, and salmon.

Florida pompano are small, delicately flavored fish with firm, rich flesh. In SHRIMP-FILLED FLORIDA POMPANO, a filling of minced cooked shrimp, cream of mushroom soup, heavy cream, and a little brandy is sandwiched between pompano fillets, which are then covered with a sherry and cream sauce and baked.

In preparing LAKE TROUT IN PASTRY, fillets of medium-size lake trout are first gently poached to remove excess oils. A mixture of wild rice, onion, and mushrooms is spread between the poached fillets, and the fish is then wrapped in pastry and baked.

The iron and copper kettles, or *chaudières*, of the early French explorers in North America had a dramatic impact on the continent's native cookery, and eventually gave a name to the seafood soups long identified with New England. CHECKERBOARD CHOWDER, like many chowder recipes, simply calls for fish of any kind—mixed or matched—and is a great way to turn end-of-season freezer remnants into a hearty, bone-warming meal.

air. Store in the lower regions of the freezer and check the glaze from time to time. Reinforce thin spots as necessary.

Block Freezing: Any container that will accommodate the fish without distorting it can be used for block freezing. Baking pans, loaf pans, ice cream or milk cartons—anything that will contain water until it is frozen will do the job. A cardboard shoebox lined with leakproof plastic bags will hold a good number of small fish, fillets, or steaks. Whole, larger fish can be block-frozen in a florist's box lined with plastic.

Line the bottom of the container with slush or chipped ice. Lay the frozen or chilled fish on the ice. Neatly arrange the fillets or head- or pan-dressed fish without crowding them, and leave a good margin around the border. Place the container in the bottom of the freezer, and pour in chilled water until the fish is well under. When that freezes, add more water to make sure the fish is well covered. The frozen block of fish may be taken from the container and wrapped for storage in the freezer. Reinforce the ice as necessary—just pour a little water on the thin spots.

Block-frozen fish may be thawed quite quickly by running cold or tepid water over the ice. When the fish is freed of ice, let it stand in clean, cold water until just thawed. Drain, wipe dry, and cook at once. Or cover the semi-thawed fish with foil or food wrap, and refrigerate until thawed; drain, wipe dry, and cook immediately.

Lean fish (and small gamebirds) have been kept at top quality for more than a year by the block-freezing method.

Gelatin Dip Glazing: A protective glazing dip helps to preserve the overall quality and extend the freezer life of any fresh fish, but it is especially valuable for rancidity-prone fatty fish with their limited keepability.

The glazing solution* contains ascorbic acid and lemon juice, which act as an antioxidant, odor inhibitor, and color stabilizer. The addition of gelatin to the solution produces a durable, adhesive film that holds the protective agents in contact with the fish while serving as a glaze, thus inhibiting oxidation (rancidity) and moisture loss.

It's important that the fish be absolutely fresh. It should be dressed and fast-frozen, or chilled down in salted ice when it comes from the water and kept chilled all the way to the freezer. Fillets, steaks, and individual small fish should be separated with plastic food wrap.

The following proportions for the gelatin dip may be scaled up or down to give the amount needed for the size or quantity of fish to be treated:

> 2 envelopes unflavored gelatin
> 2 tablespoons plus 1 teaspoon ascorbic acid
>   (buy from drug store; do not use vitamin pills)
> 4 ounces lemon juice
>   (or equivalent lemon concentrate)
> 28 ounces cold water

Mix the gelatin with 8 ounces of the water. Put the remaining water and the ascorbic acid and lemon juice in a pan and heat until the solution is just about, but not quite, boiling. Add the gelatin mixture and stir until almost clear. Let cool to room temperature.

*Developed by the North Carolina State University Seafood Laboratory and the Carteret County Extension Homemakers Nutrition Leaders of Beaufort, North Carolina.

Before dipping whole fish, trim the fatty tissue from around the cavity. Don't thaw a frozen fish to trim it; a sharp knife will cut through the soft, fatty tissue.

Dip the chilled or frozen fish in the cooled gelatin solution, turning it as necessary to completely coat the surface and cavity of the fish. (If you don't have a container big enough to accommodate your fish, improvise—line a florist's box or wallpaper-wetter with plastic.) After dipping the fish, drain off excess liquid. Wrap the fish closely in plastic food wrap, drugstore style, seal, label with species and date, and place fold down on a metal tray. Fast-freeze at the bottom of the freezer. When frozen, remove the package from the tray and store in the freezer.

For fillets, steaks, and small fish, dip and drain each piece, then package in meal-size quantities, placing plastic food wrap between the pieces. Wrap and store as for whole fish.

The recommended freezer temperature for gelatin-dipped fish is a constant $-5°$ F ($-21°$ C) or lower.

Quick rather than slow thawing is recommended. Cover the frozen fish with a seawater solution (8 tablespoons of salt in 1 gallon of water). Remove the fish as soon as it's thawed. Rinse and pat dry, and cook at once.

FISH FLESH AND HOW TO COOK IT

The most imposing of fish dishes are cooked by one of five basic methods, which are classic and universal: frying, broiling (and barbecuing), baking, poaching, and steaming. The method used depends primarily on the physical characteristics, especially the texture and size, of the fish.

Physical Characteristics

Physical characteristics such as texture (whether the fish is fatty or lean, firm or delicate), flavor, size, and even appearance have a bearing on how to cook a fish.

Texture: Fattiness, desirable in moderation, is not agreeable when excessive. Since flavor, good or bad, concentrates in the fat, it also may be unpleasantly strong in extremely fatty fish. The combination of oiliness and strong flavor is unpalatable unless the fish is cooked by a method that takes care of the problem by reducing the fat. Lean fish cooked in the same way would be dry and flavorless.

The fatty fishes bake or broil well, as the natural oils provide a built-in basting and help keep the flesh moist. They take to salt-curing and smoke-curing better than the lean. However, in moist-heat cooking, the fatty fish are poached rather than steamed. Very fatty fish are frequently parboiled to remove excessive oils and the strong flavor they carry.

The lean fishes, generally more delicate in both flavor and texture than fatty ones, cook well in dry heat but only with plenty of buttery or oily basting. By moist-heat methods, lean fish are gently steamed or poached quickly, thereby retaining their natural moisture and oils, and incidentally their flavor. If these fish are baked, it should be done under cover with plenty of moisture. Lean fish fry well in a crusty coating and they deep-fry especially well in batter.

To determine whether a particular fish is fat or lean, refer to the following table of representative edible fishes of North America. The table is divided into three habitat sections, showing those species found only in salt water; those found in fresh water as well as brackish coastal areas and salt water; and those found only in fresh water. Within each of these habitat groupings, fishes are listed alphabetically by common names of species or genus. In general, fishes in the same family and habitat have a similar fat content. For additional information about the characteristics of the important edible fishes see Chapter 9.

REPRESENTATIVE EDIBLE FISHES OF NORTH AMERICA

Species/Genus	Family	Fat Content*
Habitat: Salt Water Only		
Albacore	Mackerels/Tunas	H
Anchovies	Anchovies	H
Bluefish	Bluefishes	H
Bonitos	Mackerels/Tunas	H
Cod, Atlantic	Codfishes	L
Cod, Pacific (gray cod)	Codfishes	L
Corvinas	Drums	M
Cusk	Codfishes	L
Dabs	Flounders/Flatfishes	L
Dolphin	Dolphins	L
Flounder, Summer (summer fluke)	Flounders/Flatfishes	L
Flounder, Winter (winter fluke)	Flounders/Flatfishes	L
Flounder, Witch	Flounders/Flatfishes	L
Grouper, Nassau	Sea basses	L
Grouper, Red	Sea basses	L
Grunion, California	Silversides	L
Haddock	Codfishes	L
Hake	Codfishes	L
Halibut, Atlantic	Flounders/Flatfishes	L
Halibut, California	Flounders/Flatfishes	L
Halibut, Pacific	Flounders/Flatfishes	L
Herring, Atlantic	Herrings	H
Herring, Pacific	Herrings	H
Jacks	Jacks/Pompanos	H
Kingfishes	Drums	M–H
Little Tunny	Mackerels/Tunas	H
Mackerel, Atlantic	Mackerels/Tunas	H
Mackerel, King	Mackerels/Tunas	H
Mackerel, Pacific (chub)	Mackerels/Tunas	H
Mackerel, Spanish	Mackerels/Tunas	H
Marlins	Billfishes	M–H
Ocean Perch (redfish)	Rockfishes	H
Ocean Perch, Pacific	Rockfishes	H
Plaice	Flounders/Flatfishes	L
Pollock	Codfishes	L

*H = high in fat content; M–H = moderate to high; M = moderately fatty; L = low in fat content.

Species/Genus	Family	Fat Content*
Pompano Dolphin	Dolphins	L
Pompano, Florida	Jacks/Pompanos	H
Pompano, Pacific	Butterfishes	H
Porgies	Porgies	M
Puffer, Atlantic	Puffers	L
Rays	Rays	H
Sablefish	Sablefish	M
Sailfish	Billfishes	M–H
Sardine, Pacific (pilchard)	Herrings	H
Sardine, Spanish	Herrings	H
Sea Bass, Black	Sea Basses	L
Sea Bass, White	Drums	M
Sea Bream	Porgies	M
Searobin, Northern	Searobins	L
Skipjack	Mackerels/Tunas	H
Smelt, Whitebait	Smelts	H
Snapper, Mutton	Snappers	L
Snapper, Red	Snappers	L
Sole, Butter	Flounders/Flatfishes	L
Sole, Dover	Flounders/Flatfishes	L
Sole, English (lemon sole)	Flounders/Flatfishes	L
Sole, Petrale (brill)	Flounders/Flatfishes	L
Sole, Rex	Flounders/Flatfishes	L
Sole, Rock	Flounders/Flatfishes	L
Spearfish	Billfishes	M–H
Surfperches	Surfperches	H
Swordfish	Billfishes	H
Tomcods	Codfishes	L
Totuava	Drums	H
Triggerfish	Triggerfishes	L
Turbot, Diamond	Flounders/Flatfishes	L
Wahoo	Mackerels/Tunas	H
Weakfish (sea trout)	Drums	M
Yellowfin	Mackerels/Tunas	H
Yellowtail	Jacks/Pompanos	H

Habitat: Salt Water/Fresh Water

Bass, Striped	Temperate Basses	M
Capelin	Smelts	H
Char, Arctic	Trouts/Salmonids	H
Croakers	Drums	H
Dolly Varden	Trouts/Salmonids	H
Drum, Red	Drums	H

*H = high in fat content; M–H = moderate to high; M = moderately fatty; L = low in fat content.

Species/Genus	Family	Fat Content*
Eel, American	Freshwater eels	H
Eulachon	Smelts	H
Flounder, Southern	Flounders/Flatfishes	L
Lamprey, Sea	Lampreys	H
Mullet, Striped	Mullets	M
Perch, White	Temperate Basses	M
Pinfish	Porgies	M
Salmon, Atlantic	Trouts/Salmonids	H
Salmon, Chinook	Trouts/Salmonids	H
Salmon, Chum	Trouts/Salmonids	H
Salmon, Coho	Trouts/Salmonids	H
Salmon, Pink	Trouts/Salmonids	H
Salmon, Sockeye	Trouts/Salmonids	H
Seatrout, Spotted	Drums	H
Shad, American	Shads	H
Shad, Hickory	Shads	H
Sheepshead	Porgies	M
Smelt, Rainbow	Smelts	H
Smelt, Surf	Smelts	H
Snook	Snooks	L
Tomcod, Atlantic	Codfishes	L
Trout, Brook	Trouts/Salmonids	H
Trout, Brown	Trouts/Salmonids	H
Trout, Cutthroat	Trouts/Salmonids	H
Trout, Rainbow	Trouts/Salmonids	H
Whitefish, Lake	Trouts/Salmonids	M–H

Habitat: Fresh Water Only

Bass, Largemouth	Sunfishes	L
Bass, Rock	Sunfishes	L
Bass, Smallmouth	Sunfishes	L
Bass, White	Temperate Basses	M
Bass, Yellow	Temperate Basses	M
Bloater	Ciscos	M
Bullheads	Freshwater Catfishes	L
Burbot (ling)	Codfishes	L
Carp	Carps	L
Carpsuckers	Suckers	L
Catfishes	Freshwater Catfishes	L
Crappies	Sunfishes	L
Drum, Freshwater	Drums	H
Goldeye	Mooneyes	H
Grayling, Arctic	Trouts/Salmonids	H

*H = high in fat content; M–H = moderate to high; M = moderately fatty; L = low in fat content.

Species/Genus	Family	Fat Content*
Herring, Lake	Ciscos	M
Inconnu (sheefish)	Trouts/Salmonids	H
Muskellunge	Pikes	L
Paddlefish (spoonbill)	Paddlefishes	H
Perch, Yellow	Perches	L
Pickerel, Chain	Pikes	L
Pickerel, Grass	Pikes	L
Pickerel, Redfin	Pikes	L
Pike, Northern	Pikes	L
Pumpkinseed	Sunfishes	L
Quillback	Suckers	L
Redhorse	Suckers	L
Sauger	Perches	L
Splake (hybrid)	Trouts/Salmonids	H
Sturgeon, Lake	Sturgeons	H
Sunfishes	Sunfishes	L
Trout, Golden	Trouts/Salmonids	H
Trout, Lake	Trouts/Salmonids	H
Walleye	Perches	L
Whitefish, Mountain	Trouts/Salmonids	H

*H = high in fat content; M–H = moderate to high; M = moderately fatty; L = low in fat content.

Flavor: Whether strong or mild, good or bad, flavors are most pronounced in the skin and in the fat under the skin. Flavor can vary within a single species, and may depend on where the individual fish are caught. On the whole, fish from cold, clean waters generally have a better flavor than do those from warm, muddy, or contaminated waters.*

Undesirable or off-flavors, or just too much of a good thing, may be offset by filleting and skinning the fish and trimming excess fatty flesh. An aromatic parboiling, or court bouillon, is an effective flavor aid, especially for fatty fishes.

Size: Apart from the practical considerations imposed by the size of a fish, the smaller fishes are generally finer in texture than the monsters of the species, and more desirable on the table. With a couple of exceptions, fish of 10 pounds and under are dealt with here. Oversize fish can be made into good stews and chowders. They frequently salt and smoke well, especially the fat ones.

The following table is a general guide to the cooking methods suitable for fish of different sizes and cuts. In the kitchen anything from 5 to 10 pounds or more is considered a *big* fish.

*Contamination of fish from industrial and natural sources occurs in certain waters. Consult state and provincial authorities regarding the consumption of fish from any waters that may be contaminated.

SIZE GUIDE FOR COOKING FISH

Cut	Weight or Thickness	Cooking Method
Whole Fish		
Pan size	1 pound or less	Fry, broil.*
Small to medium	1 to 4 pounds	Split, fry, broil, bake.
Medium to big	5 to 10 pounds	Bake, steam, poach.
Big	Over 10 pounds	Cut in sections (not practical to cook whole).
Fillets		
Thin	Under 1 inch	Fry, broil, bake, steam, poach.
Thick	Over 1 inch	Bake, steam, poach; cut in chunks and deep-fry, broil, or use in chowders.
Steaks	1 inch	Pan-fry, broil, bake.
Cross Sections of Big Fish	Meal size	Bake, poach, steam whole; cut up and deep-fry or use in chowders.

*Broil includes all the direct dry-heat methods: barbecuing, spit-roasting, etc.

Cooking Times

Fish cooks very quickly and must not be overdone. It is ready to eat when it loses its translucence and the flesh flakes easily when prodded with a fork. This happens at an internal temperature of 140° to 145° F (60° to 63° C); above that temperature, the fish begins to break down and lose its juices and is on its way to overcooking and disaster. Allow the following cooking times:

- Pan-baked fish: 10 minutes plus 10 minutes per inch of thickness at thickest part in a preheated 400° F (205° C) oven.
- Poached fish: 10 minutes per inch of thickness at thickest part.
- Steamed fish: 12 to 15 minutes per inch of thickness at thickest part.

A meat thermometer is the surest guide to doneness for medium-size and big fish and for thick cuts. Insert the thermometer in the thickest part of the fish; in a whole fish this is the shoulder area just behind the gills.

How to Carve a Fish

Whether you're about to eat a 10-ounce trout, or carve a 10-pounder, the approach is much the same. It's just a matter of scale.

The flaky flesh of a fish lies against the bones in an orderly and well-defined manner with natural separations. When the fish is cooked, the flesh can be easily parted from the bones along these natural separations. Don't, however, just pull a forkful of flesh from the fish. That disturbs the orderly arrangement beyond repair. And even worse, don't try to cut through the fish with a knife.

To carve a medium-size lean fish, spoon out the stuffing. Run your carving knife along the back, with the knife tip between the flesh and backbone, from head to tail, skipping over the dorsal fin to avoid loosening the small root bones. With a fish server, lift portions of fillet from the ribs, leaving the skeleton intact. Lift the skeleton and serve the remaining fillet.

To carve a fatty fish, or a large lean one, spoon out the stuffing and carve along the back as just described, again skipping over the dorsal fin. Skin the fish if desired. Lift portions from the top (loin) fillet only — these are the choice cuts of a large fatty fish. Serve this portion first, and save the remainder for leftover fish dishes (fish pie, croquettes, etc.). Remove the skeleton, and serve the remaining loin fillet.

To dissect a small cooked fish such as a 10- or 12-ounce trout, simply run your knife along the skin over the backbone between the head and tail, revealing the separation between the two fillets. If the fish has a crisp crust, cut across it at the gills and tail. Steadying the lower half of the fish with your fork, use your knife to ease the topside fillet from the bone and simply fold it over onto the plate. Unless the fish has been overcooked, the fillet will come away from the bones in one firm piece. Now lift up the skeleton with the head and tail attached, easing it up with your fork if necessary, and set it aside. There on the plate remains the other half, or fillet, of the fish. Squeeze on a few drops of lemon juice and enjoy.

BASIC COOKING METHODS

As has already been mentioned, there are five basic ways to cook fish: steaming, poaching, baking, broiling, and frying. Each of these methods is described in the remainder of this chapter.

Steaming

A moist-heat method, steaming is used for all sizes and cuts of lean fish. Fish is steamed over boiling water in a fish steamer (or poacher), a handsome oblong utensil that has a perforated tray with handles to support the fish and to lift it in and out of the steamer.

The size or amount of the fish to be cooked in the steamer is limited by the size of the utensil, for a whole fish should not be distorted by the kettle in any way, and pieces should not be piled into the steamer.

A steamer may be improvised to accommodate a few fillets or small fish by arranging open jar rings or small cans, both ends opened, in the bottom of a deep saucepan and placing a rack or a well-perforated aluminum pie pan on the rings, keeping the water level below the perforated pan. Put the fish on a length of cheesecloth, long enough so that the ends will hang over the edges of the saucepan, to facilitate lifting the fish in and out. A similar arrangement in a roasting pan, using the rack for support, will accommodate a fairly big fish.

An old-fashioned way of dealing with an outsize fish is to steam or poach it in a copper wash boiler. The fish is slung in a hammock arrangement of linen toweling or strong doubled cheesecloth over or in the water, with the ends of the cloth tied securely to the handles of the boiler. The method still works.

Once you've got a satisfactory steaming arrangement, the procedure is simple.

Procedure for Steaming: Wipe the dressed fish with a damp cloth. Pour water into the steamer to a level just below the rack or pan, and bring to a boil. Aromatic spices and vegetables or herbs, along with white wine, may be added to the water. Lay the fish on the rack, cover tightly, and steam until the fish flakes when prodded with a fork. Cooking time depends on the size and shape of the fish. Allow about 12 to 15 minutes per inch of thickness at the thickest part.

Lift the fish out as soon as it's done. Steamed fish may be served hot or cold with one of the many sauces in Chapter 11 and with a colorful garnish, or it may be used for any recipe calling for cooked fish.

Oven Steaming: Small, unstuffed lean whole fish or small fillets, completely wrapped in aluminum foil, may be cooked in the oven; they steam in their own juices rather than bake. Oven steaming is an excellent method for preparing fish especially when a few aromatic vegetables (e.g., onion, green peppers, and celery) and a bit of wine are included in the package.

Wrap the fish loosely in aluminum foil, shiny side towards the fish, and close the package with double folds to keep the steam in. Place in a hot oven (450° F, 230° C); allow 10 minutes for each inch thickness of the fish, plus 5 minutes to let the package heat.

Poaching

Fish is poached, never boiled. ("Boil" is an improper term in fish cookery.) Two types of poaching are used here. One, for small fillets of lean fish, uses shallow liquid and is self-basting. The other is the deep court bouillon used to cook fatty and big fish. Fish may also be poached in the deep court bouillon as a flavor aid.

POACHING FILLETS, STEAKS, AND SMALL LEAN FISHES

Small fillets, steaks, and small whole lean fish may be poached in a fish stock or fumet, described later in this chapter. Delicately flavored fish are poached in salted water (1 teaspoon salt per quart) to which a little lemon juice or white vinegar is added to make acid water.

Bring the liquid to a boil. Spread the fish in a single layer on a greased rack and lower it into the liquid. Cover with a poaching parchment (a circle of cooking parchment cut to the size of the pan and with small hole in the center), or with a circle of aluminum foil or a disposable lightweight pie plate with a few pinholes to allow any steam build-up to escape. Reduce the heat to a bare simmer and cook gently until the fish flakes, about 10 minutes for 1-inch-thick cuts.

Oven Poaching: Small cuts of fish can also be poached in the oven. Spread the fish in a single layer over the bottom of a buttered or greased baking dish with a cover, season to taste with salt, pepper, minced parsley, fennel, tarragon or your favorite herb, and add a small amount of concentrated fumet or stock, enough to completely cover the bottom of the dish. (Lean white-fleshed fish and cold-smoked and salt-cured fish are poached in milk.) Cover with cooking parchment or oiled paper, put the lid on, and cook in a preheated 450° F (230° C) oven. Allow about 10 minutes for each inch of thickness of the fish and an extra 3 or 4 minutes for a glass or ceramic dish to heat through. In either case, use the remaining fumet or stock to make a thick, rich velouté sauce for the fish.

POACHING IN COURT BOUILLON

Fatty fishes should be poached in a deep court bouillon. Fish so prepared may be served immediately with a sauce or used in one of the many preparations calling for cooked fish.

The court bouillon is a "shortly boiled" aromatic liquid in which fish and shell fish are cooked, the aroma arising from any number and combination of ingredients. The term *court bouillon*, borrowed from classic French cookery, is applied rather loosely here. The court bouillon both enhances natural flavors and helps correct dietary or inherent off-flavors in the fish. (It will not, however, disguise or correct the results of inadequate care of the fish.) It is not a fish stock—though it may contribute to making one—and is most often discarded after it has done its job.

The court bouillon (see recipes below) is usually made in the vessel in which the fish is to be cooked, and then allowed to cool. Small fish, fillets, and relatively small pieces of larger fish can be cooked in an ordinary saucepan as long as it's large enough to allow them to be submerged. The fish should be tied loosely in wet cheesecloth to prevent its separating and to ease lifting.

Large fish, dressed or pan-dressed, require a large fish kettle. If necessary, a large, deep stock pot, deep roasting pan, or copper boiler may be used. Wrap the dressed fish, washed and dried, in wet cheese-cloth (dipped in the court bouillon), leaving tabs long enough to hang outside the kettle for easy handling. Lower the fish into the cool court bouillon. If the fish must be curled to fit, let the

Salmon ready for poaching.

tail take an upward curve, or truss the fish. The body of the fish must be entirely submerged. If necessary, add water and wine until it's covered.

Bring slowly to a boil, turn down the heat, and simmer gently, allowing 10 minutes per inch of thickness at the thickest part of the fish. This applies to trussed thickness as well.

Skim as much fat from the surface as possible and remove the fish as soon as it's done. If it isn't to be served immediately, leave the fish in the wet cheesecloth until it's cool. (Allowing the fish to cool in the court bouillon might enhance its flavor and moisture, but the hazards of overcooking and waterlogging outweigh the advantages.)

Parboiling: It may be desirable to parboil large (5 pounds and up), extremely fatty fish. Let it barely simmer in the initial court bouillon (or just acid water) for 10 to 20 minutes. Skim off the oily surface broth, lift out the fish, empty the kettle, and continue with a fresh, hot court bouillon or finish by steaming. Be careful not to overcook the fish.

Making Court Bouillon: The quantity of court bouillon needed depends on the size or amount of fish to be cooked and the size and shape of the pot. The court bouillon must cover the fish. Court bouillons may be concocted to one's fancy by varying the seasonings (see the following table), but always with a light hand. A *bouquet garni*, faggot, or spice bag is useful when experimenting, as it may be removed from the pot at any time. Use a white wine with white-fleshed fish. Use a very dry wine with fatty fish to cut the oiliness of the fish.

SEASONINGS FOR COURT BOUILLONS, FUMETS, AND FISH STOCKS

Aromatics and Spices	*Herbs*	*Aromatic Vegetables*
Capers	Bay leaf	Carrot
Chili peppers, whole	Dill weed	Celery
Cloves, whole	Fennel weed	Garlic
Mace	Sweet basil	Green pepper
Mixed pickling spices	Tarragon	Onion
Pepper (black and white), whole	Thyme	Pimento
		Tomato

The seasonings in the following two recipes for court bouillon may be adjusted to taste, and the quantity increased if needed.

Mild Court Bouillon

1 slice lemon
1 cup white wine
3 cups water
1 onion, sliced
3 or 4 carrot slices
1 small piece bay leaf
2 sprigs fresh parsley
1 branch fresh thyme
¼ teaspoon peppercorns
1 teaspoon salt
Dash garlic powder

Put all the ingredients into a deep saucepan, bring to a boil, and cover. (Add or delete seasonings and spices to taste.) Turn down the heat and simmer gently for about 15 minutes. Cool. Makes about 1 quart.

Aromatic Court Bouillon

¼ cup white vinegar or lemon juice
6 cups water
1 large carrot, sliced
2 stalks celery with tops, broken
2 strips green pepper
1 large onion, sliced
1 tablespoon mixed pickling spices
    tied in cheesecloth
½ teaspoon salt

Combine everything in a deep saucepan. Bring to a boil and cover. Cook gently for 15 minutes, removing pickling spices at your discretion. Cool. Makes about 1½ quarts. Recommended for robust-flavored fish.

FISH STOCK AND FUMET

Stock is called for in the preparation of many fish dishes and accessories—chowders, soups, sauces, and so on. It is the result of cooking the fish trimmings in salted water, with or without other liquid, vegetables, and seasonings. A fumet is a concentrated stock.

Whenever possible, stocks or fumets should be made from the fish that they will eventually accompany. Avoid using stocks from strong-flavored fish like mackerel in the preparation of delicately flavored fish like sole. The trimmings from the rich-fleshed fatty gamefishes make an excellent stock for soups and aspics. Stock should be made from fresh fish as soon as the fish is dressed. If the fish has been skinned for flavor improvement, don't use the skin in the stock.

Basic Fish Stock

2 to 3 slices onion
½ cup mushroom stems or trimmings (optional)
1 tablespoon chopped fresh parsley
1 teaspoon chopped thyme, or pinch dried thyme
    and/or other seasonings and spices
1 bay leaf
½ teaspoon salt
2 pounds fresh fish trimmings
    (bones, heads, fins, tails), washed
2 cups cold water
⅓ cup dry white wine
1 thin slice lemon, twisted

Put the vegetables and seasonings in the bottom of a stock pot or saucepan. (Add or delete seasonings according to taste.) Add the fish trimmings. Pour in the water and wine to cover; add the lemon.

Slowly bring to a boil, then reduce the heat and skim. Simmer uncovered for about 30 minutes. Cool slightly and strain through three thicknesses of cheesecloth or muslin that has been wrung out in cold water. Refrigerate until needed or freeze to have on hand. Use for poaching, chowders, or fish sauces.

Fish Fumet

Fish recipes involving poaching or the making of sauces frequently call for a fish fumet as part or all of the liquid. A fumet may be made from the residual juices of a baked fish; and since the fumet is simply a concentrated fish stock, it may also be made by boiling down a fish stock. This basic recipe may be freezer-stored in likely recipe quantities.

> 2 pounds fish trimmings (fins, bones, heads,
>   tails); include skins unless they have been
>   removed for flavor-improvement purposes,
>   and avoid strong-flavored trimmings from
>   fish like mackerel, skate, and mullet)
> 2 cups water
> 2 cups white wine
> 1 large onion, stuck with 1 clove
> 1 large carrot, scraped and split
> 2 celery stalks with tops, broken
> 2 tablespoons parsley
> 1 bay leaf
> ½ teaspoon cracked peppercorns
> ¼ teaspoon salt

Combine all ingredients in a large saucepan and bring to a boil. Cover loosely. Turn down the heat and simmer until the liquid is reduced by half, about 1 hour. Strain the liquid through a sieve lined with doubled cheesecloth, letting it drip undisturbed into a container for about 30 minutes.

ASPICS AND JELLIED STOCK

The stock used in making aspics and cold jellied preparations should first be clarified to give a crystal-clear liquid.

To Clarify Stock: Cool the strained stock. Lift all the grease from the surface of the cold stock.

Use the white of 1 egg plus 1 teaspoon of water for each quart of stock. Whip the egg white and water until frothy.

Put the degreased stock back on to heat. Stir in the whipped egg white as the stock warms, and continue stirring until it comes to a boil and froths up. Stop stirring and allow to boil for about 3 minutes. Strain through a sieve lined with clean, doubled cheesecloth or fine muslin. The strained stock should be crystal clear.

Pour into clean jars, cover, and refrigerate for use within days. Or fill clean glass jars two-thirds full, cover loosely, cool, and fast-freeze. Tighten covers and store in freezer.

To Make Aspic or Jelly: Reduce 1 pint of clarified stock by half. Soften 1 tablespoon of unflavored gelatin in cold water and add to the stock, stirring over the heat until well mixed. Remove from the heat, let stand until it starts to thicken but will still pour, and use as directed in recipes. This makes 1 cup of aspic.

Should the aspic set, or become too stiff to pour, melt it down and start the cooling process again. The stiffened aspic may be refrigerated and melted down as needed.

Baking

Other than baking a big dressed fish for its own sake, many fish dishes are cooked or finished in the oven. Various recipes involving baking appear in Chapter 9. General directions for baking dressed fish, both lean and fatty ones, are given in this section.

Fish of 3 pounds and up are baked whole, with or without heads and tails, or, if they're very large, cross-cut in meal-size portions. The fish may be boned or not, and baked unstuffed or stuffed.

Finding a suitable baking pan for a big fish can pose a problem in the average kitchen. With the aid of multiple thicknesses of heavy aluminum foil, any arrangement that will contain the fish and its juices without collapsing or leaking will do the job—such as fashioning a pan on a cookie sheet, covering and lining a florist's box for a 5- to 6-pounder, or lining a metal radiator cover to accommodate an 11-pound salmon (this method involved removing all the fittings from the oven except the elements in order to get the radiator cover in, then resting it on large open-ended coffee cans, but it all worked out admirably).

GENERAL PREPARATION

Thaw frozen dressed fish until they're manageable. Scale them, cut out the fins and eyes, and trim any excessive fat. Cut off the head and tail if you must, but keep in mind that fish bakes better intact—especially a lean one—as the less exposed flesh, the less moisture loss, so the end result is succulently moist inside and crusty brown outside. Wash the fish well in cold water and pat dry inside and out with paper towels.

Unstuffed Fish: Rub the cavity of the dressed fish with lemon. Tuck a few sprigs of fresh herbs (dill, fennel, thyme, savory, etc.) and onion slices into the cavity. In a fatty fish, include a quartered apple and a few strips of green pepper; in a lean one, add a few small chunks of hard butter. The vegetables and herbs are discarded before serving.

Stuffed Fish: Rub the cavity of the dressed fish with lemon. Stuff the fish lightly, about two-thirds to three-quarters full, leaving room for the stuffing to swell (see "Stuffings" in Chapter 11). Close the cavity with fine wooden or metal skewers or lacing pins and thread, or sew it up.

Place the fully dressed fish, stuffed or unstuffed, on a greased rack in a pan; or on two or three slices of pork fat, or on a layer of sturdy sliced vegetables, such as carrots, onions, or celery, in the bottom of a pan. (These vegetables flavor the drippings or stock, which can be used in making a sauce or soup.) Prop the fish's mouth open with a cork, to be replaced later with a wedge of lemon.

Preheat the oven to 400° F (205° C). Allow 10 minutes for each inch of thickness at the thickest part of the (stuffed) fish. Or cook to 140° to 145° F (60° to 63° C) by meat thermometer inserted in the shoulder behind the gills.

Remove the fish from the oven and let it rest for about 10 minutes. Carefully transfer it to a warm platter. Remove the thread and pins from stuffed fish. Replace the cork with a wedge of lemon, and put cherries or black olives in the eyes.

BAKING FATTY FISH

The general baking method should be modified somewhat for fatty fish. First, trim excessive fatty flesh along the abdomen and vent. Rub the fish well all over with butter and put in the pan. Lightly gash the skin of very fat, firm-fleshed fish, at intervals of 2 or 3 inches. Pour 1 cup of white wine over the fish. Cover loosely with a piece of aluminum foil. During cooking, baste once or twice with a mixture of melted butter and white wine. Remove the foil for the last half of baking time, dust lightly with flour, baste from the pan, and bake until the skin becomes crispy gold and the flesh is opaque and flakes to a fork.

Planked Fish: Fatty fish of around 3 to 5 pounds may be baked unstuffed on a plank. Select a 1- to 1½-inch-thick hardwood plank, unvarnished, of maple, hickory, fruitwood, or oak. If desired, the plank may be trimmed to fit a large platter for serving. "Tree" the plank by cutting grooves to branch into a central groove, ending in a shallow depression at one end to catch drippings, or place a drip pan under the plank in the oven. Making a treed plank is worth all the trouble as it can be used repeatedly and, like a salad bowl, improves with age and use.

The plank is not washed after use, but is scraped clean with a sharp knife. It is oiled and browned each time it is used. It should be stored wrapped in a clean towel (not in plastic).

The plank is used *hot*. Preheat the oven to 425° F (220° C). Rub the plank well on both sides with olive oil; place in the oven for about 15 minutes to brown well. Remove the plank, and repeat the oiling and browning.

Place the prepared fish on the hot plank and bake as directed earlier, lowering the heat to 400° F (205° C).

BAKING LEAN FISH

When baking lean fish, modify the general baking procedure by placing extra butter or bacon fat in the cavity, or stuff with a moist stuffing. Run a sharp knife along the backbone, making a slash about 1 to 1½ inches deep; insert strips of pork fat or bacon rind with fat, and hold in place with toothpicks (remove fat before serving). Or score with three or four diagonal gashes, and tuck in short strips of fat bacon.

Rub the fish with butter, dust lightly with flour, and dab well with small pats of butter. Mix ½ cup of melted butter with ½ cup of white wine and pour some of the mixture over the fish, letting it run into the pan. Cover with aluminum foil, pinching it to the edges of the pan.

Place the fish in the preheated oven. Baste frequently with the butter-wine mixture until it's all been used, and then baste from the pan. Remove the cover for the last quarter of baking time. Dust lightly with flour and baste well with the pan drippings; continue baking until the fish is a golden brown and the flesh flakes to a fork.

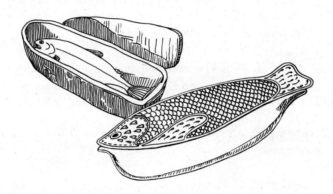

CLAY-BAKER FISH

The clay bakers of modern cookware are not far removed in principle from the ancient Indian method of wrapping a fish or fowl in mud or clay and burying it in the coals. Molded from terra cotta, the clay cookers produce a moist, nicely browned fish or bird, baked in its own juices. (The clay baker picks up scents and flavors, so don't use the same one for fish and fowl.)

The best results are obtained when the cooker is well filled. A whole 3- to 4-pound fish is about right for the average fish cooker. A bigger fish may be fitted in by removing the head and tail; or use a 2- to 3-pound center or tail cut. Two or more smaller fish may be cooked together, depending on their size.

The clay cooker and its contents should be put into a cold oven, and the temperature set at the desired degree. Small fish are cooked at a high temperature; larger fish at a lower one.

Clay-Baked Trout

Dress a 2- to 4-pound trout. Wash it well and wipe dry with a towel. Cut off the head and tail if necessary to fit the baker. Rub the cavity with a wedge of lemon, squeezing as you rub. Tuck a couple of celery tops and a few slices of onion into the cavity and add a branch of fresh dill, if handy, or a few sprigs of fresh parsley. Spread thick slices of carrot and onion over the bottom of the cooker to serve as a support for the fish. Oil the fish all over with cooking oil or melted butter or margarine and lay it on the vegetables. Put the cover in place. Place the baker in a cold oven, set it at 375° F (190° C), and bake until the flesh flakes to a fork, about 1 hour, depending on how quickly the oven heats.

Broiling

Broiling, including barbecuing, means exposing the fish directly to intense dry heat. It may be done over, under, or between heat sources. Broiling can be on any scale from a chunk of fish speared on the end of a stick and held over the coals, to the mammoth salmon barbecues (serving up to 2,400 people) in Port Madison Indian Reservation near Seattle, as well as on the kitchen or patio scale.

Fish high in fat—such as the trouts and salmons, black Alaska cod (sablefish), the mackerels, mullet, bluefish, the drums, pompanos, and striped bass—broil especially well, requiring only an occasional brush with a basting sauce. Lean fish flesh also broils well as long as the cuts are not too thin, but it requires a lot more basting than fatter fish. Dust lean fish lightly with flour to hold the basting and crust the surface, then rub or brush with melted butter or basting sauce before putting to broil; baste frequently during cooking.

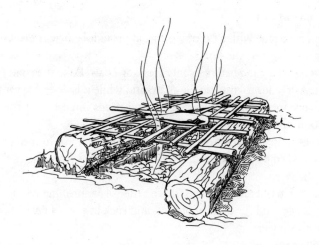

MORE TIPS ON BROILING

- Leave the skin on fillets and steaks; it holds them together. Make deep gashes in the skin of large fillets to prevent curling. Score steaks at the edges.
- Warm the rack or grill and grease it well before putting the fish on.
- Always place a dressed fish on the rack with its head toward the cook; this allows a spatula to be slid under the fish along the overlap of scales for easy turning.
- Space a number of fish on the rack, allowing for circulation of heat around the fish and a good margin of heat exposure around the edges.

- Fillets with skin on or split fish should be cooked skin-side first, then turned. They are served flesh-side up. (If you don't plan to eat the skin, the fillets need not be scaled.)
- Skinned fillets and steaks are broiled on one side, then turned and finished.
- When broiling *under* the heat, baste generously after turning the fish; when broiling *over* the heat, baste before turning.
- Broiling requires frequent-to-constant basting, depending on the fish. The basting sauce may be a mixture of melted butter and lemon juice or a more highly seasoned sauce. The sauce may first be used to marinate the fish and then heated for basting purposes.

OVEN-BROILED FISH

For best results in the oven broiler, whole fish or cuts thereof should be no less than 1 inch* and no more than 2 inches thick. Dressed pan-size fish broil well; larger dressed fish should be split. Steaks are nicest at 1-inch thickness; fillets may be up to 2 inches. Brush the fish all over with basting sauce (see tips on broiling above) and let rest while preparing the broiler.

Preheat the oven broiler to "broil." Preheat the broiler pan and grease it well with fat or oil. Place the dripping fish (skin-side up) on the rack, well spaced, and broil, oven door ajar, 2 to 4 inches under the source of heat. As soon as the top browns, turn the fish, baste, and broil the other side. Allow 10 minutes in all for each inch thickness of fish, or broil until the flesh flakes to a fork. Baste frequently as it broils.

AL FRESCO BARBECUE

The backyard barbecue with a canopy or hood provides efficient broiling over charcoal coals and excellent protection against the wind.

Fire the charcoal to a good bed of evenly glowing coals. Poke the coals occasionally to knock off any built-up ash. Ash tends to insulate the coals; and while it is desirable for the longer-lasting fire required to cook many meats, fish cooks quickly and needs intense heat for a shorter period.

Leave the hood open, back to the wind, during broiling.

Prepare and cook the fish as for oven broiling and place it in a hinged grill or on the barbecue rack, which has been warmed and greased. Broil about 4 inches from the coals. Cooking time may be shorter than in the oven.

The four-way fish basket is a handy barbecue utensil for broiling whole fish. Oil the fish's cavity, stuff with fresh parsley, dill, and green onions, and tuck in 3 or 4 small, hot stones (heated on the barbecue). Close with skewers.

Steaks and fillets are enhanced by marinating for a while in a seasoned barbecue sauce.

Turtle Cove Barbecue

In the lobby of the Turtle Cove restaurant in Port Aransas, you can get a demonstration of the art that made this seafood eatery famous along the Texas coast. You choose your fish from the catch of the day and, under the ministrations of Chef Clara Mills, watch it barbecue over a deep pit of glowing mesquite.

Chef Mills tells how to turn a whole fish—any fish—into a feast of crusty succulence: First of all, no matter how you plan to serve the fish, don't cut the head off and don't scale or scrape the fish.

---

*Cuts of fish less than 1 inch thick tend to dry out. Thin fillets (skin on) or split fish may be oven-broiled with the flesh-side up, well basted on the topside only. The skin is not eaten.

The fish's head is your handle on the whole operation, and the scales keep the skin from sticking to the rack. How big or deep a fire is needed depends on the number and size of the fish to be cooked.

Prepare a basting sauce. For the equivalent of 6 fish of about 1 to 1½ pounds each, use 1 cup of olive oil, 1 tablespoon of Worcestershire sauce, 1 teaspoon of smoked salt, freshly ground black pepper to taste, and the juice of 1 lemon. Mix well and pour into an oblong baking dish. Keep the sauce warm at the edge of the fire.

Wash the whole dressed fish and pat it dry. Turn the fish in the sauce until it's well coated, then place it on the hot greased barbecue rack, head toward you, over a deep bed of coals.

Keep an eye on the fish, advises Chef Mills. "It's ready to turn when you run your finger along the skin on the backbone and it sort of bubbles up and leaves a dent, and the meat comes away from the bone at the fins."

Baste the fish. Holding the head with one hand to steady it, slip a spatula under the head, running it along under the shingle or overlap of the scales toward the tail, and flip it over, sleek and clean. Baste again and let it cook just until the flesh flakes. Lift the fish in the same manner as before, head to tail, onto a serving platter. To eat, run a knife down the backbone, flip the top fillet over, and lift out the bone. Sprinkle with lemon juice and seasoning to taste.

Frying

Whether it's Homeric halibut deep-fried with chips in Alaska, a pan full of breakfast trout with bannock by a Canadian stream, or catfish with hush puppies in the American South, the fish fry is a North American institution.

DEEP FRYING

The whole virtue of good friture lies on the element of surprise.
—Brillat-Savarin
Physiologie du Goût, Paris, 1843

Deep frying is the immersion of food in boiling fat, which instantly forms a shell around the food, locking the moisture in and the fat out. The term in French cookery is *friture* (hence fritters), which covers both the method and the fat.

Small chunks of fish, fish cakes, and whole tiny fishes such as smelts, grunion, and whitebait are deep-fried, not to mention potato chips and hush puppies.

The fat must be deep—not less than 2 inches in the pot, and that's for small, thin pieces. The pot must be roomy and deep, for it should be no more than half filled with fat. Good results cannot be obtained by skimping. A 4-quart kettle takes about 3 pounds of fat.

The best pot or kettle for the purpose is of cast iron (Dutch oven), cast aluminum, or hammered copper. The bigger and heavier the kettle and the more fat in it, the easier it is to maintain the necessary constant high temperature as food is added. The electric deep-fry appliance, used as directed, of course, is excellent.

Other essential tools include a deep-fry basket, a slotted spoon or a skimmer, kitchen tongs, and a long-handled fork. And keep a cover handy. If the fat should catch fire, cover the kettle immediately to smother the flames. Smother with salt—never with water.

The choice of fat is important; it must be capable of attaining and holding a heat of 375° F (190° C) without burning. Of the animal fats, rendered beef suet is considered best for the purpose.

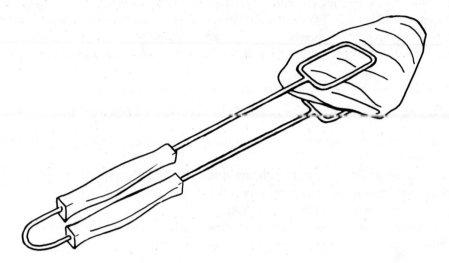

Vegetable shortening and cooking oils on the market and recommended for the purpose are excellent. Butter (or margarine) should *not* be used for deep frying.

A frying thermometer is a reliable guide for gauging the temperature of the fat. A time-honored test involves dropping a bread cube into the kettle: The fat is ready if it browns the bread in 60 seconds.

For deep-frying, the fish should be at room temperature and wiped dry of surface moisture. Cut the fillets into small pieces of uniform size. If they are more than ½ inch thick, gash the edges to allow fast and uniform penetration of heat. Before frying, the pieces are coated with crumbs or dipped in a batter.

Crumbs: Use the beaten-egg crumb dip and follow the crumbing procedure described under Pan Frying, a l'Anglaise (see page 214). Let the fish rest on a rack for 10 minutes or so. A few at a time, arrange the pieces *well-spaced* in the frying basket, and lower it into the fat so that the fish is submerged and instantly seared.

Batter: Various batters may be used for deep-frying fish. Three are given in this section; others are given with individual fish recipes. Batters should only be used for deep frying, not pan frying, for unless the entire outside surface of the batter is seared instantly, it will absorb grease.

When using batter, put the deep-fry basket into the pot of fat first. Dip the end of a fork into the hot fat, then spear a piece of fish and dip it in the batter. Holding the fish over the fat, ease it off the fork and let it drop into the hot fat so it sinks and pops up. The action must be sudden—"invasion," Brillat-Savarin calls it—a surprise attack, which instantaneously forms a crusty shell around the food.

Drop in only one piece at a time to avoid reducing the temperature of the fat. Dip the fork or tongs in the hot fat each time. Cook only a few pieces at a time; don't crowd them in the pot. Poke the pieces about gently until all are an even golden, crusty brown. Lift the basket and fish out of the fat; spread the pieces on paper and place in a warm oven until the remainder are cooked. Skim solids from the fat between batches, and let the fat return to frying temperature before cooking more fish.

Batters are best made an hour or two ahead of use, and refrigerated. The measurements in the following recipes make enough batter for 2 pounds of fish. Adjust quantities as needed.

Crisp Batter

1 cup all-purpose flour
2 teaspoons baking powder
1½ teaspoons salt
1 teaspoon sugar
1 tablespoon salad oil or melted fat

Measure, mix, and sift the dry ingredients into a bowl. Make a well in the middle of the mixture. Combine the oil with 1 cup of water and pour into the well. Mix, working from the middle, until all the flour is blended in.

Variations: Add 2 tablespoons of grated onion. Or make an herb batter by adding ½ teaspoon of minced parsley or sweet basil (or more to taste), or a pinch of powdered savory. A touch of grated lemon rind adds a nice touch to a batter.

Lemon Batter

1 egg
Juice of 1 lemon
1 cup flour
1 teaspoon baking powder

Beat the egg until light. Add ¾ cup of water and the lemon juice. Sift the flour and baking powder into a bowl, make a well in the flour, and lightly stir in the egg mixture until just smooth. This batter contains no salt, so the fish should be salted before dipping it in the batter.

Beer Batter

12 ounces beer or ale
1 cup all-purpose flour
1 tablespoon salt
1 tablespoon pepper

Pour the beer into a bowl. Sift the dry ingredients into the beer, stirring with a whisk until the batter is light and frothy.

PAN FRYING

Small dressed fish, fillets, and steaks are pan-fried. The fish are dusted with seasoned flour (*à la meunière*) or dipped in a sticking agent and rolled in crumbs (*à l'Anglaise*) before being fried.

The frying pan should be of cast iron or heavy-gauge aluminum, and large enough to hold the fish without distorting or crowding them. A large pan also holds heat more evenly.

Use bacon fat, cooking oil, vegetable oil, a mixture of oil and butter, or clarified butter for pan frying. *Don't* use regular butter or margarine.

Dressed fish under 1 pound are fried whole, or pan-dressed if necessary to fit the pan. Fish over 1 inch in thickness should be split. Fillets may be skinned or scaled, but steaks usually keep their skins during cooking. Wipe fish with a damp cloth, and pat dry between paper towels to remove any surface moisture. The fish should be at room temperature.

Flour or crumbs may be seasoned with salt and pepper. If desired, add thyme, summer savory, sweet basil, or your favorite savory seasoning, and fresh or dry grated lemon rind. Use about ⅛ teaspoon of seasoning for each ½ cup of flour or fine crumbs, or for 1 cup of coarser crumbs.

Fine, dry bread crumbs, cornmeal, crushed cornflakes, cracker crumbs, crushed potato chips, and instant dry potato flakes all make excellent coatings for pan-fried fish.

à la meunière: Combine flour and seasonings and mix well in a soup plate or paper or plastic bag. Dredge or shake the fish in the flour, a piece or two at a time, to cover all surfaces. Shake off excess coating, and let rest for at least 10 minutes before frying.

à l'Anglaise: Combine crumbs and seasoning in a paper bag. For a sticking agent, pour ½ cup of milk, a slightly beaten egg, or a combination of the two into a soup plate. Dredge the fish in flour and shake off excess, then dip each piece in the sticking agent. Put fish in the bag and shake to cover it with crumbs. Remove excess crumbs by tossing the fish lightly from hand to hand. This helps to press in the crumbs that have stuck and shakes off those that haven't. Let fish rest 10 minutes or more before frying.

To fry the fish, slowly heat fat in a frying pan to about a ¼-inch depth. The fat should be sizzling—that is, it should spit back to a flick of water and be just short of smoking. Fry the fish, uncovered, on each side until crusty brown; the flesh should be opaque, and flake when prodded with a fork. Turn only once. Slide a spatula under the fish now and then to let the fat circulate and to avoid sticking.

Do not crowd the fish in the pan. Fry a few at a time if necessary. Keep the cooked fish hot on a paper-lined platter in a warm oven until all the fish are cooked. Do not cover, and do not overcook.

Brookside Breakfast Fish Fry

Whether you cook out under the sky or in the camp kitchen, few meals are more memorable than a breakfast of bacon and fresh pan-size trout or panfish fried to a crispy turn.

Clean and wash the fish as soon after catching as possible, and lay them on a bed of fresh green leaves, or leave them spaced on a stringer, until ready to cook. If the fish are caught in the evening, keep them overnight in a cold, clean, safe place.

Cook the bacon in a large cast-iron frying pan. Transfer it to a warm platter at the edge of the fire. Drain off all but ¼ inch of the bacon fat—or drain off more and use butter or margarine to make up the ¼ inch.

In a plastic bag or on a plate, mix salt and pepper into some flour—about 1 cup for a dozen or so fish. Dredge the fish in the flour, coating well, and gently shake off the excess. Pan-fry *à la meunière*. As one lot of fish is done, add it to the bacon at the edge of the fire. Serve with hot biscuits or bannock.

SAUTEING

Sautéing is a modification of pan frying. Fish fillets or steaks are usually sautéed in preparation for serving with a sauce and for some dishes that are finished in the oven. While the pan is shaken to prevent sticking, the fish is browned quickly in very little fat over a brisk heat until barely cooked. (The word *sauté* comes from the French *sauter*, meaning "to jump about." In reference to onions and other chopped vegetables, sauté refers to light browning in butter or oil, with constant stirring.)

9

Species and Specialities

... the gentleman on my left distributed, with grateful impartiality, the white fish, delicately browned in buffalo marrow ...

—Paul Kane
Describing Christmas dinner at Edmonton
Wanderings of an Artist, 1859

The five basic methods of cooking fish flesh have considerable range when applied to the many species listed in Chapter 8, especially when combined in one way or another with the various stuffings and/or sauces appearing in Chapter 11.

The following recipes and species have been singled out as appropriate to demonstrate the adaptation of the different methods to various gamefishes across the continent. These fishes and their recipes are divided into two groups—fatty and lean—in order to guide the cook in applying the recipe to another fish of similar size or cut in the same group. Since of course there are always variables involved, the guide is not inflexible.

Species in each section appear under their common names. Where a number of species of a prestigious family generally have common culinary attributes, such as the fatty trouts (Salmonidae), the lean codfishes, and the flounders, they are included under the family name. On the other hand, where the diversities within a family are so wide that the individual species may range in size from an ounce or two to half a ton, and some may enjoy a great table reputation while others are known to be toxic, the desirable species appear under their common names, e.g., Nassau grouper and totuava among the sea basses (groupers). The name bass itself is so widely used in referring to fish of different families that these appear under their common species name, e.g., striped bass (temperate bass family); however, smallmouth and largemouth bass (sunfishes), which respond alike to cooking, are placed together. Panfishes and whitebait, which include numerous species of little consequence individually but are significant as a group, are listed under the group names in the Lean Fishes section (some fat little fishes are included in the panfishes).

Along with gamefishes are included a number of freshwater fishes generally labeled "coarse" or "trash" (carp and ling, or burbot, are just two). Either term is as misleading as it is confusing. These

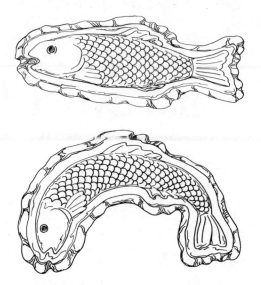

terms have little or nothing to do with table merit, referring simply to those freshwater species left over after gamefishes and commercial fishes have been so designated for regulation purposes or to any small species of no angling account.

FATTY FISHES

The following recipes for fatty species generally may be adapted to other fatty fishes of similar size and cut. Refer to the table listing representative edible fishes of North America in Chapter 8.

Albacore

If you would have good luck for the coming season, eat the heart of the first albacore catch.
— California anglers' lore

Poached Albacore Fillets with Cucumber Sauce
2 pounds albacore fillets, skinned
1 carrot, sliced
1 onion, sliced
1 quart water
½ cup vinegar
½ cup dill pickle juice
2 teaspoons salt
1 bay leaf
Cucumber sauce
Parsley

Place the albacore fillets on top of the carrot and onion slices in a large saucepan. Combine the next five ingredients and heat to a simmer. Pour the simmering broth over the fish. Cover and poach in a

400° F (205° C) oven, or on the stovetop at a constant low simmer, until the fish flakes to a fork —about 20 minutes. Lift the fish carefully to a serving dish and chill. Serve with Cucumber Sauce, garnished with parsley. *4 servings.*

Cucumber Sauce:

3 large cucumbers
2 teaspoons salt
1 pinch cayenne
1 teaspoon horseradish
1 cup sour cream
1 cup mayonnaise

Peel the cucumbers, split lengthwise into quarters, remove seeds, and chop. Sprinkle with salt, and chill for at least 2 hours. Drain well. Mix with remaining ingredients. Chill.

Bluefish

Bluefish are extremely fatty, fiercely predacious fish, which rove the Atlantic Coast from the Carolinas to Cape Cod. The freshly caught bluefish is a superb table fish, compatible with both strong and delicate herbs, and a very dry wine. Its most agreeable size is around 3 to 5 pounds, though larger blues should not be ignored. The blue bakes and broils beautifully, and its fillets make a splendid chowder. The bluefish does not freeze well, but smokes superbly.

A 4- to 5-pound bluefish baked by the basic method for unstuffed fatty fish is a fine production (see "Baking" in Chapter 8). Bake the fish on a nest of aromatic vegetables and use plenty of lemon juice.

Barbecued Bluefish Steaks

Dress a 5- to 6-pound bluefish as fresh from the water as possible. Cut the steaks from the center, a generous inch thick, and trim the fatty part at the opening. Don't discard the remainder—head, tail, and bones make a great fish chowder. Refrigerate the steaks until ready to use.

Grease the barbecue rack well and have it quite warm. Remove the steaks from the refrigerator and pat between towels. Dip each steak in a heated barbecue sauce. (Use a simple melted butter and lemon juice sauce or a more highly seasoned sauce.) Broil over the coals or in the oven, 4 to 5 minutes on each side or until the fish flakes to a fork. Brush frequently with the sauce. Don't overcook.

Cisco

The moderately fatty cisco, or lake herring, is a member of the trout family and no relation to the extremely fatty saltwater herring. It ranges from New England's fresh waters through the Great Lakes into central Canada and the midwestern states. Lake herring is but one of its aliases; others are tullibee, chub, and bloater. Its Ojibway name is *kee-we-sens*. Cisco may run to 8 pounds, but the average is about 1 pound. Pan-size cisco, or fillets, may be fried or broiled.

The following moist-heat recipe is excellent for fillets of moderately fatty fishes, and may also be used for lean fishes such as sole, flounder, walleye, and dolphin.

Kee-We-Sens

2 pounds cisco fillets, skinned
Fumet
2 tablespoons butter
½ cup chopped chives or green onion tops
2 tablespoons flour
2 tablespoons heavy cream
2 tablespoons minced fresh parsley
2 tablespoons dry sherry (optional)

Fumet:

10-ounce can mushrooms
1 cup fish stock
  (see Chapter 8, Basic Fish Stock)
½ cup white wine
A few peppercorns
Pinch thyme
½ teaspoon salt

If frozen, thaw the fillets in their wrap in the refrigerator.

To make the fumet, drain the mushrooms over a saucepan and set them aside. Add the rest of the fumet ingredients to the mushroom juice. Boil for 10 minutes, strain, and let cool. Place the fillets on a buttered plate in a large skillet. Add the fumet. Bring to a boil, turn down the heat, cover tightly, and poach very gently until the flesh flakes to a fork and takes on an opaque milky color. Carefully draining back any liquid, transfer the plate and fish to a warm oven.

Melt the butter in a saucepan. Sauté the chives in it until soft, then add the flour and cook until smooth and bubbly, stirring constantly. Add 1 cup of the fumet and stir-cook until thickened. Slice the mushrooms and stir them in along with the cream, the parsley, and, if desired, the sherry. Keep hot, but don't boil after adding the cream. Add salt to taste.

Move the fish to a warm serving platter and pour the sauce on top, or serve it on the side in a gravy boat. Serve with colorful vegetables such as spinach or green peas and baby carrots. *4 servings.*

Florida Pompano

The Florida pompano, which averages 1 to 2 pounds, is considered one of the finest fishes in the ocean. Certainly with its silvery pink skin, it is one of the most beautiful. The exquisitely flavored, firm, rich flesh of the pompano lends itself to simple cooking with understated seasonings. It is cooked whole or filleted, and is broiled or pan-fried by basic methods.

Pompano en Papilotte

Cooking fish (or meat) *en papilotte* simply means cooking it in an oiled paper package or, with a little more refinement, in cooking parchment. The method is not unlike the primitive practice of cooking in grape or papaya leaves, or cornhusks.

Preheat the oven to 425° F (220° C). For each dressed or pan-dressed fish or fillet cut a heart-shaped piece of cooking parchment, big enough when folded to encase the fish. Or use brown wrapping paper, well oiled or buttered.

Butter the fish all over and place it on the parchment heart, near the crease. Scatter around it 1 or 2 tablespoons of lobster, crab, or shrimp meat, and 2 or 3 pitted black olives. Squeeze the juice from ¼ of a lemon over the fish, and season with salt and pepper. Scatter ½ teaspoon of minced fresh parsley over the fish. Fold the parchment over the fish and crimp the edges together securely. Bake until the paper is puffed up and brown. Place the package on a warm serving plate, fold back the parchment, and serve with a wedge of lemon. *Serve 1 papilotte per person.*

Shrimp-Filled Florida Pompano

2-pound Florida pompano, scaled and filleted,
  unskinned
10-ounce can cream of mushroom soup
¼ cup heavy cream
1 cup minced cooked shrimp
1 tablespoon brandy
Salt, pepper, and paprika
¼ cup sherry

Preheat the oven to 375° F (190° C). Wipe the fillets with a damp cloth. Stir half the cream into the mushroom soup until well blended. Add the shrimp and the brandy. Sandwich the filling between the two fillets, skin-side out, and close the edges with small lacing pins. Put the fish into a well-greased shallow baking dish just big enough to accommodate it comfortably; then mix the sherry into the remaining cream and pour it over the fish. Bake until the flesh flakes to a fork, about 40 minutes, spooning the pan sauce over the top occasionally.

Serve very hot, garnished with sliced cucumbers that have been marinated in salted water with a little vinegar. *2 servings.*

Herrings

Members of the herring family of table importance are the Atlantic and Pacific herrings, the pilchard (Pacific sardine), and the American and hickory shads (see Shad). The alewife (*gaspereau* in eastern Canada) is a herring. Freshwater lake herring (see Cisco) belongs to another family and is not a true herring.

Being a little fatty fish (over 1 pound is big), the herring cures well, and salting, smoking, and kippering are still the favored methods of preparation. Fresh herring may also be pan-fried. The scaled fish cooks better if scored along the sides with gashes about 1½ inches apart (see Pan Frying in Chapter 8).

Slowpokes

6 fresh herring or alewives,
  under 1 pound each
Salt and pepper
Lemon juice
6 anchovies (optional)
1 cup vinegar plus 1 tablespoon sugar,
  or 1 cup pickle juice
1 cup sour cream
Cayenne

Preheat the oven to 325° F (165° C). Fillet the herrings (pan-size trout also may be used). Wash in cold water and pat dry between paper towels. Season each fillet with salt, pepper, and lemon juice. Roll the fillet, tucking an anchovy inside the roll, and secure with a toothpick. Arrange the rolled fillets close together in a baking dish.

Add the vinegar with the sugar mixed in, or juice from sweet pickles or pickled beets. Combine the sour cream with 1 teaspoon of lemon juice; add a trace of cayenne, and salt and pepper to taste. Pour over the fish. Bake 20 to 30 minutes or until the fish flakes to a fork. *4 servings.*

Lake Sturgeon

The lake sturgeon is the most common American member of a cosmopolitan family of prehistoric lineage. A monster of lore and legend, today's catch averages around 40 pounds. With its excessive oils removed, the flesh is excellent of flavor, described as tasting more like chicken or veal than fish.

But it's still a rich dish and is better poached than fried. Fat, coarse-grained, and flaky, sturgeon is a superior smoker and pickles well.

An average sturgeon provides about 25 pounds of bone-free fish for the freezer. Cross-cut the dressed, skinned fish into family-size portions, about 2 pounds each. Pull out the spinal cord of each piece immediately and wash the fish.

Sturgeon roe is valuable as caviar (see Chapter 10).

Sturgeon in Cream Sauce
2 pounds sturgeon, skinned and boned
Fish stock
1 large onion, chopped
2 tablespoons butter
Paprika and salt
1½ cups dry white wine
2 cups Cream Sauce (see Chapter 11)

Prepare fish stock if none is available (see Basic Fish Stock in Chapter 8).

Preheat the oven to 350° F (175° C). Slice the sturgeon into serving portions. Place in a stock pot and cover with fish stock. Bring slowly to a bubble, reduce the heat, and simmer gently for about 10 minutes. Pour off the stock and drain the fish.

Slowly brown the onion in the butter until tender, then spread it over the bottom of a baking pan. Lay the slices of sturgeon on top of the onion, season with salt and paprika, and add 1 cup of the wine. Bring to a boil on top of stove, then bake for 15 minutes.

Meanwhile, make Cream Sauce, blend the remaining ½ cup of wine into the sauce, and pour it over the fish. Continue baking the fish until it flakes to a fork, basting with the sauce from time to time. Serve with colorful vegetables. *4 to 6 servings.*

Lake Whitefish

Of long-established value in the Far North, lake whitefish is receiving long-overdue recognition as great table fare as far south as ice fishing is done.

In the summer, lake whitefish is fat and sluggish and best processed via the smokehouse. The post-spawning fish of winter is leaner, hungrier, and provides both firm tasty flesh and good sport. Winter-caught lake whitefish bakes superbly, makes great chowders, and fries and broils well. Steamed or poached and chilled, its white flesh makes a lovely salad, garnished with color (see Fish Salad).

Stuffed Lake Whitefish in Spanish Sauce

Thaw a 4- to 5-pound dressed and scaled whitefish until manageable. Leave the head and tail on the fish or cut them off, as preferred. Wash the fish and pat dry. Rub the cavity with a lemon wedge, squeezing as you rub. Preheat the oven to 400° F (205° C).

Prepare about 4 cups of a moist stuffing (see "Stuffings" in Chapter 11). Stuff the fish lightly, leaving room for the stuffing to swell. Close the cavity with a needle and strong white thread or with trussing pins and string. On the bottom of a baking dish arrange 3 or 4 slices of fat pork or bacon to serve as a rack, and place the fish on it.

Make Spanish Sauce (see Chapter 11).

While the sauce is simmering, baste the fish well with a mixture of white wine and melted butter and put it into the oven, uncovered. Baste frequently with the wine-butter mixture until the fish just begins to brown, about 20 minutes. (If the fish is browning too quickly, lay a piece of aluminum foil over it, shiny side out.) Pour half the Spanish Sauce over the fish and continue baking uncovered, basting frequently from the pan, until the fish is nicely browned and the flesh flakes readily to a fork. Carefully transfer the fish to a heated serving platter and keep it warm.

Remove the pork from the baking pan. Stir the remaining hot Spanish Sauce into the pan drippings and stir-cook for about 5 minutes.

Garnish the serving platter with fresh parsley, lemon wedges, and black olives. Serve the pan sauce in a gravy boat on the side. *6 to 8 servings.*

Mackerels

Members of the mackerel family, which includes the mackerels and tunas, range in size from a few pounds to over a hundred pounds and offer sport from child's play to big-game trophy hunting. Many vacationing youngsters wet their first line casting into a streaking school of little mackerel from a rowboat or a quiet coastal bay. (See also "Albacore.")

ATLANTIC MACKEREL AND CHUB MACKEREL

Like all the mackerel, the little Atlantic and chub mackerels are sleek and swift in the water. Running in schools, they are abundant on both the Atlantic and Pacific coasts during their inshore

COMPLETE FISH AND GAME COOKERY OF NORTH AMERICA

season. Every spring, mackerel are taken by the hundreds by East Coast anglers. Delicious when freshly caught, the oily little fish doesn't take well to freezing, and the surplus is salted down in traditional thrifty colonial fashion (see "Smoking Fish" in Chapter 3.)

Two pounds is a good size for these mackerels. Their flesh is firm, though fatty. Whole or filleted, mackerel broil and bake nicely with a zesty basting sauce. (For baking, many prefer midsummer mackerel that are not yet fully fattened up after spawning.) Pan-size mackerel are also fried *à la meunière* (see Pan Frying under "Frying" in Chapter 8).

Mackerel has a finely scaled, smooth skin. Scrape it with the blunt edge of a knife and wash the fish well before cooking.

> *Poached Mackerel with Cream Sauce*
> 2 pounds boneless mackerel fillets
> Juice and rind of 2 or 3 lemon slices
> ½ bay leaf
> ½ teaspoon salt
> A few peppercorns, cracked
> Pinch sugar
> Cream Sauce (see Chapter 11)

Cut the fillets into bite-size chunks. Tie the fish loosely in cheesecloth and put into a deep saucepan. Cover completely with cold water and add the lemon juice and rind, bay leaf, salt, pepper, and sugar. Cover lightly. Heat slowly to a bubble, reduce the heat, and simmer for about 10 minutes, or until the fish flakes to a fork.

While the fish is cooking, make Cream Sauce. If the fish is not quite ready, keep the sauce hot over hot water and stir it occasionally.

Lift the bag containing the fish, letting it drain a moment, and then arrange the fish on a heated serving platter. Just before serving, pour the sauce over the fish. Garnish with slices of hard-boiled egg, bits of pimento, and parsley sprigs. *4 servings.*

Variation: For Mackerel Florentine, blend ½ cup of grated cheddar cheese into the hot sauce. Arrange the fish on a nest of freshly cooked spinach. Pour the sauce over the fish, garnish, and serve as above.

KING MACKEREL AND SPANISH MACKEREL

King and Spanish mackerels share the family traits with the Atlantic and chub mackerels but on a grander scale. Kings can reach 100 pounds, and Spanish 20 pounds. Both are fine table fish at around 10 pounds or less. They bake and broil well, and make superb chowders.

> *Baked Mackerel in Spanish Sauce*
> 1 3-pound king or Spanish mackerel
> Cooking oil
> Salt and pepper
> ½ cup tomato juice
> 1 tablespoon finely chopped onion
> 1 cup Spanish Sauce (see Chapter 11)
> ¼ cup bread crumbs
> 2 tablespoons butter

Preheat the oven to 350° F (180° C). Rub the dressed fish with cooking oil or fat and season with salt and pepper. Place the fish in an oiled pan, pour on the tomato juice, and sprinkle with onion. Put into preheated oven for about 30 minutes, basting occasionally from the pan. Remove from the oven. Pour Spanish Sauce over the fish, sprinkle bread crumbs on top, and dot with butter. Return the fish to the oven until it is browned. *3 to 4 servings.*

—Famous Florida Recipes
Lowis Carlton

Mullet

Mullet, which goes by the name *ama-ama* in Hawaii, is a popular food fish of the southern states. In some northern regions suckers are mistakenly called mullet.

The catch averages 2 to 3 pounds. Mullet flesh has a sweet nutlike flavor and is rich in food value. Lean mullets are best broiled or pan-fried and served with a lemon-butter sauce; fatter ones may be poached and served with a wine sauce.

Fat mullets and the roes are superb smoked, a preparation that has brought fame to L. J. (Touch) Touchton and his Mullet Inn on the Clearwater-Tampa causeway in Florida. The fish are split down the back for cleaning, scrubbed thoroughly, and smoked on racks over green Florida oak for 3 to 4 hours. This treatment brings the fish to a distinctive golden-brown color and a smoky succulence. (See "Smoking Fish" in Chapter 3).

Mullet Baked in Wine

4 small mullets, pan-dressed
2 tablespoons butter
1 tablespoon diced mushrooms
1 tablespoon chopped chives
2 tablespoons finely chopped parsley
White pepper
Salt
Pinch grated nutmeg
½ cup Spanish Sauce (see Chapter 11)
Lemon juice
½ cup dry sherry or dry white wine
Anchovy essence (optional)

Wash the dressed mullets, pat dry, and place them in a well-buttered baking dish.

In a saucepan melt the butter, mix in the next 6 ingredients, and simmer for 5 minutes. Blend in the Spanish Sauce. Stir and cook until the mixture bubbles, and then add a few drops of lemon juice. Pour half the sauce over the fish, and keep the rest hot over simmering water.

Preheat the oven to 425° F (220° C), and let the fish rest while the oven heats. Bake the mullets, uncovered, basting them with their own sauce, until the flesh flakes, about 20 to 25 minutes. Remove the fish, arrange on a warm serving platter, and keep warm.

Add the sherry or wine to the pan, swishing it around to deglaze the sides, then mix it into the remaining Spanish Sauce. Add another dash of lemon juice and a few drops of anchovy essence, and pour the sauce over the fish. Serve at once, garnished with parsley sprigs. *4 servings.*

Rainbow Smelt

The fatty American, or rainbow, smelt is as delicate and perishable a little fish as will be found. Smelts require prompt and chilly processing. Netted inshore at night during their winter and spring spawning runs, the fish, generally less than 10 inches long, can be dressed and frozen under conditions favorable to culinary perfection. However, no matter how expertly and quickly they're cleaned and frozen, smelts will never taste better than when they're fresh from the water. Freshly caught smelt have a sweet fresh fragrance and flavor due to a volatile oil, which dissipates during storage.

To capture the elusive quality of smelt at its peak, cook them without delay, whether you broil them skewered on a forked pole or in a toaster rack over the coals of a wood fire on the beach, or pan-fry a mess of them at home at midnight.

Smelts are easily cleaned. Snip off the head with small scissors just below the gills, slit the fish open, and push out the insides with a thumbnail. Wash and drain on paper towels. Cook up all you can eat, and block-freeze the rest (see "Freezing Fish" in Chapter 8).

Pan-Fried Smelt

Put 1 cup of flour or a mixture of fine corn meal and flour into a bag and season to taste with salt and pepper. Put the dressed smelts into the bag a few at a time and shake gently to coat well. Put the fish on a towel to rest.

In a large frying pan, heat cooking oil, about ¼ inch deep. When the oil spits back to a flick of water but is not smoking, add the smelts, as many as the pan will take without crowding. Fry the fish, uncovered, until crisply golden on one side; then turn them immediately and brown the other side, just until the flesh flakes to a fork. Smelts cook very quickly; be careful not to overcook them.

As soon as they're cooked, remove the fish to a warm, paper-lined platter and serve at once, or keep them warm while cooking the remainder. Serve with lemon wedges.

Shad

The abundance of shad from North Carolina to the Maritime provinces in the early days of settlement was such that the well-to-do scorned them, fearful of appearing unable to afford better. Today it seems that everyone on the Eastern Seaboard is a shad lover. Introduced to the West Coast a century ago, shad now flourish there, also.

Anadromous big herrings, shad are of two species—the more plentiful American, which runs to about 8 pounds, and the smaller hickory, which averages 1 to 3 pounds. The flesh of both species is delicately flavored, light, and creamy.

The boniness of shad is legendary, and dealing with this problem has been the ongoing preoccupation of shad fanciers for a couple of centuries. In the East, lengthy baking in milk in low heat has been found to mitigate the problem, but at the risk of overcooking the fish. The California Department of Fish and Game made an in-depth study of filleting shad and published the findings in the booklet *How to Catch, Bone and Cook a Shad*, which included photographs illustrating how to bone shad in thirty-two steps. In New Brunswick, the general conclusion is that shad is best baked whole and "stuffed like a chicken" to savor the fish's sweet, creamy flesh; the bones must be picked out and special attention given to servings for young children.

Shad also makes a fine chowder. Whole or pan-dressed, the fish is tied in cheesecloth and simmered until the bones can be removed easily; the chowder is made from bone-free flesh and resulting stock.

Shad Baked in Milk

This recipe is an example of the bone-softening method used on the East Coast to render the shad's many bones soft and relatively harmless.

Preheat the oven to 250° F (120° C).

Rub the dressed shad (around 3 pounds) inside and out with a mixture of melted butter and lemon juice. Lay the fish on a large sheet of double-ply heavy-duty aluminum foil. Sprinkle about ½ cup of dry bread crumbs and a handful of chopped parsley over the top, then sprinkle about ¼ cup of lemon juice over that. Drugstore wrap, tucking the ends up to close securely. Place the shad in the bottom of a shallow baking dish (no trivet). Open the foil just enough to pour in 1 quart of milk and reseal tightly. Pour water into the pan around the package of fish to a depth of about ½ inch. Bake the fish for 5 to 6 hours, adding water to the pan as necessary to maintain a ½-inch depth.

Unwrap the fish, and carefully transfer it to a warm ovenproof serving platter. Brown under the broiler for a few minutes. The bones should now be soft. Serve with horseradish-mustard sauce. *4 to 6 servings.*

—Mary Wilson Benedict
Country Bookshop
Southern Pines, North Carolina

Planked Shad

March 11 is the day to plank a shad. Shad were called *elft*, or "eleven fish," by the early Dutch settlers, for March 11 was the day the first shad were caught and cooked on a plank in the manner learned from the Indians. If you're a stickler for tradition, see Indian-Style Planked Fish in Chapter 3. Otherwise, plank a shad as follows:

> 3- or 4-pound dressed shad
> 1½ teaspoons salt
> ¼ cup melted fat or oil
> Mashed potatoes, seasoned with thyme

Prepare a plank as described in Baking Fatty Fish under "Baking" in Chapter 8, then reduce the oven temperature to 400° F (205° C). Lacking a plank, you may use an oven-to-table platter, about 18 by 13 inches; it need only be greased and preheated in a 400° F (205° C) oven.

Clean, wash, and dry the shad. Sprinkle it inside and out with the salt. Place it on the well-greased, heated plank or platter. Brush the fish with the melted fat, and score the skin lightly in 2 or 3 places. Bake for 30 to 50 minutes, or until the flesh just flakes to a fork. Baste occasionally with melted fat.

Remove the plank or platter from the oven and arrange a border of hot mashed potatoes around the fish. Place under the broiler, about 8 inches from the heat, until the potatoes are lightly browned —about 6 to 8 minutes. Remove from the broiler and arrange two or more cooked vegetables—string beans, carrots, cauliflower, peas, onion, tomatoes—around the fish. *4 to 6 servings.*

Striped Bass

Striped bass has a long and prestigious history of feeding the North American people dating back to the Plymouth colonists who, with considerable foresight, saw fit to pass an act prohibiting the fish's use (along with that of the cod) for fertilizer. In the early 1880's some 400 striped bass were transplanted to Pacific waters, where they so flourished that today the striper roves the coastal waters from the Columbia River to Southern California. A landlocked transplanted population is fairly widespread.

An active predator, weighing up to 10 pounds or more, the striped bass is lithe in muscle and firm of flesh and is highly esteemed by cook and angler alike. A medium-fatty fish, striped bass responds magnificently to recipes for trout and salmon in the 5- to 10-pound range. The striper, a relatively bony fish, is better filleted than steaked. It bakes and poaches well whole, and excellent results are obtained from a salt-pickle and smoke cure. Scale stripers carefully to avoid tearing the skin.

Striped Bass Brandy Braise

4- to 5-pound dressed striped bass, or section
Butter
Salt and pepper
Thyme or parsley, minced
2 onions, sliced
2 carrots, sliced
2 stalks celery, cut into chunks
1 green pepper, thickly sliced
Bouquet garni
2 tablespoons brandy
1 cup dry white wine
2 tablespoons melted butter

Preheat the oven to 375° F (190° C). Prepare the fish for cooking. Rub the inside of the cavity with a mixture of butter, salt and pepper, and minced thyme or parsley. Arrange the bass in a baking pan on a bed of the onions, carrots, celery, and green pepper, and add the *bouquet garni*. Warm the brandy in a long-handled butter melter, and ignite the liquor as your pour it on the fish.

Moisten the vegetables with the dry white wine, and pour the melted butter over the fish. Bring to a boil on top of the stove, then bake uncovered for 40 to 50 minutes, or until the flesh flakes to a fork, basting frequently with the pan juices. Transfer the bass to a warmed serving platter, garnish and serve. *4 to 6 servings.*

Swordfish

Swordfish is a big gamefish (it runs 200 to 600 pounds) as much prized for its distinctively flavored, rich, firm flesh as for its angling merits. The meat of the swordfish is usually steaked or chunked and then barbecued or spit-broiled. It also bakes well.

Charcoal Broiled Broadbill Swordfish

10-ounce swordfish steaks, ¾ to 1 inch thick

Marinade:

1¼ cup garlic oil (3 cloves garlic crushed
  and soaked overnight in salad oil)

2 cups tomato catsup

2 ounces Worcestershire sauce

3 teaspoons dry mustard

1 teaspoon Tabasco sauce

6 ounces sherry

1 teaspoon monosodium glutamate

Juice of ½ lemon

2 drops liquid smoke,
  or ½ teaspoon hickory-smoked salt

Pinch thyme

Salt and pepper to taste

If the fish is frozen, thaw it in the refrigerator until just soft. Rinse it under cold water and pat dry between towels.

Skin the steaks, and trim away any excess fatty tissue along the cavity cut. (Freshly caught salmons, lake trout, ouananiche, Arctic char, and inconnu may be used instead of swordfish with excellent results.)

Combine the marinade ingredients and mix or shake well. This sauce is the secret; it brings out the wonderful flavor of the delectable fish. (Note: The amount is sufficient for 4 to 8 steaks; the marinade can be kept for 2 weeks in the refrigerator.) Pour part of the marinade into a deep bowl. Add the steaks, turning each one to coat with the sauce. Cover and refrigerate for 4 to 8 hours, turning the fish occasionally.

Make a basting brush with a tied bouquet of fresh parsley.

Lift the steaks and let them drain a moment or two. Cook on a hot greased rack over a medium-hot charcoal fire for about 20 minutes, turning the fish gently 4 times. Baste with the parsley brush at each turning, using the sauce from the bowl. Serve with rice pilaf.

—Tod Ghio
Anthony's Fish Grottos
San Diego, California

Swordfish on a Spit

2 pounds swordfish steaks, 1½ inches thick

Pitted olives, pickled onions, and/or water
  chestnuts

Marinade:

¼ cup lemon juice

¼ cup olive oil

1 clove garic, crushed

Onion juice

1 bay leaf

Parsley

Paprika and salt

Cut the fish into 1½-inch cubes, and spread them over a large glass or earthen pie plate. Combine the marinade ingredients and pour over the fish, turning the pieces so all are well coated. Cover and refrigerate for 2 or 3 hours.

Remove the fish and put the pieces on long skewers, spacing the pieces with the olives, onions, and/or water chestnuts. Lay the skewers over a dripping pan and broil under high heat (2 to 4 inches from the heat source) until crisp and golden, about 10 to 15 minutes. Turn about 4 times during cooking, basting with the marinade after each turn. The fish also may be broiled over the barbecue. Serve with lemon wedges. *4 servings.*

Totuava

Totuava is a fabulously delicious member of the drum family that migrates up the Baja California coast of Mexico. It is an exception to the general rule that fatty big fish are stronger or richer in flavor than the lean ones, and can take plenty of seasoning. The totuava, which can weigh up to 250 pounds, has moist, oily flesh and a delicate flavor—a rare combination.

In season the protected totuava is a specialty of La Perla restaurant in Tijuana, Mexico, where Chef Manuel Oceguara brushes the fillets with oil flavored with a touch of garlic, broils them quickly over charcoal, and serves them piping hot with lemon juice (see "Broiling" in Chapter 8).

Trouts and Salmons

The trouts, which include the salmons, comprise a family of fatty fishes, and those from extremely cold water are often excessively fat. Except for their cousins, the bottom-feeding lake whitefish and cisco, they are energetic predators, firm of flesh and fine of flavor. The flesh ranges in color from varying shades of pink to the fiery red of the Arctic char.

The trouts bake, poach, fry, and broil admirably, and all, especially the big ones with coarser-grained flesh, pickle and smoke beautifully.

For culinary purposes the trouts and salmons are grouped here according to size—small, medium, and big. This does not imply the average size of the catch. Put each fish into whichever size group it fits and cook accordingly. The trouts may be cooked by recipes for other fatty fishes given in this section, if the fish are of comparable size.

SMALL TROUTS (1 TO 4 POUNDS)

Small trouts, ranging from 1 to 4 pounds, include young Atlantic salmon (grilse), brook trout, young chinook salmon, young coho, sockeye, cutthroat trout, golden trout, Arctic grayling, ouananiche, kokanee, young rainbow, splake (a hybrid of lake and speckled trout), and young lakers of "keeper" size (consult fishing regulations).

Cook small trouts simply. Pan-size fish may be fried or broiled whole; others should be split, filleted, or pan-dressed and then fried, broiled, or baked. They may also be salted and/or smoked, or pickled.

Trout in Lettuce Casserole

Preheat the oven to 350° F (175° C). Choose a shallow oven-to-table casserole or baking dish large enough to accommodate 6 pan-size trout. Clean the trout, scrape the skin with the back of a table knife, wash under cold water, and pat dry between towels. Cut off the heads and tails. Rub the fish inside and out with a wedge of lemon, squeezing gently as you rub, and then sprinkle lightly with salt and pepper.

Finely shred a firm head of iceberg lettuce and put it into the casserole. Sprinkle with ½ teaspoon of salt and grind a bit of black pepper over it. Add a clove of garlic, finely chopped. Drizzle 1 tablespoon of olive oil over the top and mix to blend it all evenly.

Remove half of the lettuce and spread the remainder over the bottom of the casserole. Lay the fish on top and sprinkle a little lemon juice on them. Cover the fish with the rest of the lettuce. Cover closely with a lid or foil (pinch foil to the edge of the dish). Bake for 40 to 45 minutes. Uncover, garnish with bits of pimento if desired, and serve at once with lemon wedges. *6 servings.*

Old Southern Rainbows

Brought down from the mountains daily, individual stuffed rainbow trout are the specialty of Zavely House in Old Salem, North Carolina. Just under 1 pound is the best size, says Chef Sam Loflin, who developed this recipe.

> 4 12- to 14-ounce rainbow trout, dressed
> Stuffing
> Lemon juice
> Onion slices
> Melted butter
> Worcestershire sauce

> *Stuffing:*
> 1 small onion, finely minced
> ¼ cup melted butter
> 4 cups fine dry bread crumbs
> 1 tablespoon minced pimento (optional)
> ¼ teaspoon finely grated lemon rind
> 1 teaspoon thyme, or ¼ teaspoon tarragon
> ¼ teaspoon salt
> Dash freshly ground pepper

Preheat the oven to 375° F (190° C). Sauté the minced onion in the butter until translucent. Combine with the remaining stuffing ingredients, mix well, and let rest for about 1 hour.

Wash the fish and pat dry between towels. Rub the cavities with lemon juice. Stuff lightly, dividing the stuffing evenly. Pin loosely with poultry lacers to hold. Arrange the fish in a well-buttered, roomy baking dish, supported on slices of onion to prevent sticking. Brush the fish well with melted butter laced with lemon juice and a generous dash of Worcestershire sauce.

Bake uncovered, basting from time to time with melted butter, for about 25 minutes, or until the fish flakes to a fork and is golden brown. A very light dusting of flour after the last basting will help attain a golden crispiness. Serve hot with tartar sauce or a creamy mushroom sauce. *4 servings.*

Truite au Bleu

In Quebec fishing camps, *au bleu* is a favored method of preparing freshly caught brook or rainbow trout of around 2 pounds. All that's required to "blue" the trout is seasoned vinegar and a few standard staples.

It's the sticky film on the skin of the fish that, on contact with the hot vinegar, turns blue. Thus this film must not be disturbed. The fish is kept alive in a bucket of water from catch to kitchen. It is killed and cleaned (but not scaled or washed) only about 15 minutes before serving.

Court Bouillon:
2 cups vinegar,
  plain or seasoned with tarragon
2 cups water
1 slice lemon
1 medium onion, sliced
¼ teaspoon peppercorns
1 teaspoon salt

Put the court bouillon ingredients into a deep saucepan and bring to a boil. Cover, reduce the heat, and simmer for about 15 minutes; then bring it back to a rolling boil. (The court bouillon can be cooled and reheated to boiling when needed.) In another saucepan heat a cup of plain vinegar to a simmer.

While the poaching brew is simmering and the vinegar is heating, kill and clean the fish. Cut out the gills, but leave the head and tail. Do *not* wash the fish.

As each fish is cleaned, sprinkle it with hot vinegar and quickly plunge it into the boiling court bouillon. Reduce the heat to a simmer, and as soon as the fish, now curled and blue, flakes to a fork, lift it carefully and drain between paper towels. Let the court bouillon return to a boil before adding another fish. Serve hot, with Hollandaise sauce or hot lemon-butter on the side.

MEDIUM TROUTS (5 TO 9 POUNDS)

Medium trouts of 5 to 9 pounds may include sockeye salmon, coho, young chum and chinook salmon, pink salmon, rainbow trout, brook and brown trout, Atlantic salmon, lake trout, splake, Arctic char, and Dolly Varden. Whole fish may be baked or poached, while fillets and steaks are best poached or broiled.

The fat in a bigger fish is likely to be more objectionable than that in a small one—there's more of it for one thing. Where a small young trout or salmon may be just fine dressed in the usual manner, an older, bigger fish needs some trimming. Also, a trout from frigid deep waters is likely to be fatter than its counterpart from more temperate waters. Since there's no way of precisely tabulating degrees of obesity for all situations, the best plan is to trim any excessive fat or fatty tissue that the fish carries; trimming will improve the flavor of the fish remarkably.

Excess fat can be removed from the belly by trimming away the fatty flesh from each side of the cavity cut and from around the vent.

To remove fat near the backbone (particularly noticeable in lake trout from cold, deep waters), cut through the skin along one side of the dorsal line, leaving the dorsal fin undisturbed, or cut the fin out, as you wish. Slip the knife under the skin, folding it back. Scrape out the fatty strip over the backbone. Replace the flap of skin if the fish is to be cooked whole.

Salmon Baked in Soured Cream

1½ pounds freshly caught or frozen salmon
  or trout fillets, skinned
1 teaspoon crushed dried dill weed
1 tablespoon white wine vinegar
1 cup soured cream
Pinch cayenne
1 teaspoon salt

If frozen, thaw the fish in the refrigerator until just soft. Trim excess fat as described above. Preheat the oven to 350° F (175° C).

Soften the dill in the vinegar for about ½ hour. Blend in the soured cream and the cayenne. (Note: Be sure to use *soured* cream—that is, natural, thick pasteurized cream that has turned sour. It doesn't curdle. Results with commercial sour cream have been unpredictable).

Arrange the fillets in a large, well-buttered baking dish. Sprinkle with the salt. Pour the cream mixture over the fish. Bake for 20 to 25 minutes, or until the fish flakes to a fork. Serve with fluffy rice, a colorful green vegetable, and a dry white wine. *4 servings.*

—John McDonald
Pike Western Wine Company
Seattle, Washington

Lake Trout in Pastry

Lake trout is quite fatty, especially the winter-caught fish. This recipe calls for a gentle poaching to float off the excess oils.

5- to 7-pound thawed lake trout, filleted
  and skinned, fatty tissue trimmed
Dry red or white wine
1 teaspoon salt
1 tablespoon clarified butter
3 green onions, chopped
1 cup steamed wild rice
¼ cup sliced mushrooms
Pastry for a 2-crust pie
Salt and pepper to taste
Juice of 1 lemon
1 tablespoon butter

Place the fillets on a greased rack in a poacher. Add cold water and wine in equal amounts to just cover the fish. Add the salt, bring to a low boil, cover, and reduce to a low simmer. Gently poach about 15 minutes, or until the flesh barely flakes to a fork. Remove the fish, and let it drain a moment. Cool.

Preheat the oven to 425° F (220° C). Melt the clarified butter and sauté the onions, then combine them with the wild rice and mushrooms. Roll the pastry into a thin oblong. Place one fillet on one half, then sprinkle with salt and pepper and half the lemon juice. Heap the wild rice mixture on the fillet and spread the mixture toward the edges. Dab with butter. Season the other fillet and place it on the rice, seasoned-side down. Fold the pastry over, pinching the edges together to seal. Place on a foil-lined cookie sheet and bake for 30 to 35 minutes, or until the pastry is golden brown. Slide the foil and fish onto a warm serving platter and carefully tear away the foil. *4 to 6 servings.*

—Cathy Brown
White Gables Camp
Temagami, Ontario

Lake Trout Pojarsky with Mussels
1-pound lake trout fillet, skinned and boned
1½ cup heavy cream
Salt and cayenne
3 egg whites
White bread crumbs
1 ounce vegetable oil

Sauce:
3 tablespoons butter
1 teaspoon shallots
½ teaspoon fresh thyme, chopped
12 mussels, washed
½ cup white wine
1 teaspoon chopped parsley

Preheat the oven to 375° F (190° C). Put the fish fillet through a fine meat grinder. Mix the fish with the salt, cayenne, and half the cream. Reduce mixture to a smooth paste in a blender, or run it through a meat grinder several times until smooth.

Put the fish paste into a bowl. With a wooden spatula, work in the egg whites and the remaining cream. Shape the mixture into 4 patties about ½ inch thick. Coat with bread crumbs and brown the patties in the hot oil in a skillet. Place the pan in the oven and bake for 20 minutes. Remove the patties from the pan, and keep them warm. Discard the oil.

Make the sauce in the same pan. Heat 1 tablespoon of butter and fry the shallots and thyme for 1 minute. Add the mussels and white wine. Cover and steam until the mussels open. Take the mussels from their shells, return them to the pan, and reduce the liquid by half. Work in the chopped parsley and the remainder of the butter. Pour the sauce over the fish patties and serve.

—Gunter Gugelmeier
Executive Chef, Loews Westbury Hotel
Toronto, Ontario

Peroche (Alaskan Salmon Pie)
Uncover a collection of any Alaskan's favorite salmon recipes and you'll almost surely find a recipe for peroche. A tasty combination of salmon, rice, and vegetables encased in a flaky pastry, it probably originated with Alaska's early Russian settlers, and there seem to be as many recipes for peroche as there are cooks in Alaska.

2 cups freshly cooked or canned salmon, flaked
¼ cup fish stock or hot water
1 cup cooked rice
1 tablespoon lemon juice
1 medium onion, grated
2 stalks celery, chopped
Salt and pepper to taste
Pastry for a 2-crust pie
2 tablespoons butter

Preheat the oven to 400° F (205° C). In a bowl combine everything except the pastry and butter. Line a 2-quart casserole or deep pie dish with pastry, and fill with the salmon mixture. Dot with the butter. Cover with pastry, seal it around the edge, and score the top. Bake for 45 minutes, or until the pastry is nicely browned. A cheese sauce is suggested for the rather dry peroche. *6 servings.*

Scandinavian-Style Lake Trout

The following preparation is adapted from a 300-year-old family recipe of Berndt Berglund of Wilderness Survival, Inc., in Campbellford, Ontario.

5-pound trout, freshly caught and dressed
Fresh dill
½ cup coarse salt
½ cup sugar
2 tablespoons white peppercorns, crushed

Scrape the skin of the dressed fish (salmon or Arctic char may be used instead of trout). Wipe all over with a damp cloth—do not wash the fish in water—and dry. Remove the head and tail. Cut the fish lengthwise to the spine, separate the sides, first one then the other, and remove the backbone along with the small bones. Trim the fillets, squaring them off neatly at both ends, and remove any fatty tissue at the edges. (Use the head, tail, and bones to make a hearty fish chowder, or poach them and use the meat in a pie or patties.)

Wash the dill and shake to dry. Spread a bed of dill over the bottom of a large oblong ceramic baking dish. Chop more dill quite small, about ½ cup, and reserve. Combine the salt, sugar, and peppercorns.

Lay a fish fillet on the dill, skin-side down. Sprinkle with chopped dill, then sprinkle the salt mixture over it. Place the other slab of fish on top, skin-side up, with its thick end over the thin end of the first fillet. Spread more dill on top. Cover with a clean wooden board, cut to fit in the dish. Weight the board with a few bricks. Cover it all with aluminum foil or plastic wrap. Store the fish in a cold, dark place for at least 3 days. Turn the fish over every 6 hours the first day, then every 12 hours, replacing the cover and weights each time.

To serve the fish, transfer it to a carving board and separate the halves. With a table knife, scrape away the dill and peppercorns, and pat dry with a soft paper towel or damp cloth. Place one fillet, skin-side down, on the carving board and slice it very thinly on an angle diagonal to the tail, without cutting through the skin. Serve with the rather sharp mustard sauce given below.

Keep the remainder of the fish in a large earthen crock filled with the salt-sugar brine and chopped fresh dill. If additional brine is needed, boil 1 gallon of water and add enough salt to make the brine strong enough to float an egg; add a few more bunches of finely chopped dill, and cool. Fish prepared in this way keeps for a year in a cold, dark place.

Mustard Sauce: In a ceramic bowl combine 1 teaspoon of dry mustard, 1 tablespoon of sugar, and ½ cup of the brine that forms during salting of the fish. Blend with a whisk. Continue whisking, and beat in cooking oil, adding it a bit at a time, until the sauce is thickened.

Buffet Salmon

5- to 10-pound salmon, dressed whole
Court bouillon
½ cup potted lobster,
    or 1 3½-ounce can lobster paste
4 ounces cream cheese
Pinch cayenne

Court Bouillon:
1 bottle (26 ounces) dry red table wine
A few sprigs of parsley
1 bay leaf
1 medium onion, sliced
2 to 3 carrots, sliced
1 lemon, sliced
Dash sugar
A few peppercorns
1 teaspoon salt

Remove the eyes, leaving the head and tail on the dressed salmon. (Arctic char, lake trout, Dolly Varden, or other trout of similar size may also be used.) Trim the fatty parts around the cavity. Wrap the whole fish in wet cheesecloth, trussing if desired or necessary to fit the kettle. If the fish is excessively fatty, parboil it (see Poaching in Court Bouillon under "Poaching" in Chapter 8).

Put all the ingredients for the court bouillon in a deep kettle or roasting pan. Add 1 quart of water, bring to a boil, reduce the heat, and simmer for 1 hour. Cool the bouillon.

Carefully place the wrapped salmon in the cold court bouillon. If it's necessary to curl the untrussed fish, let the tail take an upward curve. Add enough water to cover the fish. Bring to a boil, then cover the pot, reduce the heat, and simmer gently for 1 to 1½ hours, depending on the size of the fish, until the flesh flakes to a fork — or allow 10 minutes per inch of thickness at the thickest part of the fish. Remove the pot from the heat, and let it rest for 10 minutes. Skim off the oily liquid from the surface. Transfer the fish to a platter and let it cool in the wrap. Remove the wrap, taking the skin, but leaving the head and tail intact. Gently scrape away the residual skin film with the back of a knife.

Blend the lobster and the cream cheese and cayenne into a smooth paste. If necessary, thin with sour cream.

Arrange the salmon on a large china or highly polished silver platter or tray. Put red cherries in the eyes and a wedge of lemon in the mouth. Spread the lobster-cheese mixture over the exposed flesh of the fish. Decorate with slices of hard-boiled egg and black olives, covering the seam at head and tail where spread meets skin. Garnish the platter with deviled eggs topped with a bit of anchovy, tomatoes stuffed with shrimp salad, and/or asparagus tips. Cucumber slices, radishes, black olives, and lemon wedges may be used to support the tail of the fish.

BIG TROUTS (9 POUNDS AND UP)

The big trouts, 9 pounds and up, may include the chinook, chum, coho and Atlantic salmons, Arctic char, lake trout, and inconnu. Whole or in part, these big ones may be baked or poached in a court bouillon, parboiling very fat fish first. They make great chowders, and take well to salting and/or smoking. Center cuts are at their best steaked or chunked and broiled (see Swordfish recipes).

Barbecue-Smoked Lake Trout

A large kettle-type charcoal barbecue with a hood is required for this preparation. Fill a tub (10 gallons at least) with hardwood chips—cherry, apple, pear, hickory, oak, maple, or any other unpainted hardwoods. Cover the chips with water and soak overnight. The next day, fire the entire area of the barbecue with charcoal briquettes, two layers deep; burn until all are white hot or beginning to build up ash.

Meanwhile prepare a 12- to 15-pound lake trout or other king-size fish. Dress the fish. It will likely be necessary to cut off the head and tail to fit the fish into the barbecue. Scrape the skin and cut off the fatty tissue from around the cavity, and remove the strip of fat along the backbone. Wash and wipe dry. Rub the cavity with lemon and sprinkle the fish with salt, pepper, and nutmeg (or any spices you wish) inside and out. Into the cavity tuck a sliced onion, a sliced green pepper and/or green tomato, and a few branches of fresh fennel, dill, savory, or parsley. Lay a piece of heavy-duty aluminum foil, a little larger than the fish, on the barbecue rack, and lay the fish on top of it; fold up the edges of the foil to form a pan to contain the juices.

Back to the barbecue: Remove the chips from the tub, shake off excess water, and spread the chips directly on the hot coals, smothering them entirely. This makes beautiful moist smoke. Position the rack with the fish on the barbecue over the chips. Close the cover and keep it closed—don't peek too often. (If there's no breeze, you may have to do a bit of fanning through the vents in the bottom to encourage the coals during cooking.)

A 15-pound trout takes about 3 hours to cook, about 30 minutes for each inch of thickness at the thickest part of the dressed fish. After 2 hours, look in and test it. The fish is done when the flesh flakes to a fork. Better still, before cooking, insert a meat thermometer in the thick shoulder area and cook to 140° F (60° C). When the fish is done, remove the stuffing, carve, and serve from the rack with barbecued stuffed ripe or green tomatoes and a salad. (Put tomatoes in with the fish for the last ½ hour of cooking.)

Any big fish may be smoke-cooked in this manner. Lean fishes like walleye require larding: Tuck about ¼ pound of butter in chunks in the cavity, oil the fish well all over, and lay a few thin strips of bacon on top of it.

—Lorene Wilson
Scarboro Rod and Gun Club
Scarborough, Ontario

Weakfish

Weakfish, known locally as gray weakfish, squeteague, and yellowfin, is a member of the drum family. It averages 1½ to 4 pounds, although it can go to 10 or more. On the fatty side, the flesh of weakfish is quite perishable, and the fish should be cleaned and iced as quickly as possible. Scaled, or filleted and skinned, it has a fine, delicate flavor and is excellent baked, poached, or pan-fried according to any of the basic methods in Chapter 8. Recipes for trouts of comparable size may also be used for weakfish.

Weakfish in White Wine

2 2-pound weakfish, dressed and scaled
Lemon juice
Salt
Parsley
Bouquet garni
1 small onion, thinly sliced
½ cup dry white wine
Butter
Velouté Sauce (see Chapter 11)

Preheat the oven to 350° F (175° C). Wipe the dressed fish with a damp cloth, and rub the cavity with lemon juice and salt. Tuck a few sprigs of parsley inside. Place in a well-buttered baking dish with a *bouquet garni* of thyme, fennel, parsley, summer savory, and dill (or any herbs you fancy) and onion. Pour the wine over the fish. Dab with butter, cover with aluminum foil, and bake for about 25 minutes, or until the flesh flakes to a fork. Transfer the fish to a heated platter and keep warm.

Make Velouté Sauce, using the juices from the fish and an extra dash of wine as part of the liquid. Remove the parsley from the cavity of the fish. Garnish the platter with fresh parsley or fresh fennel, and serve the sauce on the side in a gravy boat. *4 servings.*

Yellowtail

Yellowtail, a member of the jack family (which also includes the Florida pompano on the East Coast), is common around Los Angeles County and the upper Baja California. A big beautiful fish, the yellowtail is probably famed more for its spirit on the end of a line than for its merits on the table. Californians bake, broil, or smoke it.

Baked California Yellowtail

1 pound yellowtail fillets, skinned
2 tablespoons butter
½ cup water
1 tablespoon Worcestershire sauce
Savory salt, thyme, and tarragon to taste
1 onion, thinly sliced
2 tomatoes, thinly sliced
12 asparagus tips, fresh cooked or canned
Parmesan cheese
1 cup mild barbecue sauce

Preheat the oven to 350° F (175° C). Wash the fillets, and dry with paper towels. Cut into serving portions.

In a glass, flame- and oven-proof dish, melt the butter over a medium heat on top of the stove, and sauté the fish in it for 1 to 2 minutes on each side. Add the water, Worcestershire sauce, and seasonings. Place overlapping slices of onion and tomato on top of the fish, and crown with asparagus tips. Sprinkle Parmesan cheese over everything and pour on the barbecue sauce. Cover and bake for 15 to 20 minutes, or until the fish flakes to a fork. *2 to 4 servings.*

LEAN FISHES

Following are some favorite North American recipes for lean fishes. They may be adapted to other species of similar size, cut, and texture. Refer to the table listing representative edible fishes in Chapter 8.

Carp

A fish esteemed by emperors of the ancient world, carp has not earned the general high regard on the North American table that it has enjoyed in other areas of civilization. Indeed, many regret that the fish was ever introduced to this continent. A muddy bottom feeder, the carp's untidy habits have been considered detrimental to the habitat for more desirable fishes and the cause of the disappearance of wild rice from some Ontario lakes. Certainly its habits are not conducive to fine flavor in fish.

However, with proper preparation carp still provide the excellent, coarse-grained fish flesh enjoyed by kings of old and North Americans of European tradition today, who keep carp alive in fresh water for days to rid the fish of its muddy taste. Carp angled from fresh, clear lake waters should present no flavor problem if killed, dressed, and skinned immediately, then cooked in a court bouillon by an aromatic moist-heat method (see "Poaching" in Chapter 8). Carp make excellent soups and stews, being also a favorite for gefilte fish. Though a lean fish, carp smoke well.

Fisherman's Carp Stew

This recipe is adapted from a Mediterranean fisherman's stew called taillevent. Literally, a four-cornered mainsail, in the old French idiom *taillevent* meant a well-fed person. For that reason, it was the nickname given a famous 14th-century French chef who made a right hearty fish stew.

> 1 fresh carp, 3 to 4 pounds or more
> Salt and pepper
> 1 lemon
> ¼ cup olive oil
> 4 large onions, sliced
> 1 clove garlic, crushed
> 1 large green pepper, cut in rings
> ½ cup fresh herbs (parsley, thyme,
>   summer savory, etc.), crushed
> 4 firm ripe tomatoes, sliced
> 1 cup white wine

Fillet and skin the carp. Tie the head, tail, and bones in cheesecloth and put in a deep saucepan. Cover with 4 to 5 cups of water, add a little salt and pepper, and squeeze in half the lemon. Squeeze the other lemon half over the fillets and let stand. Throw both lemon rinds into the saucepan, bring to a gentle boil, and cook for about 1 hour. Remove the bag of trimmings and lemon rinds, and boil the stock down to about 2 cups and reserve.

Heat the olive oil in a large iron skillet or Dutch oven. Add the onion, garlic, pepper rings, and herbs. Sauté until the onion is translucent. Remove the vegetables with a slotted spoon and discard the garlic.

Cut the fillets in chunks and add to the hot oil in the pan. Cook lightly until the fish just begins to turn color. Return the cooked vegetables, add the tomatoes, stock, and wine. Test and adjust for seasonings. Cover tightly and cook over a low heat until the fish flakes to a fork. Serve with garlic bread. *4 servings.*

Catfish

In a little booklet, *Country Catfish*, put out by the U.S. Department of Commerce, this favorite fish of the American South is described as having "an unusual appearance." That's putting it kindly. One suspects that the downright homeliness of the catfish has much to do with its lack of popularity in other areas of North America. But the beauty of this fine and plentiful fish is under the skin. There lies the firm sweet flesh that has given catfish a prominent place in southern cookery and has earned it such respect in the South that parks, streams, and other points of interest—not to mention sports' notables and numerous small boys—have been named after it.

Of the many fine ways to cook catfish, probably the most famous is the southern fish fry of catfish and hush puppies.

Tar Heel Catfish and Hush Puppies

This recipe is for whole fish of about 1 pound—one fish per serving. Larger fish may be filleted and prepared by the same method.

> 6 catfish, pan-dressed and skinned
> ½ cup evaporated milk
> 1 teaspoon salt
> 1 cup flour
> ½ cup yellow corn meal
> Pepper to taste
> 2 teaspoons paprika
> 12 slices bacon
> Hush Puppies (see Chapter 11)

Thaw fish if frozen. Wash the dressed catfish and pat dry between towels. Combine the milk and salt in a soup plate. Combine the flour, corn meal, pepper, and paprika in another dish. Dip each fish in the milk and then roll it in the flour mixture, coating it evenly.

Fry the bacon in a heavy pan until crisp, remove, and drain on absorbent paper. Fry the fish in the hot bacon fat for 4 minutes. Turn carefully and fry the other side for 4 to 6 minutes, or until the fish is brown or flakes easily to a fork. Drain on absorbent paper. Serve hot with the bacon and hush puppies and cole slaw on the side. *6 servings.*

Creole Catfish Gumbo

> 1 pound skinned catfish fillets
> ¼ cup melted fat or cooking oil
> ½ cup chopped celery
> ½ cup coarsely chopped green pepper
> ½ cup coarsely slivered onion
> 2 cloves garlic, finely chopped
> 1 teaspoon brown sugar
> 2 cups fish stock (see Basic Fish Stock
>   in Chapter 8), or 2 beef bouillon cubes
>   dissolved in 2 cups boiling water
> 4 or 5 firm ripe tomatoes
>   or 1 20-ounce can tomatoes
> 1 10-ounce package frozen okra, sliced
> 2 teaspoons salt
> ¼ teaspoon pepper
> ¼ teaspoon thyme
> 1 bay leaf
> 1 tablespoon lemon juice
> Dash hot pepper sauce
> 1½ cups hot cooked rice

Cut the fish into 1-inch chunks.

Sauté the celery, green pepper, onion, and garlic in hot oil until tender. Sprinkle sugar over the vegetables. Add the fish stock, tomatoes, okra, seasonings, lemon juice, and sauce. Cover and simmer for 30 minutes. Add the fish. Cover and simmer for 15 minutes longer, or until the fish flakes to a fork. Remove bay leaf.

Place ¼ cup of rice in each of 6 soup bowls. Fill with gumbo and serve. *4 to 6 servings.*

Codfishes

The codfish family includes the cods of the Atlantic and Pacific — but not Alaska black cod (sablefish) or lingcod — as well as cusk, haddock, hakes, pollocks, tomcod, and the freshwater burbot, or ling. Scrod is the young codfish.

The recipes given here for the Atlantic and Pacific cods are applicable to other species of the family of the same size or cut.

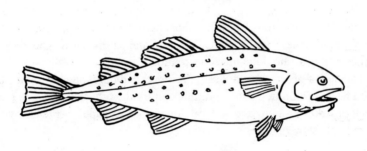

ATLANTIC COD AND PACIFIC COD

Cod is unlike other fish, say the cod experts. Called the "beef of the sea," its flesh is rich and gelatinous without being fatty. The cod is a predaceous feeder, and its flesh is firm of texture and fine of flavor. It lends itself not only to all methods of cooking but also to efficient salt and smoke cures. The cod's unique propensity to rehydrating was considered most valuable in the early days when shipping of fish was dependent on salting.

Shediac Bay Codfish Bake
1 good friend
1 rowboat
Jigging tackle
1 cooler, half full of crushed ice,
   half full of beer
1 midsummer afternoon on the bay

Jig contentedly, replacing the beer with cod. That done, head for home. Clean the fish. Select one of about 4 pounds and set it aside on ice. Freeze or distribute the remainder among your neighbors. Bake your cod.

Scale the dressed cod, and cut out the gills. Wash the fish and pat it dry between towels. Stuff it with a bread dressing (see Basic Stuffing in Chapter 11), well seasoned with summer savory fresh from the garden, and sew it up. Rub the cod with lots of butter and put it in a baking pan. Add a little water, a half cup of white wine, a handful of summer savory, and a few slices of onion to the bottom of the pan. Cover and bake in a 400° F (205° C) oven for about 30 minutes. Remove the cover, baste the fish from the pan, and let it brown until the flesh flakes. If you like, make a sauce from the drippings and serve it hot. *4 servings.*

—Clorice Landry
Shediac Bay, New Brunswick

Cod au Gratin

1 pound fresh cod fillets
(or freshened salt cod)
2 cups Cream Sauce (see Chapter 11)
Trace tarragon (optional)
½ cup grated cheddar cheese
Dry, browned bread crumbs

Thaw the fillets if frozen, and wipe with paper towels. Poach the fillets in salted water (see "Poaching" in Chapter 8).

Preheat the oven to 425° F (220° C).

Prepare medium-thick Cream Sauce, adding tarragon if desired, and into the hot sauce mix half of the cheese until it's melted and evenly blended. Break the cooked fillets into chunks and arrange them in a casserole. Pour the sauce over the fish. Mix the remaining cheese with the bread crumbs and sprinkle over the top. Bake for about 10 minutes, until nicely browned. Don't overcook. *4 servings.*

Soup to Take Sailing

This seafood soup may be made a day or so ahead, and frozen for travel.

3 or 4 pounds fresh cod, haddock,
or cusk, dressed
2 medium potatoes
½ pound salt pork, diced
1 onion, chopped
1 pint of fresh shucked clams and juice
1 pint of fresh peeled shrimp (optional)
2 12-ounce cans evaporated milk
Salt and freshly ground pepper to taste

Cover the dressed fish with water. Bring to a boil, skim, and reduce the heat. Simmer until the flesh flakes. Remove the fish and reserve the stock. Dice and cook the potatoes separately and drain them.

Brown the salt pork in a Dutch oven along with the onion. Strip the meat from the fish, breaking it into chunks and removing any bones, and put it in the Dutch oven, along with the potatoes and reserved stock. Add the clams (if fresh ones are not available, use a couple of small cans of baby clams with their juice) and the shrimp, if desired. Stir in the evaporated milk and heat the soup, but don't let it boil. Taste-test along the way and add salt and pepper to taste.

Let the soup cool off, and then pour it into a plastic bowl and freeze it hard. Wrap it up and take it aboard the boat. If the soup is stored in the galley fridge, by the next day it will be thawed enough to heat in a saucepan—but don't let it boil.

—Mrs. Ross McKenzie
Halifax, Nova Scotia

Fried Cod Tongues

1 pound fresh cod tongues
1 tablespoon strained fresh lemon juice
¾ cup flour
½ teaspoon salt
A few grains black pepper
¼ pound lean salt pork, with rind removed,
  cut into ¼-inch dice

Put the cod tongues in a sieve or colander and wash under cold running water. (Cheeks and jowl or throat may be included, also.) Pat dry with paper towels. Sprinkle evenly with lemon juice. Combine the flour, salt, and pepper in a large paper bag and set aside. In a heavy skillet, fry the salt pork over moderate heat until crisp and brown. Discard the dice. Drop the cod tongues into the flour mixture and shake the bag vigorously to coat well. Shake the excess flour off the tongues and fry uncovered, over moderately low heat, for about 10 minutes on each side or until they're delicately browned. Drain the tongues briefly on paper towels and serve at once from a heated platter. *4 servings.*

BURBOT (LING)

Ling is the popular name for the burbot (not to be confused with turbot), a freshwater cod occurring in abundance through the border states northward. It usually runs 3 to 5 pounds, but has been known to grow to 40 pounds in the north, where it is called loche.

Unprepossessing in appearance at any time, the ling in summer has a characteristic muddy taste and soft flesh. Since the ling is a late-winter spawner, it is at its vigorous best during the ice-fishing season. Then the flesh is firm and the muddy taste is minimal—any there may be can be eliminated by prompt dressing and skinning.

The loin, or upper fillet, of the ling is a delicacy and may be prepared according to recipes for fillets of cod, flounder, or any other fine lean fish. Ling makes a great chowder (see Chapter 10). Ling has a very rich, oily liver, which was much prized by upper Great Lakes' commercial fishermen in earlier days.

Dolphin

The dolphin is a favorite of sportsmen and epicures along the Atlantic Coast, and along the Pacific, where it is known by its Hawaiian name, *mahi-mahi.*

Dolphins yield 5 to 10 pounds of firm flesh, on the lean side but rich. Delicious in flavor, dolphin is best cooked simply, according to the basic methods for lean fish of its size. Red snapper, flounder, freshwater pike, and walleye recipes may be used for dolphin.

Island Mahi-Mahi

4 dolphin steaks, 1 generous inch thick,
  or skinned fillets
½ cup butter
Worcestershire sauce
½ lemon
Heaping tablespoon freshly chopped parsley
Hollandaise sauce

Preheat the oven to 375° F (190° C). Wipe the fish with a damp cloth. Make lemon-parsley butter: Melt the butter over moderate heat. Add a dash of Worcestershire sauce, squeeze in the juice from the lemon, and stir in the chopped parsley.

Brush the steaks with some of the warm melted butter mixture. Place the steaks in a hinged, well-oiled grill or wire toaster and put under the broiler. Quickly broil both sides until the fish shows grill marks—just enough to sear well. If broiling over charcoal, put the steaks directly on the greased grill.

Arrange the pieces in one layer in a heated, well-buttered oven-to-table shallow baking dish. Pour the butter mixture over the fish. Bake for about 8 to 10 minutes, until the flesh flakes to a fork, spooning butter from the pan over the fish once or twice during that time. Garnish with lemon wedges and parsley sprigs. Serve at once with Hollandaise sauce. *4 servings.*

—Marty McCombs
The Warehouse
Marina del Rey, California

Flounders

The flounder family, including the flounders (flukes), halibut, plaice, soles, and turbot, accounts for many of the world's most valuable fisheries. Flounders come in sizes from a few inches to 10 feet long. All are lean and quite bony. Their white flesh has a fine flavor and a delicate and—in some species—a fragile texture. Within a size range, recipes for various flounders are interchangeable.

SUMMER FLOUNDER AND WINTER FLOUNDER

Summer flounder and winter flounder are also known as fluke or plaice. The common catch inshore and in the bays is around 2 to 5 pounds, perhaps larger. The flesh is superb, though bony, and is well worth the trouble of filleting. Poached, steamed, or baked by simple basic methods and served with a fine sauce, fresh flounder is a dish of elegance. It pan-fries beautifully.

Fillets of Flounder with Mushrooms
2 pounds boneless flounder fillets
½ cup butter
2 or 3 thin slices onion
2 cups sliced mushrooms
3 green pepper rings
2 pimento pepper rings
Salt and white pepper
1 tablespoon lemon juice
2 cups dry white wine
¼ cup flour
½ cup cream
Dash cayenne
A few fresh chives, chopped
1 hard-boiled egg, sliced
4 or 5 black olives, sliced

If frozen, thaw the fillets in refrigerator. (Halibut, red snapper, dolphin, pike, and walleye also may be cooked by this recipe.) Preheat the oven to 375° F (190° C).

Grease a large baking pan with *half* the butter. Spread the onion slices, mushrooms, and pepper rings on the bottom of the pan. Place the fish on the vegetables, salt and pepper lightly, and drizzle the lemon juice, wine, and 1 cup of water over the fish. Closely cover with foil and poach in the oven for 15 to 25 minutes. (The cooking time can be affected by the length of time it takes the dish to heat, so prod the flesh with a fork after 15 minutes to see if it flakes.) Carefully remove the fish to a heated serving platter and keep it warm.

Melt the remaining butter in another saucepan, and blend in the flour, stirring until it bubbles. Reduce the broth from the baking pan by half, strain (reserving the vegetables), and stir into the roux. Cook until thickened. Blend in the cream and cayenne and let the sauce heat through. Add salt and pepper to taste. Add the strained mushrooms and onion, and pour the sauce over the fillets. Garnish with chives, slices of hard-boiled egg, sliced black olives, and the pepper rings if they aren't too limp. *4 to 6 servings.*

HALIBUT

Halibut is a highly prized table fish on both the East and West coasts, and it commands the highest price of the flatfishes in inland markets. The halibut most commonly taken by sportsmen are relatively small, about 5 to 10 pounds, which is the finest table size. The glossy white flesh of the predatory halibut is firm and flavorful. Halibut are filleted or steaked. Either way, they are best cooked simply and are splendid deep-fried in beer batter.

Poached Halibut de Pesca
4 10-ounce halibut fillets, skinned
2 medium potatoes, peeled and quartered
2 bay leaves
1 teaspoon pickling spice
¼ teaspoon salt
¼ teaspoon monosodium glutamate
3 ounces olive oil
1 teaspoon chopped parsley
1 lemon
Freshly ground pepper

If frozen, thaw fillets in refrigerator until they're soft enough to separate. (Red snapper, whitefish, trout, or salmon may be used instead of halibut.) Rinse fillets under cold water, and pat dry between towels.

In a large, deep skillet, bring 1 quart of water to a boil. Add the potatoes, spices, salt, and MSG, and boil for 5 minutes over medium heat. Add the fish. Reduce the heat and simmer for 10 minutes or until the fish flakes to a fork. Remove the fish and potatoes to individual plates or a large shallow casserole (heated). Pour the olive oil over the fish and potatoes. Sprinkle with the parsley and douse generously with lemon juice and fresh pepper. Serve with butter, and half a lemon wrapped in cheesecloth. For a colorful presentation, serve with baby carrots and creamed spinach on the side. *4 servings.*

—Tod Ghio
Anthony's Fish Grottos
San Diego, California

Homeric Fish and Chips
1½ to 2 pounds halibut fillets
1 cup Bisquick
1 bottle beer

Cut halibut into approximately 2-inch cubes.

Add enough beer to the Bisquick to make a thick batter. Make more as needed. Dip the halibut in batter and let dry for about 1 hour. Fry 5 or 6 pieces at a time in hot, deep fat for about 2 minutes, or until golden brown. (Drink remaining beer while you wait for fish to be ready to fry.)

Serve with French-fried potatoes.

—Homer Homemakers
Cooking Up a Storm in Homer, Alaska

SOLES

More pages of cookery seem to have been written under the title *Sole* than any other basic item of food, except perhaps sauces. The extensive mileage appears to be the result of countless permutations and combinations of soles, basic cookery methods, and sauces.

Actually, the best of the North American table soles are not of the true sole fraternity, but are right-handed flounders—that is, their eyes are on the right side. Most plentiful on the West Coast, these are the butter sole, Dover, petrale (brill), English (lemon), rex, and rock soles, as well as the diamond turbot. The winter flounder and witch flounder of the Atlantic are also right-eyed flounders; the delicate flesh of these small fish is comparable to that of the fine soles, and they are cooked by the same recipes. In fact, both are also called gray sole. Summer flounder or fluke, in the same cookery class, is left-eyed and a little bigger than the winter flounder. For that matter, the term *sole* is applied rather loosely to many small members of the flounder family.

Small soles may be pan-dressed and cooked whole; large ones are filleted and skinned like other flounders. Delicate in flavor and texture, the soles should be cooked by the simplest of methods and handled tenderly. Pan-fry *à la meunière* or quickly sauté and finish in the oven, with one of the many fine white or cream sauces for fish. Sole is excellent gently poached or steamed, and served with a sauce. It is superb deep-fried in a crisp batter. Create your own combination and add to the list. Whatever you do with sole, don't overcook it. Garnish sole dishes with an eye to color.

Dutch Sole with Bananas

This recipe from Holland was contributed by Betty Van der Ree of The Taste Guild, Inc., Toronto, to my earlier book *Fish Cookery of North America*. It has since been found to be superb for fillets of freshwater walleye.

4 thick fillets of sole
Seasoned flour
Clarified butter (see Glossary)
2 to 3 firm yellow bananas
2 ounces cognac
½ cup slivered almonds (or macadamia nuts)
Lemon juice

Wipe the fillets with a damp cloth and dust with the seasoned flour. Melt the butter to about a ½-inch depth in the pan. Cook the fillets quickly in the butter, then carefully transfer them to a heated oblong fish-baking dish. Lay a piece of aluminum foil over the top, and place the dish in a warm oven. Peel and split the bananas in half, then quarter each piece. Dust lightly with flour. In the same hot butter used to cook the fish, brown the bananas until golden all over, turning them gently. Arrange the bananas over the fish in the oven.

Warm the cognac by pouring it into a small pitcher and letting it rest a minute or two in a bowl of hot water. Brown the nuts in the remaining hot butter. Remove the fish from the oven and sprinkle the nuts on top. Season lightly with lemon juice. Pour the warm cognac over the fish, ignite, and bring the flaming feast to the table. *4 servings.*

Poached Fillet of Sole Florentine

1½ to 2 pounds sole fillets
Salt
Juice of ½ lemon, or ½ cup white wine
2 pounds fresh spinach,
    or 2 10-ounce packages frozen
2 cups Bechamel Sauce (see Chapter 11)
3 tablespoons white wine
½ cup grated cheddar or Romano cheese

Preheat the oven to 375° F (190° C). Wash, dry, and cut the fillets into serving portions. Poach the fish (see "Poaching" in Chapter 8), adding the lemon juice or white wine.

Meanwhile, wash and cook the spinach lightly in a tightly covered pot with only the water clinging to it. When barely tender, drain and chop coarsely. Spread over the bottom of a buttered, shallow, oven-to-table baking pan.

Make Bechamel Sauce as directed. Blend in the 3 tablespoons of wine. Add the cheese, saving a little to sprinkle over the top later. Stir until melted and evenly blended. Keep hot over hot water, stirring now and then.

Place the poached fish on the spinach, pour the sauce on top, and sprinkle with remaining cheese. Bake until bubbly and gold, about 15 minutes, or put under the broiler until browned. *4 servings.*
This recipe is also excellent for walleye or other lean, white-fleshed fish.

Largemouth Bass and Smallmouth Bass

The most popular freshwater game basses, the largemouth and smallmouth, are not basses at all but belong to the sunfish family. Distributed widely over North America, they are known by a profusion of local names.

Generally weighing 2 to 4 pounds, these lean, scrappy gamefishes have excellent firm flesh. The skin may have a bitter taste, especially in the largemouth, and for this reason the fish is usually filleted and skinned, and then pan-fried or baked according to the basic methods for lean fish. Larger bass make magnificent soups and chowders (see Chapter 10).

Baked Fillets of Bass in Lime Juice and Sour Cream
> 2 pounds bass fillets, skinned
> 1 large lime
> ½ pint sour cream
> Salt and pepper

Preheat oven to 350° F (175° C). Arrange the fillets in a buttered baking dish. Squeeze the juice from the lime and grate the rind. Season the sour cream with salt and pepper to taste and mix in the lime juice. Pour over the fish and sprinkle the top with grated lime rind. Bake in preheated oven for about 30 minutes, or until the fish flakes to a fork.

> —Kathryn Tucker Windham
> *Treasured Alabama Recipes*

Nassau Grouper

One of the family of sea basses, the Nassau grouper is about the most popular sport and food fish around the Florida coasts, where it is called simply grouper. The general catch is about 5 to 15 pounds. Steaked or filleted, grouper is best skinned. It is excellent deep-fried and in chowders (see Chapter 10). Recipes for other lean fishes of comparable size may be used for grouper.

Psari Plaki (Nassau Grouper in Red Sauce)

A traditional dish of the Greek community around Tarpon Springs, Florida, *psari plaki* may vary in content and method according to the cook. The following is a specialty of Louis Pappas, as it is prepared for the Pappas Restaurant in Tarpon Springs or for the family. Freshly caught grouper from local waters is Louis Pappas' choice, though mullet, red snapper, mackerel, lake whitefish, pike, and bass (freshwater and stripers) may be used instead.

> 2 to 3 pounds grouper fillets or steaks
> Salt
> Olive oil
> Lemon juice
>
> *Red Sauce:*
> ¼ cup olive oil
> ¼ cup finely minced garlic
> 2 onions, sliced
> 1 bell pepper, diced
> 2 medium carrots, diced
> 2 stalks celery, diced
> 2 cups canned tomatoes,
>   or 6 or more peeled ripe tomatoes
> 1 cup hot water
> 2 tablespoons tomato paste
> ½ teaspoon each oregano, basil, fresh parsley,
>   fresh chopped chives
> 1 teaspoon freshly ground black pepper
> Salt to taste

Wash the fish and cut it into serving portions. Salt it well, put it into a strainer, and let it drain for 10 minutes. Brush with olive oil and place in an oven-to-table baking dish. Dribble a little lemon juice over the fish. Cover and refrigerate while making the sauce.

Preheat the oven to 350° F (175° C).

Heat the olive oil in a deep saucepan. Add the garlic and onions and cook for about 5 minutes. Add the diced pepper, carrots, and celery. Sauté gently for about 15 minutes. Add the tomatoes, hot water, tomato paste, and seasonings, and blend well. Bring to a boil, then reduce the heat, cover, and cook gently until the vegetables are mushy and the stock is quite thick. Purée by pushing the mixture through a sieve or potato ricer, or process in a blender until smooth. Keep over hot water until needed.

Put the baking dish into the hot oven just long enough for the fish to heat through and firm up —about 10 minutes. Pour the sauce over the fish. Add a little water to the dish to keep the sauce moist. Scatter more sliced onion and thinly sliced tomato over the top. Bake just until the fish flakes to a prod with a fork. *4 to 6 servings.*

Minuta a la Cazulla

Fresh grouper in casserole with shrimp and clams in a wine sauce is a specialty of the Don Quixote Restaurant in Ybor City near Tampa, Florida. A family operation, the relatively small restaurant is noted for its Spanish cuisine. Chef Maria Zapico uses grouper in the following recipe, but says that any fine white-fleshed fish, such as flounder, halibut, or walleye, may be used with excellent results as long as it's fresh.

> 1½ to 2 pounds grouper fillets, cut into chunks
> 4 live clams, scrubbed
> 16 shrimp, peeled and deveined
>
> *Sauce:*
> 2 tablespoons olive oil
> 8 to 10 cloves of garlic, finely minced
> 1 or 2 small hot red peppers, seeded and minced
> 2 tablespoons flour
> 1½ cups chicken stock
> 2 to 3 tablespoons sherry

First make the sauce: Heat the olive oil in a deep saucepan, add the garlic and pepper, and sauté lightly. Add the flour and stir until bubbly; then pour in the chicken stock, and continue stirring until the sauce is smoothly thickened. It should be medium-thick. Stir in the sherry. Simmer for about 10 minutes, stirring frequently.

Add the fish fillets to the sauce. Cover and cook gently for 10 minutes, moving the fish around in the sauce occasionally to keep it from sticking. Add the clams (in the shell) and cook for 5 minutes, then add the shrimp and cook for 5 minutes more. By this time the fish should be flaky and the clams opened.

Serve in 4 small, deep bowls, dividing evenly, 4 shrimp per bowl, and crown each serving with a clam. Top with freshly cooked green peas. Garnish with asparagus tips, a slice or two of hard-boiled egg, and bits of pimento.

[248]

Northern Pike

Northern pike, also called great northern or just pike, can grow to 40 pounds or more. Those of 6 to 8 pounds and less are best for the table, though the bigger pikes make fine stews and chowders.

Pike is cooked by basic methods for lean fish. The flesh has an excellent flavor, and fine texture according to size. The fish is very bony, making filleting a tricky operation but worth the trouble. Fillets of pike simply baked under a winy cream sauce and served with colorful fresh vegetables make a superb meal. (Pike are salt-cured to preserve the catch, taking care of the bone problem at the same time.)

Fillets of Northern Pike with Wine Sauce
4 pounds pike fillets
½ cup flour, seasoned with salt and pepper
3 tablespoons cooking oil
¾ cup chopped onion
½ cup peeled, chopped tomatoes
½ cup dry white wine
½ cup sautéed sliced mushrooms
2 tablespoons chopped parsley

Roll the fish in the seasoned flour. Sauté the fillets and onion in hot oil until they are browned on both sides and flake easily. Remove the fish to a heated platter and keep warm.

Add the tomatoes and wine to the onions in the skillet and cook 5 minutes. Stir in the mushrooms and parsley. Heat through. Pour the sauce over the fish, sprinkle with parsley, and serve. *6 to 8 servings.*

—Jean Power
Beaverton, Ontario

Panfishes

The panfishes are those tasty *little* sportfishes too small to be considered gamefish and small enough to fit into a frying pan. They are usually well under 1 pound. For cooking purposes, small gamefishes of "keeper" length may be considered panfish if they fit the pan.

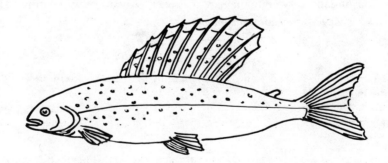

As said earlier, the group includes lean and fatty fish. Hence the panfishes here include the small herrings, cods and scrods, whitings, grunts, snappers, butterfish, and flyingfishes, as well as the surf-perches, the freshwater perches of the temperate bass family, the basses of the sunfish family (which includes the pumpkinseed, bream, crappies, and bluegills), the perch family itself, and the pickerels of the pike family. Brown bullheads (mudcat, mudpout, catfish, madtom) may be considered pan-fishes if they fit the pan. The fatty rainbow smelts are dealt with separately, earlier in this chapter.

Such small fish are very perishable. The essence of their goodness is in their freshness. They require prompt, on-the-spot cleaning and cooling, followed by cooking or freezing. For more on panfish, see Pan Frying under "Frying" in Chapter 8.

Dilled Panfish

6 pan-dressed panfish, fresh or frozen
Salt and pepper
½ cup clarified butter or margarine
 (see Glossary), or cooking oil
1 tablespoon crushed dillweed,
 preferably fresh, or dill seed
Juice of 1 lemon

If frozen, thaw the fish in the refrigerator. Wash fish in cold water and pat dry between towels. Cut through the ribs to one side of the backbone and flatten the fish. Sprinkle with salt and pepper. Melt the butter in a frying pan. Add the dill and heat until the butter bubbles. (Capers or wild sorrel may be substituted for the dill.)

Fry 2 or 3 fish at a time, depending on pan space. Place the fish flesh-side down in the hot butter and fry for 2 or 3 minutes until lightly browned, turn the fish and continue frying until the flesh flakes, another 2 or 3 minutes. Lift to a warm serving platter and keep warm while frying the rest of the fish. When all have been cooked, turn the heat under the pan to low and stir the lemon juice into the dilled butter. Pour over the fish and serve at once.

Perch

Perch are generally dropped into that catchall of small fishes called panfish (see above) and fried without further thought—and very good they are that way. However this plentiful little cousin of the highly esteemed walleye rates more imaginative treatment.

Mrs. Sweeney's Salt-Fried Perch

I cook other fish—whitefish, trout, or bass—like this, but, oh, those fresh, sweet little perch, they're the best.

—Mae Sweeney
Thessalon, Ontario

Clean a dozen or so freshly caught perch, cut off the heads, and skin the fish. Wash in cold water, and drain between towels on a tray. Spread a layer of fish over the bottom of an earthen or glass bowl large enough to accommodate a few layers of fish. Don't use metal. Sprinkle the fish generously with salt, add another layer of fish, more salt, and so on, until all the fish are in the bowl; finish with a layer of salt. Cover the bowl with a plate and refrigerate it for at least 12 hours.

When you're ready to cook the fish, take them out of the brine and drain them well in a colander. Don't wash them. Dredge each fish in flour seasoned with black pepper (they're salty enough), and gently shake off the loose flour.

In a large, heavy frying pan, pour enough olive (or corn) oil to come halfway up the fish, and heat it slowly until it's moderately hot. Add the fish, as many at a time as the pan will take without crowding. When one side is done to an even light gold, turn and cook the other side, but only until the color is gold and the flesh flakes to a fork. Drain the cooked fish on thick paper towels and eat them while they're hot.

Red Snapper

The red snapper grows to 30-odd pounds. A superb table fish in any size, it is generally preferred under 10 pounds. A lean fish with firm, rich, delicately flavored flesh, it bakes beautifully. Both head and throat are very gelatinous and much in demand for aspics and chowders. The throat flesh is particularly rich and delicate.

Huachinago Veracruzano (Red Snapper Veracruz Style)

This dish is a favorite throughout Mexico, where it is usually served with boiled potatoes. Red snapper is the traditional fish for this recipe, but any firm white-fleshed fish may be used.

> 6 red snapper fillets (about 2½ to 3 pounds)
> Salt and pepper
> 4 tablespoons fresh lime or lemon juice
>
> *Sauce:*
> 3 cups canned or fresh tomatoes,
>   peeled and diced
> 2 tablespoons cooking oil
> ¾ cup coarsely chopped onions
> 2 cloves garlic, minced
> 3 to 4 pickled jalapeño chilis, seeded,
>   rinsed, and cut into strips
> ¼ cup pimento-stuffed olives, sliced
> 1 teaspoon salt
> Pinch cinnamon
> Pinch cloves

Sprinkle the fish fillets with salt and pepper, brush with lime or lemon juice, and let stand while you prepare the sauce. Mash the tomatoes or purée them in the blender. Heat the oil in a skillet and sauté the onions and garlic until tender and golden. Add the tomatoes and the remaining ingredients and cook gently over moderate heat for about 5 minutes. Place the fish fillets in a greased casserole. Pour on the sauce, cover, and bake in a preheated 350° F (175° C) oven for about 20 to 30 minutes, or until the fish flakes easily with a fork.

To serve, transfer the fish to a heated platter and pour sauce over all. *6 servings.*

—Victor J. Bergeron
Trader Vic's Book of Mexican Cooking

Fairhope-Style Red Snapper
4-pound red snapper, dressed
1 teaspoon salt
Stuffing
1 cup melted butter

Stuffing:
4 tablespoons butter
2 tablespoons chopped celery
4 tablespoons chopped onion
1 bay leaf
1 teaspoon salt
⅓ teaspoon pepper
3 cups cubed stale bread
3 tablespoons chopped cucumbers

Preheat oven to 400° F (205° C). Wipe the fish with a damp cloth and rub inside with 1 teaspoon of salt.

Melt the butter in a heavy skillet. Add the celery, onion, and seasonings and sauté lightly. With a slotted spoon remove vegetables from the skillet and reserve, discarding the bay leaf. Add the bread crumbs to the skillet and toast them in the remaining butter. Return the celery and onion, add the chopped cucumbers, and mix well.

Fill the fish with the stuffing and sew it up. Put the fish in a shallow baking pan and pour the melted butter over it. Bake in preheated hot oven for 45 to 60 minutes or until the flesh flakes to a fork. Baste frequently from the pan while baking.

—Kathryn Tucker Windham
Treasured Alabama Recipes

Walleye and Sauger

The walleye, or doré as it's called in Quebec, is an attractive, succulent fish. Its firm, white, flaky flesh places the lean walleye and its smaller cousin, the sauger, among the most desirable of table fishes.

The sauger, known also as sand pike and sand pickerel, is not the popular gamefish that the walleye is. Although its even more delicate flesh is considered the better by many, others find it too bland.

Both fishes respond to the basic methods for cooking lean, fine fish, either whole or filleted, according to size and recipe. Walleye is superb deep-fried in batter. (See also recipes for sole and flounder.)

Baked Walleye Fillets Amandine

4 2-pound walleyes, filleted and skinned
¼ cup butter or margarine
¼ cup finely minced onion
¼ cup chopped parsley
1 cup sliced mushrooms
2 tablespoons finely sliced almonds
Salt and pepper
¼ cup dry white wine
1 tablespoon flour
½ cup 10% cream
Paprika
Chopped parsley

Preheat the oven to 375° F (190° C). Wash the fillets under cold water, then pat dry between towels. Melt half the butter in a saucepan and gently sauté the onion, parsley, and mushrooms for about 10 minutes, stirring frequently. Add the almonds and mix.

Place 4 of the fillets on the bottom of a large (9 × 14 inches) well-buttered oven-to-table baking dish. Sprinkle lightly with salt and pepper. Spread the sautéed mixture evenly over the fish. Top with the remaining 4 fillets and sprinkle lightly with salt and pepper. Pour the wine on top and dot with the remaining butter. Bake uncovered for 15 minutes, until fish is partly cooked. Remove the fish from the oven, but don't turn off the heat. With a basting syringe or a spoon, draw off as much of the pan liquid as possible and reserve. Keep the pan of fish warm.

Put the flour into a small saucepan and gradually stir in the cream. Mix until smoothly blended. Blend in the reserved pan liquid. Cook slowly, stirring constantly, until thickened. Pour this sauce over the fillets. Return the fish to the oven for about 5 minutes, or until it flakes to a fork. Don't overcook. Sprinkle with paprika and parsley. *4 servings*.

Stuffed Walleye

A 4- to 5-pound walleye (pickerel) is in fine form when stuffed, simply baked, and served with a flourish. This recipe calls for a whole dressed fish of about 5 pounds.

Make Fruity Stuffing with wild rice (see Chapter 11) while the walleye thaws in the refrigerator.

Preheat the oven to 400° F (205° C). Wash the fish under cold running water and pat dry, inside and out, between towels. Remove the eyes, leaving the head, tail, and dorsal fin intact. Rub the cavity with a lemon wedge, squeezing the wedge as you rub. Lightly stuff the fish about ⅔ full (excess stuffing may be baked separately in foil). Sew or lace the edges of the cavity together with strong thread or string and lightly gash the skin at 2- to 3-inch intervals on both sides.

Put a bed of thick onion and carrot slices in the bottom of a baking pan, and arrange the fish on top (the vegetables will act as a rack). Put a candied cherry in the topside eye socket and a cork in the mouth. Combine equal parts of white wine and melted butter. Brush the fish with this mixture and place in the oven. Estimate baking time by allowing 10 minutes for each inch of thickness at the thickest part of the fish, plus an extra 10 minutes. Or insert a meat thermometer into the shoulder behind the gills and bake to a reading of 140° F (60° C).

Baste with the wine-butter mixture from time to time. If the fish starts to brown too quickly, lay a piece of foil over it. About 20 minutes before the end of the cooking period, remove the foil,

COMPLETE FISH AND GAME COOKERY OF NORTH AMERICA

dust the fish very lightly with flour, and baste from the pan. Continue baking until the skin is a crusty gold and the flesh flakes to a fork. Don't overcook. Transfer the fish to a warm serving platter. Take out the cork, and replace with a lemon wedge. Remove lacing and garnish the fish with fresh parsley, lemon wedges, and stuffed green olives or cherry tomatoes. *4 to 6 servings.*

Whitebait

Smaller still than the panfish is a group of fishes generally termed whitebait (bait-size). These are the tiny, little more than 1- or 2-inch long members of the herring family, as well as the anchovies, silversides, whitings, minnows, and the fry of other fishes.

California grunion (a silverside) is one of the more fascinating of the group. In late spring, predictable almost to the hour, the grunion run en masse onto the beaches of southern California to spawn by the light of the moon. During the brief spawning period, it's open season on grunion, but California regulations prohibit the use of any tackle other than one's bare hands and a bucket. Grunion gathering is a popular California sport.

Deep-fried whitebait is an epicurean delight, rare because it is seasonal and the little fishes must be out-of-the-water fresh, and preferably alive.

Deep-Fried Whitebait

Wash the freshly caught fish and pat dry between towels. Put into a bag containing flour, and shake to coat the fish lightly. Place in a small-mesh deep-fry basket. Shake again to remove excess flour. Plunge the basket into deep, hot fat (see "Frying" in Chapter 8) for about 30 seconds, or until the little fish are crisp. Drain on paper towels. Serve hot, heaped on a napkin. Sprinkle generously with salt, and garnish with lemon wedges.

10

More Fish Dishes

From the angler's point of view, much of the merit of many great fish dishes is that they just call for "fish." Any fish, as long as it's edible and fresh, will qualify.

—Anon

The recipes in this chapter, most of which "just call for 'fish'," are arranged for convenience into several groups: soups, stews, chowders, and casseroles; chopped, ground, and flaked fish; pickled and marinated fish; salt-cured fish; and roe.

With the exception of the roes, all the recipes are preparations of fish flesh. Where a recipe mentions a species, it is because the recipe is a specialty of the region where that fish is abundant. It may be used for other species as well.

SOUPS, STEWS, CHOWDERS, AND CASSEROLES

Ocean Reef Chowder

1 fresh grouper, about 5 pounds
1 gallon water
1 tablespoon salt
1 large onion, coarsely chopped
4 whole cloves
1 bay leaf
1 large stalk celery, chopped
1 medium onion, finely chopped
¼ pound butter
1 teaspoon curry powder
½ teaspoon each rosemary, oregano,
  and leaf thyme
1½ cups flour
2 teaspoons monosodium glutamate
Light cream, about 1 quart

Clean the grouper and cut off the head. Skin the fish. Place grouper and head in a large kettle with the water, salt, coarsely chopped onion, cloves, bay leaf, and celery. Bring to a boil, reduce heat to simmer, and cook about 12 minutes, or until fish flakes when pierced with a fork. Take the pot off the heat; strain and reserve stock. Remove fish meat from the bones and cut into bite-size pieces.

Sauté chopped onion in butter in a saucepan until it's tender but not brown. Add the curry powder, rosemary, oregano, thyme, and flour, stirring until smooth. Stir in the strained reserved stock and monosodium glutamate. Stir until smooth, then reduce to a simmer and cook 20 to 25 minutes.

Using one-third as much cream as fish stock, bring the cream to a boil in a separate saucepan. Pour it into the chowder; add the grouper chunks. Reheat and serve at once. Do not boil after adding cream.

Makes 20 servings—enough for a chowder party.

(Tip: Freeze leftover chowder and reheat, but do not boil.)

—Lowis Carlton
Famous Florida Recipes

Checkerboard Chowder

Fish have a way of complementing each other, big and small, lean and fat, red and white, that makes for a great soup. The following could be called an end-of-season freezer-clearance chowder, for that's how it came about. No one knows exactly why it's called checkerboard.

3 to 4 pounds fish fillets, any kind,
   mixed or matched
½ cup olive oil
½ green pepper, diced
1 medium carrot, diced
2 medium onions, diced
3 cloves garlic, minced
20-ounce can tomatoes
1 bay leaf
2 quarts hot water
1 or 2 cans clams and juice,
   or 1 pint fresh shucked clams
1 cup white wine
1 tablespoon lemon juice
¼ cup minced fresh parsley
1 small can pimentos, chopped
1 teaspoon fennel seed
¼ teaspoon freshly ground black pepper
Salt to taste

Thaw the fish in its wrapping in the refrigerator just until you can cut it into chunks. Over a low heat, gently cook the green pepper, carrot, onion, and garlic in the olive oil for about 10 minutes, stirring often. Add the fish, tomatoes, bay leaf, and hot water. Bring to a boil, reduce the heat, and simmer for 20 minutes. Add the remaining ingredients, bring to a boil again, reduce the heat, and simmer for about 30 minutes. A few cooked shrimp may be added if handy.

Put-and-Take Fish Soup

A characteristic of soup-making is that the larger the quantity, the better the soup. This recipe should serve 18 to 20 people. A smaller or larger quantity may be made by adjusting the amounts accordingly.

The flexibility of the following recipe endears it to the camp cook. Packaged dry vegetable flakes or soup mixes may be substituted for the fresh vegetables if necessary. The juice from a bottle of sweet pickles may be used instead of the spices, sugar, and vinegar. Dill pickle juice adds a touch. Add a can of clams and juice if handy, or fresh clams if you're by the seashore.

3 to 4 pounds dressed fish
¼ cup mixed pickling spices
3 or 4 garlic cloves
½ cup butter or margarine
¼ cup bacon fat or cooking oil
1 cup each chopped onion, celery,
  and green pepper
1 teaspoon dried fine herbs
1 teaspoon sugar
2 tablespoons vinegar or lemon juice
2 quarts boiling water
2 19-ounce cans tomatoes
1 48-ounce can tomato juice
½ cup tomato catsup or chili sauce
1½ cups quick-cooking rice
Salt to taste
Dash Tabasco sauce
Worcestershire sauce to taste

Fillet and skin the fish. Cut the fillets into chunks and set them aside. Tie the trimmings (heads, tails, bones, and skin), pickling spices, and garlic securely in cheesecloth.

In a large soup kettle, melt the butter and bacon fat. Add the chopped vegetables and herbs. Sprinkle the sugar on top. Gently stir-cook until the onions are soft. Add the vinegar, boiling water, tomatoes, tomato juice, catsup, and the trimmings bag. Bring to a boil and simmer for about 20 minutes. Stir in the rice and cook gently for another 10 minutes, or until the rice is cooked. Stir the chowder up from the bottom from time to time. Add the fish, then add the salt and Tabasco to taste. Mix in Worcestershire sauce, starting with a scant tablespoonful. Continue to cook gently until the fish flakes to a fork. Test and adjust the seasoning. Remove the trimmings bag and serve.

Fisherman's Stew Cioppino Style

Cioppino is a California coastal fisherman's *bouillabaisse* containing whatever the catch provides. Originating with the early Italian fishermen of San Francisco, the dish has become a traditional seafood preparation down the coast. Subtle seasoning is generally preferred in the Italian cioppinos around San Francisco. The stew takes on a slightly hotter Mexican flavor as it approaches the southern border.

Versions of cioppino are as numerous as the cooks who make it, but on one thing all appear to agree: An authentic cioppino can be made only where fresh seafoods are at your doorstep, especially live crab, which the purists claim is essential to the brew.

The tomato-based stew is highly adaptable to meaty freshwater fishes, such as pike, bass, trouts, and catfish, when combined with quality shellfishes in frozen or canned form available at inland markets. In the following adaptation, varieties and amounts given for shellfishes may be varied according to taste or availability.

2 pounds fish fillets, skinned
1 cup clams, fresh, canned, or frozen
1 cup crabmeat, fresh, canned, or frozen
12 large shrimp, fresh, canned, or frozen
2 tablespoons olive or other salad oil
1 large onion, chopped
1 clove garlic, minced
6 to 8 large ripe tomatoes, or 1 20-ounce
   can tomatoes, chopped; or 1 10-ounce can
   tomato sauce plus 10 ounces water.
2 teaspoons Worcestershire sauce
2 drops Tabasco sauce
1 bay leaf
¼ teaspoon oregano or thyme
1 teaspoon sugar
½ teaspoon salt
Freshly ground pepper to taste
½ cup white wine

If the fish and shellfish are frozen, thaw them in refrigerator until soft. Heat the oil in a Dutch oven or deep kettle and sauté the onion and garlic until the onion is translucent. Add the remaining ingredients (but not the fish and shellfish) and bring to a bubble, then simmer slowly for about 1 hour, or until the sauce is reduced by half. Remove the bay leaf.

Cut the fish into chunks and bury them in the sauce. Add the juice from the clams. Cover and simmer for about 15 minutes, until the fish is just ready to flake to a fork. Add the clams. Drain and add the crabmeat and shrimp. Heat through over a very low flame. Don't let it boil. (The processed shellfish are already cooked and must not overcook.) Adjust salt and pepper, and serve with garlic bread.

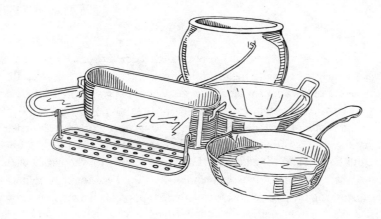

American-Style Bouillabaisse

4 to 6 frozen lobster tails
3 pounds frozen fish fillets
¼ cup diced carrots
1 cup minced onions
1 clove garlic
½ cup olive oil
2½ cups canned tomatoes
1 bay leaf
2 quarts hot water
1 cup shrimp or crabmeat
1 quart whole clams
1 cup white wine
1 tablespoon lemon juice
¼ cup minced parsley
½ cup canned pimentos
¼ teaspoon saffron
1 tablespoon salt
¼ teaspoon pepper
8 to 12 slices hot browned garlic bread

Thaw the lobster tails and fish fillets enough to cut. In a Dutch oven or large kettle, cook the carrots, onion, and garlic in the olive oil over low heat for 10 minutes. Cut the fish fillets in 2-inch pieces; and add them along with the tomatoes, bay leaf, and hot water. Bring to a boil and simmer for 20 minutes over very low heat. Add the lobster tails (split lengthwise in their shells), shrimps, and clams.

Bring back to a boil, add the remaining ingredients, and simmer for 30 minutes. Place a slice of garlic bread in each soup plate. With a slotted spoon, heap fish, vegetables, and shellfish on the bread, and moisten well with the broth. Follow with a good salad, a mild cheese, and a light desert. Include large dinner napkins with the services. *8 to 12 servings.*

—Madame Benoit
Encyclopedia of Canadian Cuisine

Doré en Chaudière (Walleye Chowder)

The word *chowder*, which has come to mean a fish or seafood soup, derives from the French word *chaudière*, a large iron kettle. Doré, or walleye, is a favorite for chowder in Quebec, and the following recipe is a specialty of that province.

You will want a couple of 2- to 3-pound walleye, or one big one, for this chowder, which should serve 6 to 8 hungry anglers. Clean and fillet the fish. Skin the fillets and tie the skin, bones, heads, and tails in a cheesecloth bag, then set it all aside while you get on with the basics of the chowder.

Put the iron kettle (or Dutch oven) on the fire to heat up. Dice about ¼ pound of salt pork and sear it in the kettle, turning the pork with a long-handled spoon until it's golden brown on all sides. Remove the pork and set it aside to drain on a paper towel. Slice 2 or 3 onions and lightly stir-brown them in the remaining hot fat until translucent.

Add the following (measurements are for guidance only—adjust to taste):

> 3 or 4 medium potatoes, peeled and sliced
> 1 or 2 stalks celery, diced,
>   or ½ teaspoon celery seed
> 3 or 4 medium carrots, sliced or diced
> 1 green pepper, diced
>   (or a bit of dry pepper flakes)
> 1 bay leaf
> 2 teaspoons salt
> ½ teaspoon pepper
> 2 quarts boiling water

Add the fish trimmings to the kettle. Bring to a slow boil and cook until the vegetables are almost tender, about 15 to 20 minutes.

Cut the fish fillets into chunks and add to the soup along with the browned salt pork. Boil gently for 5 to 10 minutes, until the fish flakes to a fork and the vegetables are cooked. Add 2 cups whole or evaporated milk and heat through, but don't boil after adding the milk. Lift and discard the bag of fish trimmings. If the soup is too thin, blend in instant mashed potatoes until the desired consistency is reached. Garnish with parsley flakes or fresh wild mint, and serve immediately with hot biscuits.

This recipe may also be used to make a chowder of carp, bass, and other lean fish. Where skins may impart an undesirable flavor, as in the case of carp and bass, discard them.

California Fish Casserole

The following recipe is used for fishes of subtropical waters such as sea bass, rockfish, albacore, yellowtail, tuna, or totuava — the whole fish or fillets, depending on the size of the fish. The method adapts well to freshwater fishes such as carp, walleye (pickerel), bass, and whitefish, which are lean to moderately fatty. Lake trouts and salmons, which are fatty fishes, should be trimmed of excessive fat along the belly and over the backbone. The freshwater fishes may be cooked with the skin on, except when the skin is undesirable.

> 4- to 5-pound whole pan-dressed fish,
>   or 2 to 3 pounds fillets
> 2 to 3 tablespoons olive or vegetable oil
> 1 medium onion, chopped
> 2 cloves garlic, minced
> 3 sprigs parsley, minced
> Pinch thyme
> 20-ounce can tomatoes
> 2 ounces sherry
> ½ teaspoon freshly ground black pepper
> Salt to taste
> 3 potatoes, peeled and thickly sliced

Preheat the oven to 350° F (175° C). Heat the oil in a saucepan, and sauté the onion and garlic until golden brown. Add the parsley and thyme and cook for a few minutes longer. Chop and add the tomatoes and juice and cook for 10 minutes over lowered heat. Add the sherry and ½ cup of water and cook for another few minutes; add the pepper and salt.

Grease a shallow baking dish, 15 by 9 inches, and spread the potatoes over the bottom. Lay the fish on the potatoes and pour the sauce over the fish. Bake uncovered for 45 minutes or until the fish flakes to a fork. Baste frequently from the pan, adding water as necessary to keep it all well moistened.

—Tod Ghio
Anthony's Fish Grottos
San Diego, California

Fish Fillets with Shrimp Sauce
1½ pounds fish fillets, skinned
⅓ cup minced onion
1½ cups milk
3 tablespoons margarine
3 tablespoons flour
½ teaspoon salt
¼ teaspoon pepper
⅓ cup grated cheddar cheese
1 cup cooked shrimp
2 tablespoons sherry
Dash pepper
1 tablespoon minced fresh parsley

Preheat oven to 400° F (205° C). Place the fillets in a greased baking dish, sprinkle the minced onion over them, and pour on milk to cover. Put into the hot oven for 25 minutes, or until the fish flakes to a fork.

Meantime melt the margarine in the top of a double boiler. Stir in the flour, salt, and pepper. When the fish is done, remove it from the oven and pour off the milk into the roux in the boiler top. Cook over boiling water, stirring constantly, until smooth and thickened. Add the cheese and stir until it melts. Add the shrimp and sherry and blend. Pour the sauce over the fish and return it to the oven for about 5 or 10 minutes, or until lightly browned. Grind a little pepper over the top and garnish with parsley.

—Kathryn Tucker Windham
Southern Cooking to Remember

CHOPPED, GROUND, AND FLAKED FISH

Fish Pilaf

2 cups leftover fish, fried or baked
4 strips bacon, cut in pieces
1 large onion, chopped
2 cups white rice, uncooked
½ teaspoon each crushed thyme and marjoram,
   or herbs to taste
20-ounce can tomatoes
4 cups strong chicken, veal, or fish stock
Salt and pepper
Butter
¼ cup slivered almonds
¼ cup black olives, halved and pitted
Fresh parsley, crushed

In a large, heavy cook-and-serve skillet or a Dutch oven, cook the bacon until crisp and then drain on a paper towel. In the remaining fat, sauté the onion until translucent. Stir in the rice and brown lightly. Add the herbs, tomatoes, and stock, stirring once to blend, and season with salt and pepper to taste. Bring to a boil, cover, and reduce heat to a simmer. Cook covered for 15 minutes, or until the rice is tender but not soft. Blend in the fish and heat it through. Heap in the middle of a large, hot platter and keep warm.

In a little butter, lightly sauté the almonds and olives. Sprinkle over the pilaf along with the bacon bits and a little crushed fresh parsley. Surround the rice with fried mushrooms and tomato sauce, or crayfish or shrimp in a butter sauce.

Gefilte Fish

Gefilte fish is a delicious fish-forcemeat preparation traditional to Jewish cookery. Recipes are many and various fishes may be used (depending on local supply), often in combination.

Gefilte fish is usually prepared in the form of little cakes, but a whole fish skin may be stuffed with its own meat. It is an excellent way to transform the flesh of big fish, or so-called coarse fish like carp, into a delicacy. The author of the following recipe prefers the light flesh of whitefish and pike.

5 pounds whitefish and pike
1 pound onions, chopped
1 teaspoon salt
½ teaspoon freshly ground black pepper
1 teaspoon sugar
5 eggs
1 large carrot
1 large onion
½ teaspoon salt
Peppercorns

Fillet the fish and reserve the bones. Put the fish through a food chopper or blender, and mix it well with the chopped onions, seasonings, sugar, eggs, and ½ cup of water.

Into the bottom of a deep kettle, slice the carrot and onion. Add ½ teaspoon of salt and a few peppercorns or a dash of pepper, then add the fish bones. Add 2 cups of water. Boil gently for ½ hour.

Meanwhile, with wet hands shape the fish mixture into patties and carefully pile them into the kettle on top of the vegetables. Cover and bring to a boil. Reduce the heat and simmer for 2 hours. Serve hot on bread. Strain the sauce in which the fish was cooked and pour it over the fish balls. Or serve cold with lots of red horseradish.

—Anne Butovsky
Ottawa, Ontario

Potted Fish

Potted fish is not far removed from the fish pemmican made by the Indians of Eastern Canada. Its modern preparation with the kitchen blender is little more than a refinement of the old ways. (The result, however, is not as durable.)

Fillet, bone, and skin a 2- to 3-pound fish. Generously salt the fillets on both sides. Put them on a plate, cover, and refrigerate overnight.

The next day, preheat the oven to 250° F (120° C). Rinse the fish in cold water and pat as dry as possible between paper towels. Place the fillets side by side on half of a sheet of oiled aluminum foil, shiny side down; bring the other half of the foil up and over the fish, but don't seal. Bake until the flesh flakes easily. Shred the fillets, removing any remaining small bones.

Starting with about ½ cup of fish, break it down in a blender, adding butter or margarine until the mixture is moist and velvety smooth. Add more fish and more butter until all the fish has been processed. Blend in 2 tablespoons of brown sugar, then season lightly with salt, white pepper, a scant ¼ teaspoon of ground mace, allspice, or cloves (or a combination of any or all), and a good pinch of cayenne. Don't judge the spices by taste—they'll develop during storage.

In small, clean earthen bowls or glasses, pack the fish paste firmly to about ½ inch from the top, pressing and smoothing it against the sides to eliminate air pockets. Fill to the top with clear rendered beef fat or melted butter. If the fat cracks or shrinks when cold, add more melted fat. Cover with aluminum foil and store in a clean, dry, cold place. Use after 7 to 10 days. (To store for more than 2 weeks, freeze.)

Fish that's been salt-cured and smoked has an extra-long life, as well as a nice flavor, when potted by this method.

Fish Salad

Red-fleshed or snowy white fish makes an attractive, refreshing salad. The fish may be poached for the purpose, or leftover poached or baked (but not fried) fish may be used.

2 cups poached fish, boned and coarsely shredded
¼ cup finely diced celery heart

Dressing:
1 cup commercial sour cream
1 tablespoon granulated sugar
2 tablespoons lemon juice or lime juice
1 teaspoon prepared horseradish (freshly opened)
Pinch cayenne
½ teaspoon salt
¼ teaspoon white pepper

Combine the dressing ingredients and mix well. Refrigerate several hours or overnight. About 1 hour before serving, fold the dressing into the prepared fish and celery, blending evenly. Refrigerate until needed. Serve on lettuce leaves and garnish with sliced black olives or pimento-stuffed olives, and a thin slice of lemon or lime.

Whitefish Prairie Mousse

1 tablespoon unflavored gelatin
¼ cup cold water
¼ cup boiling water
1½ teaspoons salt
1 cup stiffly whipped cream
2 cups flaked steamed lake whitefish
1 tablespoon prepared horseradish
½ cup finely diced celery
2 tablespoons finely diced sweet gherkins
1 tablespoon lemon juice
Dash white pepper
1 cucumber, washed and very thinly sliced

Soak the gelatin in the cold water. Add the boiling water and salt. Stir well and let cool. Fold in the whipped cream, and then the whitefish. Add the next five ingredients and blend.

Lightly oil a 3-cup fish mold. Pour in ⅓ of the fish mixture, cover with a layer of cucumber slices; repeat; and then end with a layer of fish. Chill until firm. Turn out onto a serving plate and garnish with greens, adding a few black and green (stuffed) olives.

PICKLED AND MARINATED FISH

Recipes for pickling fish in Apicius' *Roman Cookery*, believed to be the first cookbook in the Western world, are practically the same as those in use today. That should speak for their value and excellence. The enduring recipes call for good judgment in preparation and taste rather than exact measurement.

Nearly all firm- or coarse-fleshed fish pickle well—the fatty ones better than the very lean. Those of fragile texture, like the flounders (soles) and sauger, are best avoided. In Minnesota, where

Scandinavian tastes lean towards salty fare, coarse fish such as suckers, buffalo, and tullibees (cisco) are pickled in quantity. A few general points apply to all pickling procedures:

- Fish should be fresh and of top quality.
- Water, if hard, should be boiled and cooled before use; otherwise use distilled water.
- Vinegar should be at least 4% strength.
- Salt should be the pure canning or pickling type.
- Spices should be used fresh and *whole* for best results.
- Storage should be in a refrigerator at a maximum temperature of 40° F (5° C). Pickled fish should be used within 4 to 6 weeks.

Pickled Fish

2 to 3 pounds fish fillets, cut into small chunks
Brine: 1½ cups canning or pickling salt
   to 4 quarts water*
White vinegar (at least 4% strength)
Pickling solution
Sliced onions
5 to 6 pint sealers

Pickling solution:
8 bay leaves
3 cups white vinegar
1 cup white wine
2½ cups sugar
4 teaspoons mustard seed
2 teaspoons each whole cloves, whole allspice,
   and black peppercorns

In a bowl, soak the fish in the brine. Refrigerate for 48 hours. Drain. Cover with vinegar. Refrigerate another 48 hours. Combine the pickling ingredients and boil 5 minutes. Cool. Drain the fish and pack in sterilized pint sealers, layering with sliced onions. Pour the pickling solution over the fish. Cover and refrigerate at a maximum temperature of 40° F (5° C) for at least 2 days before using. Use within 4 to 6 weeks.

Wine-Marinated Fillets

Any firm-fleshed fish may be used with this recipe, including small trout or pink-fleshed catfish; it's a matter of color.

*If water is hard, boil and cool before using; or use distilled water.

5 or 6 small fish (about 2 pounds each),
    freshly caught and filleted, skin on or off
1 medium carrot, thinly sliced
1 medium onion, thinly sliced
1 teaspoon peppercorns
A few heads fresh dill, or ½ teaspoon dill seed
1 bay leaf
1 to 2 pounds pickling salt
White wine

In the bottom of a deep earthen bowl, arrange a layer of carrot slices and onion rings; add a few peppercorns, a bit of dill, and a fragment of bay leaf, and sprinkle salt on top. Add a layer of fish fillets. Repeat layering until all the fish is in the bowl, ending with a layer of vegetables and salt. Pour wine over the fish until covered. Lay a clean plate on top for light pressure, cover the bowl, and refrigerate undisturbed for 1 to 2 weeks.

Fish en Escabeche

2 to 3 pounds fish fillets, skin on or off
Salt and black pepper
Flour
Cooking oil, preferably olive
2 medium onions, thinly sliced
½ sweet red pepper (pimento), thinly sliced
A few peppercorns
2 or 3 bay leaves
White vinegar

Wash the fillets in cold water and pat dry between towels. Cut into bite-size chunks. In a soup bowl, mix salt and pepper in the proportions of 4 parts salt to 1 part pepper. Rub the mixture into the fish on all sides. Put some flour into a plastic bag and season it with the same salt-and-pepper blend. A few pieces at a time, shake the fish in the flour to lightly dust. Toss the pieces back and forth in your hands to shake off excess flour, then place on a towel.

In a large frying pan, heat oil deep enough to pan-fry the fish. When the oil just sizzles to a flick of water, quickly fry the fish on both sides, a few pieces at a time, until barely colored. As the pieces are fried, arrange them closely in a layer in the bottom of a deep earthen or glass bowl.

To the hot oil, add the remaining ingredients, including the vinegar. (Use as much vinegar as you estimate it will take for the whole mixture to completely cover the fish in the bowl. The amount will depend on the depth of the fish and the shape of the bowl.) Reduce the heat and simmer for about 5 minutes. Pour the hot mixture over the fish. If it does not completely cover, heat more vinegar and add it to the bowl. Weight lightly with a clean plate, cover the bowl, and let cool. Refrigerate for at least 24 hours before eating. (The dish will keep for up to a week in the refrigerator.) Serve as a cold entrée, an hors d'oeuvre, or a snack.

SALT-CURED FISH

Salt curing as a preservative is excellent for both lean and fatty fishes. Fatty fish require more salt and spend less time in the brine than do leaner fish but their oils provide a moister texture. The salt cure is especially good for bony fish, as the bones soften in the process.

Salting is a drying process. The purpose of a salt cure is to draw fluids from, and leave salt in, the flesh and thus to inhibit spoilage. Improved refrigeration permits lighter salting and less drying, resulting in a more flavorful, palatable product.

Preparing Fish for Salting

Only three things are required for salting fish: a suitable receptacle in which to do the job, salt, and fish.

The container may be an earthen crock; a clean wooden tub or barrel; or a new, clean, covered plastic pail or garbage container. (Only wood or plastic containers, spoons, etc., should be used.) The salt should be as pure as can be obtained—dairy salt, pickling salt, or noniodized table salt.

The fish should be freshly caught and dressed according to their size, with the gills removed. Small fish are generally kipper-split (split down the back and cleaned and flattened). Larger fish are split into two fillets; the backbone is removed and the skin left on. The dressed fish are scrubbed until they glisten and then wiped dry.

Thick fillets should be scored on the flesh side with cuts about ½ inch deep (but not to the skin), and 1 or 2 inches apart to facilitate the penetration of salt. Fillets of extra-large fish may be cut into chunks. Very small fish, up to 8 ounces, are generally gibbed (cleaned and eviscerated through the gills) and salted whole.

There are no hard-and-fast rules for salting to cover all situations. Expertise comes with experience. Generally speaking, fatty fish require more salt than lean fish; heavier salting is required for spring and summer catches where storage conditions depend on the weather. (The heavy salt can also be a matter of taste.) The autumn catch, where a cold winter lies ahead, may be lightly salted. With refrigerated storage, salting may be done at any time. Storage should be in a well-ventilated, clean, dark place, not more than 50° to 60° F (10° to 16° C). After 3 months, or at the first sign of fermentation, the brine should be changed. Salted fish should be stored no more than 9 months in all.

The two following salting recipes are from experts. One, in the Atlantic tradition, is from a collection of old family mackerel-salting recipes from residents of the Cape May area; the other is from a northern Ontario Great Lakes fisherman. Both recipes may be applied to fish generally.

Cape May Salted Mackerel

Fillet the fresh-caught mackerel. Wash them thoroughly, making sure no blood remains on the fillets.

Use a clean porcelain or stone crock about 18 inches deep and 12 inches wide. Place a layer of mackerel on the bottom of the container and sprinkle a little bit of kosher salt on it. Repeat this arrangement until all the mackerel are in the container. Don't be too heavy on the salt—it might burn the fish.

Put a heavy porcelain or wooden plate on top of the final layer of salted mackerel and weight it with a clean, heavy stone, or use a gallon jug filled with water, if no other weight is available. Cover the container with clean muslin or cheesecloth and let it set for 2 to 3 weeks. A brine will rise, completely covering the mackerel, and the fish will take on the salted taste.

After soaking the mackerel in fresh water overnight, bake or sauté in a pan for a very delectable meal. Or dredge the fillets in bread crumbs and fry them.

—Joe Bisch
Philadelphia, Pennsylvania

Great Lakes Salt Cure

Difficult-to-bone freshwater fishes, such as pike, pickerel, perch, and suckers, are commonly salted.

Clean, scale, and head-dress or fillet the fresh fish, depending on size, and wipe dry. Use a clean plastic or wooden bucket or a crock big enough to accommodate the fish.

Cover the bottom of the crock with a layer of pickling (noniodized) salt. Add a layer of fillets, flesh down, on the salt. Repeat layers of salt and fish, finishing with a good layer of salt over the top. Cover the fish with a plate weighted with a clean glass or plastic gallon jug filled with water. Leave for a week, until the fish are under brine and no more forms. Remove the fish and discard brine. Wash the crock.

Prepare a new brine of cooled boiled water, enough to fill half the crock, adding salt until it will float a raw egg.

Scrape each fillet or fish clean of drawn blood, wipe with a cloth, and return to the crock. Add a few peppercorns, cracked. Pour the fresh brine over the fish. Cover again with a weighted plate. The fish must be well under the brine. If necessary, make more brine. Cover with clean muslin. Leave in a well-ventilated, cold, dark place and use after 2 weeks. The fish should keep in this manner through the winter.

—Harry Souci
Sault Ste. Marie, Ontario

Cooking Salted Fish

Salted fish are freshened before cooking. Scrape or scale the skin. Rinse under cold running water. Cover with fresh cold water and let stand overnight. Rinse, drain, and pat the fish dry between towels.

The freshened fish are then cooked like similar cuts of fresh fish: pan-fried, poached, baked, or made into fish soups or chowders. Salted fish is also excellent in casseroles. Reduce or omit salt from recipes for fresh fish; it's a matter of taste.

Keep in mind when cooking salt-cured fish that it is practically cooked already and requires very little further cooking. Salted fish, freshened or right out of the brine, well drained and dried of surface moisture, is delicious when quickly heat-smoked (see "Smoking Fish" in Chapter 3).

Salted Fish Fritters

2 cups salted fish, diced
4 cups raw potatoes, diced
Boiling water
2 eggs, well beaten
3 tablespoons butter or margarine, softened
Black pepper
Fat for deep frying
2 cups Spanish Sauce (see Chapter 11)

Rinse the fish well in cold running water. Put into a saucepan with the potatoes, barely cover with boiling water, and cook until the potatoes are tender. Drain well. Return the mixture to the pan and shake over low heat to dry off remaining moisture. Transfer to a mixing bowl and mash finely. Add the eggs, butter, and pepper to taste. Beat with a fork or mix in a blender until light and fluffy.

Deep-fry in hot fat by dropping the fish mixture a tablespoon at a time into the fat and frying until golden, about 2 minutes. Don't crowd the fritters in the fat. Drain on paper towels and serve very hot with Spanish Sauce.

Salted Fish Hash

1 cup salted fish
2 tablespoons butter
1 large onion, minced
2 cups cooked potatoes, diced
Salt and pepper to taste
Parsley

Soak the fish overnight to freshen, changing water once or twice depending on saltiness desired. Drain and shred the fish. Heat the butter in a large skillet and sàuté the onion until translucent. Add the fish, cover, and cook gently for about 5 minutes. Add the potatoes, season to taste, cover, and cook until lightly browned on the bottom. Turn the hash, add a tablespoon of boiling water and a little minced parsley, and cover and cook until lightly brown. Turn with a spatula a few times. Serve with vegetables and a white or cream sauce.

ROE

Caviar, the celebrated preparation of roe of sturgeon, has rather overshadowed any claim to fame by lesser producers of fish eggs, or any other preparation thereof. However, while Imperial Europe was teasing its impeccable palate with the salted delicacy, Indians of North America, who had never heard of caviar, were weaning babies on fish eggs, including sturgeons'.

Used at the prespawning stage, fish roes should be wholesome-looking, clear, and well formed, with no sign of shriveling or cloudiness. The sac should be firm and clear, smoothly and closely filled with a translucent mass of eggs. Failure to meet these qualifications may indicate contamination, and such roes should not be eaten.

Roes of fishes other than sturgeon—for example, salmon, cod, haddock, tuna, mullet, whitefish—may be salted into a caviar product every bit as delicious as the more usual preparations. Paddlefish roe yields a fine caviar. Warning: The roes of some fishes (for example, puffers and gars) are toxic.

Caviar in the Kitchen

Always use roe of prespawning fish. Roe is extremely perishable and thus should be taken from the fish as soon as it is killed, and processed at once. Cleanliness is vital throughout the processing. Keep hands clean and sterilize all utensils and equipment with the care given an infant's bottles.

You will need a screen or sieve of a size to allow the eggs just to pass through without breaking; a glass or boilproof plastic bowl; a French wire whisk; small glass jars with covers; and 1 ounce of fine, noniodized salt for every 2 pounds of roe.

Put the roe on the sieve or screen over the bowl. Gently moving them about with the whisk, separate the berries from the sac and fluid and let them fall into the bowl. Wash the berries gently in several cold waters, moving them around with the whisk as necessary until all the frothiness can be drained off and the clean, whole berries remain. Let them drain for a few minutes on thick paper toweling or a clean linen towel.

Rinse out the bowl and return the berries to it, alternating a layer of berries with a layer of salt in the proportions given above, finishing with a layer of salt. Increase the salt in warm weather—up to 1 ounce salt to 10 ounces roe, but no more.

Immediately pack the caviar in prepared small jars, making sure it's level with the top so that there is no air space. Cover. Store in the bottom of the refrigerator for 2 weeks, at which time it will be ready to use and at its best. The salted caviar may be kept several weeks at a near-freezing temperature, but must not be allowed to freeze or the berries will break. (It should also be kept in darkness.) Upend the bottles every few days to prevent oil from settling at the top.

To keep the caviar at peak quality, pack it in small jars and, once opened, use it all. Don't store caviar again once it's been opened.

Cooked Fish Roes

Roes must not be overcooked or, like other eggs, they become tough. A light poaching or parboiling, until they just begin to coddle or turn opaque, helps float off some of the oiliness and makes it easier to apportion the roe.

To parboil, wash the roe and pat dry between towels. Drop the roe into boiling salted water to which lemon juice has been added—about 1 tablespoon to 1 quart of water. Reduce the heat and cook until the roe just begins to turn opaque. Lift with a slotted spoon and plunge into cold water. Drain. Separate the roe into pieces.

Pan-fried roe à la meunière: Dip each piece of parboiled roe in beaten egg, dust with seasoned flour, and lightly pan-fry in clarified butter (see Glossary) until crisp and brown, turning once. Serve on toast, topped with hot melted butter with a dash of lemon juice and onion juice mixed in.

Baked roe: Place parboiled roe in a buttered baking dish. For 1 pound of roe, brown 1 tablespoon of fine herbs in browned butter (see Glossary). Pour over roe. Add ¼ cup of sherry. Cover and bake in a 375° F (190° C) oven for about 10 minutes. Serve on dry toast, spooning the sauce over the roe.

Poached roe: Large roes, such as those from sturgeon and paddlefish, are poached. Bring a kettle of water (enough to cover the roe) to a boil. Add salt to taste and lemon juice or vinegar, about 1 tablespoon to 1 quart of water. Drop the roe into the boiling water, lower the heat, and simmer for about 10 minutes — until the roe is opaque. Drain the roe. Break the sac and serve the eggs.

Soft roes: The soft roe, or milt, is the sperm of the male fish. A smooth white substance, it is considered a nourishing and highly digestible delicacy. Much favored are the milts of carp, herrings, mullet, and mackerels. To prepare soft roes for cooking, wash them well in cold water, drain, and strip the small vein found on one side. Cook and serve the soft roes like other roes: Poach quickly or parboil for about 2 minutes, then pan-fry, bake, or oven-brown.

Fish roes are a rich dish and should be served on dry toast with a tart, piquant sauce or condiment like green tomato pickle. Tabasco or Worcestershire sauce adds a nice touch. Otherwise, serve with nothing more than sliced tomatoes, a green salad, and a dry white wine.

PART FIVE

Potpourri

A confused collection; a miscellaneous mixture; a medley;
a hotchpotch . . .

Webster's New Twentieth Century Dictionary

11

A Miscellaneous Mixture

From its preparation in the kitchen to its service on the table, there are various things that enhance a game dish along the way. This chapter of such miscellanea includes a selection of great stuffings, sauces, fruity confections, and some accessory items such as corn breads, bannocks, and wild rice traditional to serving game in North America.

STUFFINGS

A savory preparation for filling the cavity of a fish or fowl is called a *stuffing* to avoid confusion with procedures for the dressing and care of the game. Stuffings when cooked should be light, moist, and fragrant. Like all accessories, they should complement rather than overpower.

Bread should be dry enough that it crumbles between the fingers, and wild rice should be pre-cooked to a dry fluffiness, its kernels separated in little curls (see Wild Rice section at end of this chap-

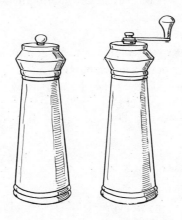

ter for cooking directions). Brown or white rice (no relation to wild rice) is often used as a substitute for bread; it, too, should be dry and fluffy. Corn bread should be light and crumbly.

Stuffings are best prepared 1 hour or more in advance and allowed to rest so the flavors have a chance to blend. Cavities of the game should be filled with a light hand—no more than two-thirds to three-quarters full—to allow for swelling. Unless otherwise noted, the following stuffing recipes make about 2 cups of stuffing, enough to stuff a 5- to 6-pound fish or a brace of grouse.

Herbs for Stuffings

Pungent	Medium	Mild
Oregano	Basil	Chervil
Sage	Caraway	Parsley
Tarragon	Marjoram	
Winter savory	Rosemary	
	Summer savory	
	Thyme	

Basic Stuffing

1½ cups stale bread crumbs or cooked wild rice
1½ teaspoons thyme or other herb
⅛ teaspoon salt
Pinch pepper
2 tablespoons chopped celery (optional)
1 tablespoon minced onion
2 tablespoons clarified butter
   or delicate cooking oil
¼ cup warm stock or milk

Toss the bread crumbs or rice together with the seasonings. Sauté the celery and onion in the butter until translucent, add to the mixture, and toss gently but well. Sprinkle the stock over the stuffing and toss again to blend (for dry stuffing, omit the liquid).

In this recipe, thyme, a medium savory, is used as an example; but herbs may be varied or mixed according to taste or supplies. The stuffing may be more or less highly seasoned by switching or blending herbs, or by using more or less of them.

A Miscellaneous Mixture

Corn Bread Giblet Stuffing

Southern-style roast turkey is distinguished by its traditional corn bread stuffing.

¾ cup chopped onion
1 cup chopped celery
¼ cup butter or margarine
4 cups crumbled corn bread
4 cups stale bread cut in small cubes
1 cup chopped, cooked turkey giblets
¾ teaspoon salt
½ teaspoon poultry seasoning
¼ teaspoon pepper
1 egg
1½ cups stock or water

Sauté the onion and celery in butter until translucent. Add the corn bread and bread cubes. Cook, stirring, until lightly browned. Add the giblets and mix well. Add the salt, pepper, and poultry seasoning. Beat the egg slightly, add to the stock, and pour the liquid over the stuffing, mixing well.

Stuff the turkey lightly and cook as usual, or bake the stuffing in a greased pan at 375° F (190° C) for 30 to 40 minutes and serve separately.

Makes about 6 cups.

Wild Rice Mushroom Stuffing

1 tablespoon grated onion
½ cup finely diced celery
¼ cup diced mushrooms
2 tablespoons clarified butter
1½ cups cooked wild rice
Salt and pepper to taste

Sauté the onion, celery, and mushrooms in the butter until light gold, and mix with the cooked rice. Add salt and pepper and toss lightly to blend. Use for fish or small birds.

Wild Rice and Partridge Stuffing for Fish

2 cups steamed wild rice
1 cup thick mushroom sauce, or
  1 10-ounce can cream of mushroom soup
1 cup cubed cooked partridge or
  other wildfowl (or chicken)
1 small onion, diced and sautéed
1 teaspoon chervil, parsley, or other mild herb
Dash mace or allspice
Salt to taste

This moist stuffing is good for both fatty and lean fishes.

Mix everything together, let it rest for an hour or so, then stuff the fish very lightly and sew it up. Extra-fresh mushrooms, diced and sautéed, may be added to the stuffing.

Potato Stuffing

The Pennsylvania Dutch actually call this potato filling. It can be served as a side dish with any meat, or used as a stuffing for fish or fowl.

> 6 to 8 medium potatoes, peeled
> ⅔ cup milk (approximately)
> ¼ cup butter or margarine
> 1 medium onion, finely chopped
> 1 small stalk celery with top, finely chopped
> 2 slices stale white bread, coarsely crumbled
> 1 large egg
> 2 tablespoons minced parsley
> 1 tablespoon flour
> Salt and pepper to taste

Boil the potatoes in salted water until fork tender; drain well and mash, adding about ⅔ cup of milk, or enough to give a smooth, light texture.

Meanwhile, melt the butter and sauté the onion and celery until the onion is translucent. Combine with the remaining ingredients and mix well. Add the mixture to the mashed potatoes and blend thoroughly. A little more milk may be added if the mixture seems too thick, but don't let it get too wet.

For a side dish, heap the stuffing into a well-buttered baking dish. Brush lightly with melted butter and bake at 350° F (175° C) for about 1 hour. Or stuff a fish or fowl, filling no more than two-thirds full to allow space for swelling, and cook.

Fruity Stuffing

> ¼ cup slivered almonds
> 1 ring candied pineapple, finely sliced
> ½ cup candied cherries, red and green, sliced
> 1½ cups cooked wild rice or stale bread crumbs
> ½ teaspoon summer savory or thyme
> 1 teaspoon celery salt
> ½ teaspoon sweet basil
> ½ teaspoon salt
> Dash white pepper
> 1 small onion, finely chopped
> 2 tablespoons clarified butter or cooking oil

Combine the nuts and fruit with the bread crumbs and seasonings, mixing well. Sauté the onion in the butter until it's translucent and add to the mixture. For a moister stuffing, add ¼ cup of warm meat stock. Use to stuff fish or fowl.

Tom Schirm's Famous Chestnut Stuffing for Wild Turkey

Tom Schirm is famous throughout the hunt camps of Huntingdon County in Pennsylvania for his chestnut stuffing. Generations of hunters have set such store and appetite by his stuffing that they bring domestic turkeys into camp as insurance.

½ pound chestnuts in the shell
4 cups dry bread crumbs
½ teaspoon salt
Pepper
Celery, finely chopped
Thyme or savory (optional)
¼ pound butter, melted

This recipe makes enough stuffing for a 12- to 15-pound turkey. Adjust quantities as needed for a larger or smaller bird.

Score the nuts across the bottom end of the shell, drop into boiling water, and cook for 10 to 15 minutes. (This softens the hull and loosens the inner skin, making the nuts easy to peel.) Chop the skinned nuts quite finely. Using your fingers, mix the bread crumbs and nuts together in a large bowl. Add salt, a good dash of pepper, and just a little bit of finely chopped celery — too much will kill the taste of the chestnuts. Add a pinch of thyme or savory if desired. Add the butter to the stuffing and mix lightly with the hands until evenly blended. Cover the bowl with a towel, and let the stuffing rest for an hour or two.

When the turkey is ready to stuff, spread a little butter around the inside of the cavity, then stuff with a light hand. (The chestnut stuffing also enhances wild goose as well as such upland game-birds as grouse and pheasant.)

Apple Stuffing

¼ cup diced bacon (4 slices)
½ cup chopped celery
½ cup chopped onion
¼ cup chopped parsley
½ cup sugar
5 medium-size tart apples, sliced
1 cup fine dry bread crumbs
½ teaspoon salt
⅛ teaspoon pepper.

Fry the bacon until crisp. Remove it from the pan and drain on paper. In the hot bacon fat sauté the celery, onion, and parsley for about 3 minutes. Stir in the sugar. Cover, reduce the heat, and cook slowly until the vegetables are tender. Remove the cover and cook for about 2 minutes until the vegetables are glazed. Crumble the bacon and stir it in, along with the bread crumbs, apple slices, and seasonings. Mix well.

This recipe makes about 4 cups of stuffing, and is delicious with goose and ducks.

—Pauline Woychesko
Foam Lake, Saskatchewan

Peanut Stuffing for Ducks
1½ cups cracker crumbs
1 cup shelled peanuts (unsalted)
1 cup heavy cream
2 tablespoons melted butter
A few drops of onion juice
¼ teaspoon salt
Pepper to taste
Pinch cayenne

Put the cracker crumbs and shelled peanuts through a food chopper. Add the cream, melted butter, and onion juice, and mix gently but well. Season with salt, pepper, and cayenne. Mix lightly. This moist, rich stuffing is enough for 2 ducks, 2½ to 3 pounds each.

—Mrs. W. F. Gray
Ottawa, Ontario

SAUCES

A sauce should not disguise but enhance the flavor of the meat or fish it accompanies. Fine sauces are neither complicated nor costly, and they are certainly not mysterious. Most are made in a matter of minutes from the juices of the meat or fish involved, or from a basic sauce or stock that may be prepared in advance and kept on hand in the refrigerator or freezer. The making of a successful sauce requires the chef's undivided attention, little enough when one considers the trouble taken to get the game to the kitchen.

Use a saucepan of an even-heating, fast-conducting metal, such as cast aluminum or tin-lined copper, enamel, or ceramic-coated iron. White sauces requiring no browning may be made in the top part of a double boiler. If the sauce is to contain wine, lemon juice, or vinegar, avoid using aluminum or tin, which might cause some discoloration of the sauce. For stirring, a wooden spoon or a whisk will allow you to scrape without scratching the bottom of the pan and to stir without bruising the sauce.

Before getting down to work, make sure all your equipment and measured ingredients are ready and within easy reach. Any interruption of the cooking-stirring process can ruin the sauce. Work with a deft, gentle touch and a constant eye.

SEASONINGS FOR SAUCES AND MARINADES

Aromatics and Spices	Herbs	Aromatic Vegetables
Allspice	Basil	Carrot
Capers	Bay leaf	Celery
Cayenne	Chervil	Chive
Celery seed	Dill weed	Garlic
Chili	Marjoram	Green pepper
Cloves	Oregano	Onion
Commercial seafood	Parsley	Pimento
seasoning	Rosemary	Tomato
Cumin	Sorrel	
Curry	Tarragon	
Dill seed	Thyme	
Fennel seed		
Juniper berries		
Mace		
Mustard, dry		
Mustard seed		
Paprika		
Pepper (black and white)		
Pine nuts		
Saffron		
Turmeric		
Wintergreen,		
natural oil of*		

*Must be *natural* oil of wintergreen to be edible. Buy it from a pharmacist for the purpose.

Brown Pan Gravy

Brown pan gravy is made in the roasting pan on top of the stove, from the juicy, dark, unscorched drippings of roasted meats. It is unseasoned except for salt. The finished gravy should be deep brown, rich and nutty in flavor, smooth in texture, and rather thin, with no grease floating on top. It is made quickly, with concentrated attention, and should never need to be strained.

Water in the drippings can cause flour to lump instead of to brown. In the first stages of the roasting, the added liquid and basting prevent the drippings from burning; then the final bastings are done with the pan juices, allowing extra moisture to cook away. If drippings have burned in the bottom of the pan, forgo the pan gravy and make another sauce.

After removing the cooked roast from the pan, skim off excess fat from the drippings (that is, as much clear fat as can be spooned off), leaving only a surface coating over the browned drippings.

You'll need 1 part flour to 4 parts drippings. Make a conservative guess as to the amount of flour required (it will not be possible to measure all the drippings accurately). Each tablespoon of flour requires about 1 cup of hot liquid, so make sure you have plenty on hand. Potato water, wild rice water, meat stock, leftover marinade, and/or hot water are all suitable. For a thicker gravy, reduce the amount of liquid added.

Place the pan and drippings over a fairly high heat. Let boil a moment to allow any traces of water to evaporate. Sprinkle half the flour over the surface, constantly stirring and scraping the browned bits up from the bottom of the pan. Add the remaining flour, and stir and scrape until the mixture is well blended and browned and gives off a nutty bouquet.

Just as the mixture threatens to smoke, turn the heat down to medium, and stir in the hot liquid. Start with ⅓ of the estimated requirement, stirring and cooking until blended and thickened before adding more. Keep adding liquid until the desired consistency is reached. Season with salt to taste. Keep at a low simmer until needed, stirring occasionally. Do not boil. Serve in a heated gravy boat.

Wildfowl Giblet Gravy

Cook the neck and giblets in a saucepan, covered with salted water, until tender. (They should be put on to cook while the birds are being prepared for the oven.) Shred the meat from the neck and chop fine with the giblets in a food chopper or blender. Use the stock to make a thin brown pan gravy, stirring the ground giblets in when it thickens. Test and adjust for seasoning. Serve hot in a heated gravy boat.

Brown Sauce

Brown sauce is the base for many fine hot sauces for meat. In principle, it is made by thickening a concentrated seasoned meat stock with a brown roux. This simple recipe yields about 1 cup.

2 tablespoons fat
2 tablespoons flour
1 cup hot strong stock
¼ teaspoon salt
Dash freshly ground black pepper

Make a brown roux: Melt the fat in a saucepan over medium heat until golden, and just beginning to turn brown. Sprinkle the flour over the fat, stirring and scraping up from the bottom of the pan until the mixture is nicely browned (but not scorched) and smooth and thick. Gradually add the hot stock, stirring until thickened. Add salt and pepper to taste. Turn the heat very low and simmer for ½ hour or more. Stir occasionally, adding a bit of hot stock as necessary to maintain the desired consistency.

Brown sauce may be made in larger amounts, sealed in clean, hot recipe-size jars, and stored in the refrigerator for up to a week. Quickly chilled and fast-frozen, the jars of sauce may be freezer-stored indefinitely—but don't screw down the jar tops until the sauce is frozen.

Pepper Sauce

1 cup Brown Sauce
2 teaspoons wine vinegar
1 small onion, grated
1 tablespoon chopped chives
½ teaspoon minced parsley
Pinch thyme
1 bay leaf
½ teaspoon freshly ground black pepper
¼ teaspoon salt

To the Brown Sauce add the other ingredients. Simmer, stirring occasionally, over low heat for 20 minutes. Strain, or simply remove the bay leaf. Serve with venison steaks or chops.

Madeira Sauce
2 cups Brown Sauce
Bouquet garni
Salt and pepper
1 small onion, sliced
Pinch nutmeg
1 clove
3 tablespoons Madeira wine

To the hot Brown Sauce, add all the other ingredients except the wine, and cook over a very low heat for 1 hour. At serving time, add the Madeira. Strain through a sieve into a heated gravy boat and serve at once.

Spanish Sauce
½ cup fresh light olive oil
5 cloves garlic, finely chopped
2 green peppers, coarsely chopped
3 onions, coarsely chopped
2 cups canned tomatoes
10½-ounce can tomato puree (sauce)
2 bay leaves
¼ teaspoon oregano
1½ teaspoons Worcestershire sauce
Juice of 1 lime
Salt and pepper

In a saucepan, heat the olive oil and cook the garlic and green peppers until the latter are almost tender. Add the onion and cook until tender but not browned. Stir in everything else. Simmer until slightly thickened and well blended, about 20 minutes, stirring occasionally. Makes about 2½ cups. (What you don't need, freeze for future use.)

—Lowis Carlton
Famous Florida Recipes

Velouté Sauce
2 tablespoons butter
2 tablespoons flour
2½ cups hot white stock
   (from white meat or fish)
Salt and white pepper to taste
Mushroom stems and skins (optional)

The stock should, of course, be compatible with the sauce's host. Use a fish stock or fumet with fish; never with fowl or meat.

Melt the butter in a saucepan or the top of a double boiler and stir in the flour. Stir over low heat until the mixture is a smooth, bubbly liquid, just about to turn golden. Add the hot stock and stir until thickened, stirring up from the bottom of the saucepan. Add the seasonings and mushroom bits. Lower the heat and simmer for 1½ hours, or cook over gently boiling water in the double boiler. Stir and skim the sauce frequently. As the stock is usually seasoned, the sauce may not need any additional flavoring; this is a matter of taste. Strain if necessary before serving.

The velouté may be made in advance and refrigerated for future use as a base for other sauces. Store in recipe-size covered containers, brushing the surface of the sauce with melted butter. Cover tightly. Refrigerated, the sauce should keep for up to 2 weeks as long as the container is not opened. For fish or fowl.

Fine Herbs Sauce
2 tablespoons butter
1 tablespoon diced mushrooms
1 tablespoon chopped chives
2 tablespoons finely chopped parsley
Salt and white pepper to taste
Pinch grated nutmeg
½ cup Sauce Espagnole or Velouté Sauce
Lemon juice

Melt the butter, mix in everything but the last 2 ingredients, and simmer for 5 minutes. Blend in the Espagnole Sauce or Velouté Sauce. Stir until it bubbles. Add a few drops of lemon juice. Remove the sauce from the heat, and keep hot in a double boiler. This is a fine sauce for baked fish.

White Wine Sauce
2 cups Velouté Sauce
½ cup dry white wine
½ cup white stock (from white meat or fish)
Pinch cayenne
1 tablespoon lemon juice
½ cup butter

Combine the Velouté Sauce, wine, and stock; add the cayenne. Bring to a boil, turn down the heat, and reduce the sauce by half. Stir frequently. Remove from heat and stir in first the lemon juice and then the butter. Blend well. Stir until the desired consistency is reached. For fish or fowl.

Béchamel Sauce
2 tablespoons butter
2 tablespoons flour
2 cups warm milk
1 onion stuck with 1 clove
Small piece bay leaf
Pinch of parsley or thyme or other savory herb
Salt and pepper

Make a white roux: Melt the butter over medium heat and stir in the flour. Cook, stirring constantly, until the mixture is pale gold and smooth and bubbly. Gradually stir in the warm milk, continue to stir until the sauce is thickened. Add the onion and herbs, and season to taste with salt and pepper. Simmer over very low heat for ½ hour. Strain and serve.

An extra-smooth texture may be obtained by scalding and slightly cooling the milk before adding it to the roux. See the next recipe for many variations.

Cream Sauce
1 tablespoon butter
1 tablespoon flour
1 cup 10% cream
Salt and pepper
Parsley, chopped (optional)
Garlic (optional)

Make a white roux by melting the butter over medium heat and stirring in the flour; cook, stirring constantly until the mixture is smooth and bubbly and pale gold. Gradually add the cream and stir until thickened. Season with salt and pepper to taste. Add a bit of chopped parsley and a trace of garlic if desired.

Both Béchamel Sauce and Cream Sauce can be modified to produce many versatile variations, which are used extensively in preparing and serving various fish, fowl, and lean small-game dishes. Use 1 cup of Béchamel Sauce or Cream Sauce as the base for the following sauces.

Caper: Blend in 2 or 3 tablespoons of chopped capers.

Cheese: Heat the sauce over hot water and blend in 2 or 3 tablespoons of grated cheddar cheese.

Egg: Blend in a finely chopped hard-boiled egg.

Lobster: Blend in ½ cup of cooked, chopped lobster meat, including coral (ovary).

Mushroom: Lightly sauté thinly sliced mushrooms in 1 tablespoon of butter. Add 1 tablespoon of sherry. Remove from the heat. Blend into the hot sauce.

Parsley: Blend in 2 or 3 tablespoons of chopped parsley.

Shrimp: Blend in ½ cup of cooked, chopped shrimp.

Soubise (onion): Boil 4 or 5 large onions until mushy. Drain, mash the onions well, and combine with the sauce. Return the mixture to the saucepan, sprinkle with 1 tablespoon of *beurre manié* (see Glossary), and blend well over medium heat. Add ½ cup of evaporated milk or cream and stir until it bubbles. Serve with salted fish.

Wine: Blend 2 or 3 tablespoons white wine into the sauce.

Mustard Sauce

2 tablespoons olive oil
2 teaspoons granulated sugar
2 tablespoons dry mustard
Pinch salt
¼ teaspoon turmeric (optional)
1 tablespoon flour
⅓ cup light cream or evaporated milk
¼ cup vinegar

Heat the oil in the top of a double boiler over gently boiling water. Thoroughly mix the sugar, mustard, and salt. If a yellow color is desired for this otherwise pale sauce, add turmeric to the mustard mixture. Set aside. When the oil is heated, add the flour, stirring for a minute or two until blended. Remove from the heat. Add the mustard mixture and blend well. Gradually stir in the cream or evaporated milk. Replace over boiling water; stir and cook until smooth and thickened. Let cool. Add the vinegar and blend well. Pour into a dish, cover, and keep cool until needed.

The sauce should be made several hours in advance and allowed to develop. It may be refrigerated for 2 or 3 days. Good with all manner of cold fish and meats, and with tongue.

Mustard Dill Sauce: To 1 cup of Mustard Sauce add 1 tablespoon of zesty, Dijon-style prepared mustard. Mix well. Add 2 tablespoons of minced fresh dill. Let the sauce rest an hour or two. Serve with smoked fish.

Curry Sauce

2 onions, sliced
1 clove garlic, slivered
2 tablespoons cooking oil
2 tablespoons curry powder
½ teaspoon sugar
1 cup canned tomatoes, or 3 fresh
   tomatoes, peeled and chopped
2 apples, peeled and sliced
½ bay leaf
2 cloves
Salt to taste
½ cup white stock or water
1 tablespoon cornstarch

Sauté the onion and garlic gently in the oil until the onion is translucent. Add the curry powder and mix. Sprinkle the sugar over the top. Mix in the tomatoes, apples, bay leaf, cloves, and salt. Cover tightly and simmer for about 10 minutes. Add the stock. Bring to a boil, cover, and cook gently until the apples and onion are mushy, stirring occasionally. Put through a sieve or fine potato ricer. Test for seasoning. Mix the cornstarch in ½ cup of water, and blend into the sauce. Heat and stir until thickened.

This sauce is good with all fatty fishes and game meats. It is an excellent sauce in which to heat leftovers, especially waterfowl.

Chili Pepper Sauce: Substitute chili powder for the curry. Serve with Venison Burgers with Herbs.

Orange Sauce

3 tablespoons bland cooking oil
3 small green onions with tops, minced
¾ teaspoon crushed tarragon
1¼ cups fresh orange juice
3 tablespoons shredded orange rind
¼ cup tart crabapple jelly
¼ teaspoon dry mustard
Pinch salt
1 tablespoon white corn syrup

Heat the oil in a saucepan, add the onion and tarragon, and sauté over low heat until the onion is translucent (2 or 3 minutes). Add the other ingredients in the order given, blend well, and simmer for about 10 minutes.

This sauce is excellent poured over pot-roasted pheasant or duck—leave cover off and allow to glaze in a hot oven. Or use as a basting for broiled birds. Serve the remainder hot in a gravy boat.

Game Sauce

1 cup tart jelly
½ teaspoon dry mustard
¼ teaspoon onion juice
⅛ teaspoon ground ginger
½ teaspoon grated orange peel
½ teaspoon grated lemon peel
½ cup orange juice
2 tablespoons lemon juice

Melt the jelly, stirring in the mustard, over low heat. Add the onion juice, ginger, and grated peels. Mix well. Stir in the juices and simmer over low heat, stirring constantly, until well blended. Leave over very low heat until needed, at least 10 minutes. Use as a final basting, or serve as a hot sauce with roasted or broiled fat game—bear, beaver, possum, etc.

Sweet and Sour Sauce

1 cup pineapple juice
1 tablespoon brown sugar
2 tablespoons malt vinegar
⅛ teaspoon powdered garlic
½ teaspoon soy sauce
½ cup diced pineapple
½ green pepper, chopped
1 tablespoon chopped pimento (canned)
1½ tablespoons cornstarch
2 tablespoons cold water

Combine the first 5 ingredients in a saucepan and bring to a boil. Add the pineapple, green pepper, and pimento. Mix the cornstarch and water and blend into the sauce. Cook and stir until clear and thickened. Keep over low heat 10 minutes. Serve hot with broiled cuts of young bear or fat small game—beaver, raccoon, woodchuck—or with roast or broiled duck.

Barbecue Basting Sauces

Heated barbecue sauces are used for the constant basting required during dry-heat broiling or barbecuing. The sauces may be used cold to marinate the meat first, but they should then be warmed for basting.

Sauce No. 1:
1 cup red table wine
2 tablespoons vinegar
½ cup olive oil (may be part vegetable oil)
Dash sugar
1 large onion, grated
1 clove garlic, bruised
½ teaspoon pepper
Pinch cayenne
Bouquet garni

Sauce No. 2:
4 tablespoons lemon juice
½ teaspoon finely grated lemon rind
3 tablespoons honey (liquid)*
2 tablespoons soy sauce*
2 tablespoons salad oil
1 tablespoon sherry
1 clove garlic, bruised

Prepare either formula several hours or a day in advance. Following the order in which they're listed, blend all ingredients in a glass jar with a screw top. Shake until the sugar is dissolved. Cover and let stand, shaking from time to time. Remove the *bouquet garni* and/or garlic, and heat in a saucepan when ready to use.

Creamy Horseradish Sauce
½ cup heavy cream, whipped
Pinch salt
1 tablespoon prepared horseradish, drained

Into the whipped cream, fold the horseradish and salt. Refrigerate for an hour or two. Serve with cold aspics, smoked or spiced fish, jellied tongue, etc.

*Maple syrup may be substituted for the honey and soy sauce except when the barbecue sauce is to be used with fish.

A Miscellaneous Mixture

Beetroot and Horseradish Sauce
1 cup Velouté Sauce
½ cup prepared horseradish
½ teaspoon dry mustard
3 tablespoons vinegar
½ teaspoon sugar
½ teaspoon salt
½ cup grated cooked beets

Heat the Velouté Sauce in a double boiler, then add the horseradish, mustard, vinegar, sugar, and salt. Cook for about 10 minutes over boiling water, stirring frequently. Add the cooked beets, and heat for another few minutes. Chill. Serve with cold steamed or poached fish or aspics of white-fleshed fish.

Cold Mayonnaise Sauces
These sauces are all good served with fish.

Mustard: Combine 1 cup mayonnaise with 1 teaspoon each of hot English mustard, anchovy paste, sharp cucumber relish, chopped capers, and chopped herbs (thyme, parsley, sorrel).

Tarragon: Combine 1 cup of mayonnaise with 1 teaspoon of crushed fresh tarragon, 1 teaspoon of lemon juice, and a pinch of lemon rind.

Tartar: Combine 1 cup of mayonnaise with 1 tablespoon each of chopped capers, sliced stuffed olives, chopped sweet cucumber pickle, and chopped parsley.

Cold Green Sauce
Handful watercress
Handful spinach
1 teaspoon dry chervil
Pinch dry tarragon
1 cup mayonnaise

Wash the watercress and spinach and put into a small, covered saucepan with only the water clinging to them. Cover tightly and simmer gently for 4 to 5 minutes; add the chervil and tarragon, and simmer another minute or two. Put everything in a blender and reduce to a smooth puree. Incorporate this into the mayonnaise, blending well. Chill and serve.

FRUIT CONDIMENTS

Condiments of wild berries and fruits are natural accompaniments to game. Tart wild berries—chokecherries, pin cherries, Saskatoons, lingonberries, cranberries (high bush and low), currants, wild grapes, etc.—each a delight in itself, can be easily made into gem-clear jellies, spicy preserves, or more-or-less tart sauces.

A few of these condiments are given here. Edible wild fruits and plants are book-length subject matter. Recommended reading is *Wild Plants of Missouri* by Jan Phillips (Missouri Department of Conservation); and *The Edible Wild* and *Edible Wild Plants*, both by Clare E. Bolsby and Berndt Berglund (Pagurian Press Ltd., Toronto; Charles Scribner's Sons, New York).

As to which wild fruit is best served with any particular game, it is basically a matter of taste and/or availability. Probably the best guideline is to avoid the very tart strong fruit condiments when serving wines at the table, and to use instead the blander sweeter preparations.

Spiced Cranberries

4 cups cranberries
2 cups brown sugar
½ cup vinegar
½ cup water
1½ teaspoons cinnamon
1½ teaspoons ground allspice
½ teaspoon ground cloves

Combine everything in a deep saucepan and bring to a boil. Reduce the heat and simmer gently for about 2 hours, stirring occasionally, until a bit of the sauce jells loosely on a cold saucer. Pack in clean jars, cover, and store. Serve with all types of game.

Spiced Grapes

4 pounds blue grapes
2½ pounds granulated sugar
1½ cups cider vinegar
1 teaspoon ground cloves
1 teaspoon allspice
½ teaspoon cinnamon

Wash the grapes. Remove the skins and set aside. Put the pulp in a saucepan and bring to a boil. Simmer for 5 to 10 minutes, stirring to break down the pulp. Press the pulp through a potato ricer or colander to remove the seeds. Put the pulp and skins into a heavy preserving kettle and add the other ingredients. Bring to a boil, stirring lightly with a wooden spoon. Boil until a spoonful thickens or jells *slightly* when dropped on a cold saucer. Stir up from the bottom occasionally during cooking to prevent scorching.

Pour into clean, hot, small jars, and seal with melted paraffin, and cover. Store in a cool, dark place 2 to 4 weeks (to allow the spices to develop) before using. This recipe is moderately to highly spiced; spices may be increased if desired. This is an excellent accompaniment to any game. This recipe yields 5 or 6 8-ounce jars.

Rosewater Glaze for Wildfowl

To make rosewater, fill a deep saucepan with washed wild-rose petals, letting them settle somewhat. Add water to barely cover. Bring to a boil, reduce heat, simmer gently for about 5 minutes. Drain off the rosewater, pour into a bottle, and refrigerate.

To make the glaze, combine 1 tablespoon of rosewater with 3 tablespoons of honey and 2 tablespoons of melted butter. Mix well and brush the fowl occasionally with the glaze as it roasts or broils.

Cranberry-Rosehip Sauce

In a saucepan over medium heat, dissolve ½ cup of sugar (or more to taste) in 1 cup of water. Add about 1 cup each of highbush cranberries and rosehips. Bring to a boil, lower the heat, and cook, stirring occasionally, until all berries have popped (5 to 10 minutes). Blend in a dash of lemon juice. Serve with game meats and wildfowl.

Lingonberry Sauce

1 quart lingonberries
1½ cups sugar
½ cup water
1 tablespoon lemon juice

Wash and pick over the berries. Put into a saucepan along with the remaining ingredients. Bring to a boil, stirring gently until the sugar has dissolved. Reduce the heat and simmer for 15 minutes. Serve with game meats.

BREADS

Buttermilk Corn Bread

3 cups cornmeal
3 teaspoons baking powder
1 teaspoon baking soda
1½ teaspoons salt
⅓ cup shortening
2 cups buttermilk
2 eggs, unbeaten

Preheat the oven to 425° F (220° C). Combine all of the dry ingredients. Melt the shortening in the baking pan in which the corn bread will be baked. (Use a large shallow pan if crisp corn bread is desired; use a 9-inch square cake pan for thicker, cakier bread). Combine and add the melted shortening, buttermilk, and eggs to the dry ingredients; beat only until smooth.

Return the batter to the baking pan. Bake for 25 to 30 minutes. Cut into squares and serve hot.

Sweet Milk Corn Bread

2 cups fresh milk or reconstituted
  evaporated milk or dry milk
2 tablespoons vinegar or lemon juice
3 cups cornmeal
3 tablespoons flour
3 teaspoons baking powder
1½ teaspoons salt
⅓ cup shortening
1 egg, beaten (optional)

Put the vinegar into a 1-pint measuring cup, add the milk, and let stand for 10 to 15 minutes to clabber. Combine the dry ingredients and proceed as for Buttermilk Corn Bread, using the clabbered milk instead of buttermilk.

Favorites with fish chowders, game stews, and pot roasts, corn breads may also be served very hot with butter and maple or corn syrup.

Hush Puppies

Hush puppies and their name are said to have originated when hunters dropped bits of corn-cake batter into frying fat and then tossed the cooked morsels to the hungry, noisy dogs, pleading, "Hush, puppies."

Prepare batter according to the Buttermilk Corn Bread recipe. Dip a spoon in cold water, scoop up a spoonful of batter, and drop it quickly into hot deep fat (370° F, 188° C). Dip the spoon in cold water before each addition. Hush puppies are a favorite accompaniment for fish dishes, especially catfish and chowders.

Basic Bannock

Bannock o' bear-meal,
Bannock o' barley,
Here's to the Highlandman's bannock o' barley.

— Robert Burns

Bannock is a fast-rising hearth bread of Scottish origin, quickly made by cooking on a griddle directly over a deep bed of glowing coals. The original bannock was made with barley, oat, or pease meal. Today it is usually made with flour or a mixture of flour and meal. Any good baking-powder biscuit recipe, or biscuit mix, may be baked bannock style. Bannock is used as a substitute for bread and potatoes with any kind of fish or game.

4 cups flour
1 teaspoon salt
1 teaspoon baking soda
3 teaspoons baking powder
¼ cup butter or shortening
1 egg, beaten
1 cup buttermilk*

*Buttermilk makes the lightest, best-flavored bannock. If you must use fresh, evaporated, or powdered milk, clabber it as directed under Sweet Milk Corn Bread, and omit the baking soda from the recipe.

Preheat the oven to 425° F (220° C). Sift together the flour, salt, baking soda, and baking powder. Cut in the butter or shortening and rub with the fingers to a coarse, mealy texture. Combine the beaten egg and buttermilk. Make a hole in the flour and add the liquid. Stir quickly, just enough to mix. (Stir *deiseal*, or clockwise, which is the lucky way. *Widdershins*, or counterclockwise, is unlucky according to old Druid belief.) Turn the dough out onto a floured board and knead with floured hands; knead as little as possible—just enough to form into a round soft cake. Flatten the cake with your hands. Put into a floured skillet or cake pan and bake for about 15 minutes, until nicely browned. Serve warm.

Open-Hearth Variation: Unless the fireplace is well protected, arrange a reflector of heavy aluminum foil to windward. Place the pan of bannock close to a deep bed of coals, with a low flame, to heat through and brown the bread on the bottom—2 or 3 minutes—then raise the pan to prevent burning. When the bannock has risen, slip small peeled green hardwood sticks under one side of the bread to tilt it off the bottom of the pan and allow it to bake through without burning on bottom. When it's firm on top, turn the bannock out of the pan and prop it toward the fire to brown the top. If using a rack, simply turn it over the coals for a moment to brown.

Wood-Stove Variation: Remove the stove lid. Start the bannock in a pan right over the deep coals, using a roomy canopy of aluminum foil over the pan as a reflector if necessary. After 2 or 3 minutes, replace the stove lid and finish baking on top of the stove in the same manner as for the open hearth. Brown over the coals on a wire toaster. If the stove has a very hot oven, the bannock may be baked. Bannock requires close watching. If the bottom crust becomes scorched, just slice it off and serve topside up.

Campfire Variation: Roll bannock dough into fat finger-thick strips. Wind a strip over a small peeled green maple or hardwood pole and hold over the coals to cook, turning until done.

Woodsman's Bannock

2 cups flour
2 teaspoons baking powder
½ teaspoon salt
3 tablespoons porcupine or bear fat,
    or bacon fat
Shortening

Combine the flour, baking powder, and salt. If no flour sifter is handy, toss together lightly with two forks to mix and aerate. Cut in the fat, and rub quickly and lightly with the fingers to a coarse mealy texture. Sprinkle ¼ cup of cold water over the top and stir until evenly moistened. Turn the dough out on a floured board or paper, and knead very lightly for about 30 seconds. Heat shortening, ¼ inch deep, in a frying pan. Tear off bits of the dough and ease into the hot fat. Fry until golden brown on the bottom, then turn and brown the other side. Serve warm.

Variations: Lightly grease a frying pan. Shape the dough into a ball and flatten it into a round cake. Bake it in a frying pan over hot coals. Place a hood of aluminum foil or an aluminum pie plate over the top of the pan, a little off center. When the dough has risen and the bottom crust has browned, turn the bannock and brown the top. This may be done directly over the coals. Woodsman's Bannock, like Basic Bannock, can also be cooked campfire-style.

WILD RICE

The delicate, smoky, nutlike flavor and distinctive chewy light texture of wild rice make it naturally compatible with game, especially the wild waterfowl of the Midwest, which feed on it. However, this world-famous delicacy is not rice at all, but a tall, aquatic grass which grows wild in the shallow waters throughout much of central North America.

Basic Wild Rice

Pick over the wild rice carefully on a white plate to remove any grit that may be in it. Wash in a sieve under cold running water until the water is clean.

The wild rice may be steamed or boiled. Both methods yield 4 cups of cooked rice to 1 cup of raw. Steaming is a much lengthier procedure but retains more flavor and drier texture.

Steamed: Cover the washed rice with cold water and soak overnight. Drain but do not rinse. Spread the soaked wild rice over the bottom of a steamer and sprinkle lightly with salt. Steam over boiling water, covered, for 1 to 2 hours, until the wild rice is fluffy and the kernels are tweedy dark brown and gray and separated in light, fat curls. Remove from the steam, giving it a gentle shake, and let the rice dry in the pan. Use in stuffing or any dish calling for cooked wild rice.

Boiled: For 1 cup of wild rice, bring 4 cups of water to a boil in a saucepan. Add the washed wild rice, stir, and return to a boil. Cover and boil gently for 5 minutes. Remove from the heat. Let stand, covered, for 1 to 2 hours. Reheat to a boil. Cook covered for ½ hour, until tender and fluffy. Drain, saving water for stock or sauce.

Empress-Style Wild Rice

¼ pound wild rice
2 ounces bacon, diced
¼ cup diced green onions
⅓ cup sliced mushrooms
1 stewed tomato or 1 fresh tomato,
   peeled and chopped
Pepper to taste
½ clove garlic
Salt to taste
Parmesan cheese
Butter

Wash the wild rice well with cold water. Cook as directed for Basic Wild Rice. Drain well. Fry the bacon lightly, add the green onions and mushrooms, and sauté lightly. Cool slightly and mix with the wild rice, adding the chopped tomato, juice included, pepper, and garlic mashed and mixed with the salt. Place in a well-buttered casserole. Sprinkle with Parmesan cheese, dot with butter, and bake in a 350° F (175° C) oven for 15 to 20 minutes.

—C. E. Butler
Chef, Empress Hotel
Victoria, British Columbia

Glossary

ACID WATER: A slightly acidic solution containing ¼ cup of vinegar or lemon juice per 1 gallon of water.

BARDS: Slices or thin slabs of pork or beef fat, or fat salt pork or bacon, applied to the surface of meat or fowl as larding. The crackling removed from a baked ham makes a good bard for a roast of venison or for a bird.

BEURRE MANIÉ (kneaded butter): Butter worked into flour until mealy. One tablespoon of butter takes up about 2 tablespoons of flour. An excellent last-minute thickening for meat stews and sauces: Sprinkle the beurre manié over bubbling liquid and stir until thickened.

BLANCHED BACON: Bacon is excellent for larding. However, the characteristic taste of smoked bacon is undesirable in delicate fowl, and may also be considered objectionable in other game meats. Blanching the bacon removes this taste while leaving the fat for larding. *Method*: Place strips of bacon in a shallow saucepan, and cover with cold water. Bring to a bare simmer and leave over very low heat for about 10 minutes. *Do not boil.* Drain well.

BOUQUET GARNI: A bundle of fresh or dried branches of herbs tied together with thread or string. Used in court bouillons, fumets, marinades, and any moist-heat cooking procedures.

BROWNED BUTTER: Clarified butter heated until it's nut brown. Also called "noisette" butter.

CLARIFIED BUTTER: Clarifying butter removes the whey, a whitish sediment in ordinary butter which scorches before the butter becomes hot enough for frying or browning. *Method*: Melt the butter (or margarine) in chunks in a small saucepan until it bubbles up. Remove from the heat, skim the froth, and pour off the clear butter, leaving behind the sediment that settles in the bottom of the saucepan. In small amounts, the melted butter may be strained through a sieve, lined with a single facial tissue, into the sauté pan or saucepan in which it is to be used. (The problem of scorching butter can also be solved by using equal parts of butter and cooking oil or fat instead of all butter. Such a mixture will brown without scorching.)

CROUTONS: Small cubes of stale bread fried in hot clarified butter until crusty gold; served with soups and thin stews. Also refers to rounds of stale bread fried and served with very small birds.

FAGGOT: Herbs and spices sandwiched between two chunks of celery and tied securely. The faggot may be easily removed without straining at any stage to avoid overseasoning. *Method*: Use pieces of celery 2 to 3 inches long. Lay the desired herbs in one piece, burying small spices in the middle. Top with the other piece of celery and tie securely with thread or string. The faggot should be quite closely filled.

FINE HERBS: A mixture of medium and/or mild herbs, used as directed in recipe.

LARDING: The application or addition of fat to lean meats. This can be done in various ways such as by rubbing the outside of the meat (especially steaks) with oil or fat, or by adding the fat, usually in the form of diced salt pork, directly to the pot (stews, casseroles) or to the meat (minced). See also BARDS, LARDING NEEDLE, and PIQUE METHOD.

LARDING NEEDLE: A tubular needle by which long thin strips of chilled, dry pork fat (lardoons) are drawn through the meat so that nodules of fat are left on the surface of the meat. Lardoons may be rubbed with garlic and/or soaked in brandy.

MIREPOIX: A dice of aromatic vegetables—carrots, celery, green peppers, sweet red peppers, onion—sautéed in oil or butter.

PICKLING SPICES: A mixture of aromatic spices consisting of allspice, celery seed, tiny chili peppers, cloves, mustard seed, bay leaf, and others as desired. Tied in a cheesecloth bag, the spices may be removed when the desired flavor is attained. A packaged mixture of pickling spices is available in many stores.

PIQUE METHOD: A larding method in which slits are pierced in the meat at frequent intervals and strips of chilled fat are pushed in, leaving a nodule on the surface of the meat.

ROUX: A mixture of equal parts of fat and flour cooked together, forming the base of a flour-thickened sauce. A light (white) roux, usually used in sauces for fish and small fowl, is made by adding flour to melted fat and cooking, stirring constantly until smooth and bubbly, just short of coloring. For a dark roux, used with meats and fowl, stir flour into melted fat and cook, stirring constantly until smooth and brown, just short of smoking. (If butter is used for fat, it is best to clarify it first.)

SEASONED FLOUR: Flour seasoned with salt, pepper, and other seasonings as desired. Mix in proportions of ½ teaspoon of salt and ¼ teaspoon of pepper to each ½ cup of flour.

STOCK: Stock is called for in the preparation of many fish and meat dishes and accessories (stews, soups, sauces, gravies, etc.). Fish stock is described in Chapter 8. Meat and fowl stocks are prepared by slowly cooking meat and bones in water with or without other liquid, vegetables, and seasonings, and then reducing the liquid. Heavy meat bones are usually "sweated" first in a hot oven. In many recipes the stock required is produced in the process of preparing the dish. The various game soups involve stock making.

Index